ADVANCE PRAISE FOR
IT TAKES A COUNTER-REVOLUTION

"Larry Klayman is a fearless advocate who defeated special counsel Mueller's 'deep state' attempt to have me testify against President Trump by threatening me with prosecution if I did not lie under oath. I am eternally grateful to him! He is a true champion of justice!"

—DR. JEROME CORSI, *NEW YORK
TIMES* BESTSELLING AUTHOR

"I have known Larry Klayman for many years as a friend and as my lawyer. He's a straight shooter and a patriot. We need more people like Larry in the legal profession."

—SHERIFF JOE ARPAIO

"Larry Klayman is a uniquely public-spirited lawyer. He has never lost sight of the fact that the responsible activity of individual citizens, seriously seeking to exercise their God-endowed rights, is the indispensable energy source for all our institutions of self-government."

—AMBASSADOR ALAN L. KEYES, FORMER UN
AMBASSADOR AND PRESIDENTIAL CANDIDATE

"Larry Klayman is my hero because he has integrity—enough to prevent him from blind loyalty to party or ideology...That's because he is fearless and relentless in the pursuit of justice... There were other men like Larry early in American history. Their names were Washington, Jefferson, Madison, and Henry."

—JOSEPH FARAH, CEO, WWW.WND.COM

"That *Time* magazine has yet to name Larry Klayman 'Man of the Year' is a failure of *Time*, not Klayman's."

—JACK CASHILL, BESTSELLING
AUTHOR OF *RON BROWN'S BODY*

"Larry Klayman stood in the stead for my family and me under very trying circumstances. He is persistent, loyal, and a great believer in the Constitution, as my sons and I are as well. I respect his wisdom and strength and cherish his friendship."

—CLIVEN BUNDY, NEVADA RANCHER

"While others talk of corruption and injustice in our federal courts, Larry Klayman is a man who has done something about it. As founder of Judicial Watch and Freedom Watch, Larry Klayman became a household name to those of us who want to stop the runaway power of federal judges and restore honesty and integrity to our federal court system. Echoing the sentiments of our Founding Fathers like Thomas Jefferson and James Madison, Larry Klayman has fought for a return to the principles and foundation of our Constitutional Republic wherein people are the source of all power. With over forty years of experience in the practice of law, Larry Klayman has represented defendants across America in defense of their right to 'life, liberty, and the pursuit of happiness.' Larry is a valiant warrior for truth and justice, and a man I am proud to call my friend. I hope that you will enjoy his noble work, *It Takes a Counter-Revolution!*"

—CHIEF JUSTICE ROY MOORE

"Klayman's work *It Takes a Counter-Revolution* is brilliant, however unorthodox. But Larry is always right!"

—BEN STEIN, LAWYER, ACTOR, WRITER

"As the father of Navy SEAL Ty Woods, who was killed at Benghazi, I highly recommend this book. Just as Ty was a warrior as a Navy SEAL, as a fellow lawyer and as his friend I can attest to Larry being a warrior in the courtroom."

—CHARLES WOODS, FATHER OF
NAVY SEAL TY WOODS

"I admire Larry, because he is first and foremost a patriot. He not only believes in the words of the Constitution, he practices those words in all of his endeavors. He was there when I needed him."

—LAURA LUHN, SEXUAL ABUSE
VICTIM OF ROGER AILES

"Larry Klayman is one of the most principled and intellectual minds in the world of litigation. He believes in fighting for justice at all costs to protect our constitutional freedoms! I am honored to be able to call him a friend and mentor. God brings people into your life for different reasons. I believe that God connected us because he wanted me to have a big brother to encourage me to maximize my potential and guide me in the right direction. Thank you, Larry!"

—SERGEANT DEMETRICK PENNIE, PRESIDENT OF
THE DALLAS FALLEN OFFICER FOUNDATION

"Larry Klayman was the only attorney who had the guts to stand beside us and go against the government to get answers when our son, Michael, was killed in Afghanistan aboard Extortion 17 on 08/06/2011. Larry is a bulldog in the courtroom! He helped us win against the NSA, the first time in American history!"

—CHARLES STRANGE, GOLD STAR FATHER
OF PO1 MICHAEL STRANGE (DEVGRU)

"Larry Klayman shows what a true American is. Standing up for what's right even if it isn't popular. His steadfast support and work has been paramount during this insane time, of the FBI and the Biden regime trampling the rights of myself and many other Americans."

—SIAKA MASSAQUOI, JANUARY 6,
2021 PEACEFUL PROTESTER

IT TAKES A
COUNTER-REVOLUTION
WAKE UP AMERICA!

Larry Klayman, Esq.
Founder of Judicial Watch and Freedom Watch

ISBN: 978-1-63758-525-2
ISBN (eBook): 978-1-63758-526-9

It Takes a Counter-Revolution:
Wake Up America!
© 2022 by Larry Klayman, Esq.

Cover design by Ethan Stone

Published in the United States of America
1 2 3 4 5 6 7 8 9 10

DEDICATION

It Takes a Counter-Revolution: Wake Up America! is dedicated to our most farsighted of Founding Fathers, Thomas Jefferson. Jefferson's superior intellect manifested itself in many ways, as a lawyer, writer, politician, philosopher, architect, farmer, educator, and most particularly in his common-sense understanding of human nature. He understood that the new republic would over time enter into another revolutionary state, thanks to the natural evolution of corruption in society. He forecast that the "blood of patriots" would inevitably have to be spilled, primarily as a result of a federal judiciary, which he opposed. Jefferson warned that if put in place by the framers of the Constitution, federal judges would become despots, as they would be unelected by and thus not answerable to We the People. This especially rings true today. My book is therefore a clarion call on ways to wage a peaceful revolution and try to avoid Jefferson's prophecy, which may yet come to pass.

TABLE OF CONTENTS

FOREWORD

By Alan L. Keyes

As a young lawyer, speaking to a gathering characteristic of the youth of a nation almost as young as he was, Abraham Lincoln praised its founders for erecting "a political edifice of liberty and equal rights," which each succeeding generation had only to preserve and transmit to posterity. Given his youth, we may forgive his carefree dismissal of the specter of foreign conquest. But our nation's history, up to and including the fateful crisis we presently endure, has time and again confirmed the accuracy of this, with which he identified the persistent, existential danger to our nation's survival.

At what point then is the approach of danger to be expected? I answer, if it ever reaches us, it must spring up amongst us. It cannot come from abroad. If destruction be our lot, we must ourselves be its author and finisher. As a nation of freemen, we must live through all time, or die by suicide.

In the twentieth century, the United States passed through the trial of foreign war and international economic depression. Far from destroying us, that trial confirmed the extraordinary force of character, ingenuity, and material power generated by our way of life. We overcame those challenges, so that, far from being killed, we became, for several decades, the preeminent nation on earth.

Of course, Lincoln's life also reminds us of the contest that, more than any other, *confirmed the truth* of his youthful prediction. Like the leading founders of the United States, young Lincoln foreshadowed the existential trial that had to come if the nation was to erase the palpable contradiction between the rightful obligations of humanity—by God endowed—and the inhuman curtailment of those obligations that all forms of slavery involve.

In our day, some Americans decry America's founding generation because they upheld the standard of God-endowed right as the premise of our self-government, even as they degraded it by continuing, expanding, or tolerating the practice of slavery. But who deserves greater opprobrium: people who acknowledge the standard right that impels good conscience to condemn their wrongdoings or people who construe the murder of helpless innocents as righteousness, upholding no standard of right except physical power?

As I write this foreword, the people of the United States face an existential trial that could prove to be their last hurrah. Exploiting the threat of virulent disease, the same people who have made the ritual murder of their posterity a rite of passage now seek to terrorize our whole nation into accepting the permanent sacrifice of true right, including liberty, as the only path to safety. Behind the blatant pretense of respect for life, they have abruptly suspended the rights the Constitution of the United States exists to secure, including especially the primordial rights rooted in our obligation to revere God and, by His command, perpetuate ourselves and our humanity.

These obligations, and all those proper to our natural existence, are our first belongings—the first properties of humankind, by God endowed. It is rightly our first labor and responsibility to secure and preserve them. As we fulfill natural calling—freely choosing to do right by God's authority, we exercise the species of freedom no mere human power has any license to curtail. The American Declaration calls this right exercise of freedom, by the name of liberty, placing it, just after life itself, at the head of the unalienable rights God's living will bequeaths to all humanity.

This simple logic is the first premise of our liberty as a nation. It is the ground for our claim to self-government, saving only the majesty of our Creator, God. In our day, it is willfully neglected—except by the remnant of hardy souls, unwilling to let go of our adherence to the logic of God that upholds its self-evident truth. But for this logic, we must cease to be a free people. We shall slip again into the deep mire of terror, dictatorship, and the contest of power in which few prevail—oppressing many—so that all lose sight of the God-intended humanity they are supposed to have in common.

Larry Klayman is one of those who remain faithful to this logic of God: the basis on which the people of the United States may claim also to be believers. Because of his good faith, he has always resisted the temptation, prevalent among the elites of our day, to discard the premise of equal justice, logically connected with God's endowment of human right. We are not all equal in strength, intelligence, or fortitude. We will, therefore, never be simply equal in the results of our individual endeavors. But the terms of God's endowment of right equally oblige us all to use the capacity for choice that distinguishes us in nature, to fulfill, as best we can, the provisions of His will.

Larry Klayman is a uniquely public-spirited lawyer. He has never lost sight of the fact that the responsible activity of individual citizens, seriously seeking to exercise their God-endowed rights, is the indispensable energy source for all our institutions of self-government. As a people, we do not purport to govern directly.

Instead, we elect others to represent us in government. This fact has misled many to assume that our self-government depends on superior "leaders," a belief more consistent with the "führer" principle of Nazi Germany than the Constitution of the United States.

During all the years I have known him, Larry Klayman has acted as one who understands that what the elected officials in government represent in the performance of their duties ought to be what people themselves first present in their hearts, minds, and actions as citizens. He has taken seriously the institutions of government that directly call for individual involvement at the local level, including especially the practice of indictment and trial by jury, wherein the people, acting as judges of fact, also have the responsibility to form judgments about the law in order to correct provisions that neglect or misrepresent the obligation to do right by God's will. That obligation is, after all, the ultimate source of authority for their self-government.

It has been some decades since the phrase "information is power" came into vogue as a mantra of our nation's Machiavellian elitists. They play on the disregard for truth this mantra tacitly involves. As the word implies, information is more about what people *accept as true* than what *is* true. Lies can form consciousness, sometimes more effectively than facts, especially if they more immediately rouse forceful passions. When justice becomes a matter of information, accusations and trials become tests of ingenuity. Indoctrination in education or the media overrides the exposition of truth. Verdict becomes edict. Justice gives way to arbitrary will, cunningly narrating its way to power.

Well-intentioned people who apprehend this danger have striven through my lifetime, as our nation's founders did, to use existing institutions to obstruct this disdain for truth. In this book, Larry Klayman continues the effort to do so, as he has throughout his career. The task is harder now than it has ever been. The inordinately ambitious, deceitful character of America's elitist faction has deeply poisoned the environment for public discourse. Discouraged by this, many of our citizens have lost patience with reasoning. They have lost sight of the assumption of good character that has, at critical moments, allowed our nation's institutions to weather the storms of false, self-righteous passion, fomented by would-be tyrants. Such a storm is raging now. By manipulating resentment, anger, hatred, and especially fear, they aim to terrorize Americans into discarding their responsibility of care and leadership for our institutions of self-government. They have already commenced constructing the totalitarian and technological controls that will replace them.

As he has consistently sought to do in the past, Larry Klayman challenges people to recognize and repel this assault on our decent liberty. Appealing to what Lincoln called "the better angels of our nature," he seeks to reawaken the civic courage that has, more than once, impelled us to reclaim the path of strenuous citizenship vital to the survival of our national hope. Most importantly, Larry Klayman refuses to lose sight of the source of that courage—the adamantine faith in God, who even now still sets before us life and death; blessings and curses; evident truth and self-idolizing deception, trusting in us to choose the path of right that his fresh footsteps show the way to tread.

PRELUDE TO A COUNTER-REVOLUTION!

"They who would give up an essential liberty for temporary security, deserve neither liberty nor security."

—Benjamin Franklin[1]

Since I first penned and had published my earlier version of this work on October 27, 2020, *It Takes a Revolution: Forget the Scandal Industry!* much has happened and not for the better. As my former father-in-law from Rome, an Italian Rodney Dangerfield, used to quip, "Appreciate today because tomorrow will be even worse."

With the highly questionable and to this day only an alleged defeat of President Donald J. Trump in the 2020 elections, ascending to the throne of the current government was one Joseph Robinette Biden and his affirmative-action sidekick, Kamala Harris, chosen as a vice presidential candidate not based on stature or for that matter intellect, but primarily because she is both black and a woman. This less-than-dynamic duo, who—along with House Speaker Nancy Pelosi—has become the three stooges of a radical

1.   Benjamin Franklin. *Quotations of Benjamin Franklin* (2003).

Left comprised of radical socialists and communists; blacks; radical Muslims; the Marxian Jewish left; radical feminists; radical gays, lesbians, transgenders and transsexuals; and last but hardly least radical atheists and anarchists, all bent on destroying the foundations of our Judeo-Christian society and installing in its place an eventual Soviet-style socialist if not communist dictatorship. Their goal: to create a godless state where their form of government takes the place of and squeezes out of our lives the Father and His Son.

As a result, during the last year after our severely mentally diminished and intellectually deficient current president was sworn in on the Capitol steps, along with the constantly laughing cackling witch of an alleged vice president, the nation as we knew it has all but been destroyed, causing our Founding Fathers to turn over in their graves.

The Left's plan, while hardly original for socialists, communists, and other leftist radicals, was this:

First, use the COVID-19 pandemic to take near total control over the populace, initially with house quarantines—effectively house arrests—and then vaccine mandates, all the while attempting to force down our throats a medical "experiment" that has not been thoroughly tested for short-, medium- and long-term side effects and very harmful to pregnant women, blacks, and Hispanics in particular. Not content with subjecting adults to the so-called vaccines, the Left then moved on to injecting children, our nation's treasure, with it.

Second, stoking fear and quelling any dissent to the total leftist takeover implemented after the presidential election, by using my once-proud alma mater, the U.S. Department of Justice (DOJ) and its Federal Bureau of Investigation (FBI), as Biden's, Harris's and the Left's own private Gestapo, terrorizing and hunting down, indicting, incarcerating pending trial, and convicting even the peaceful protesters who came to Washington, D.C. and the

Capitol Building on January 6, 2021, in support of then-President Trump. As will be chronicled in this book, the compromised and corrupt federal judiciary, particularly in the District of Columbia, both Democrat- and establishment-Republican-nominated and confirmed, fearing for their own lives, have slavishly followed suit, rubber-stamping the Department's reign of terror, by throwing the peaceful protesters in prison while they await trial, likely conviction, and sentencing. According to the third-rate poor excuse of the chameleon-like FBI director Christopher Wray and mouse-like attorney general Merrick Garland, and their "Fuhrer Joe Biden," the biggest problem and threat to democracy in the country today are so-called white domestic terrorists. As for Biden, he is so mentally gone that perhaps he no longer knows that he is white and thus qualifies as a racist and domestic terrorist by his and the Left's own definition.

The uprising of January 6, 2021, was predictable, the citizenry having experienced the rising and cancerous corruption in all three branches of government for decades. But the frustration exploded, albeit mostly peacefully, when The Donald could not even get a fair hearing, much less any hearing at all, from his own handpicked justices on the Supreme Court, underscoring that indeed the judicial branch is the most endemically and systematically—a favorite adjective of the Left when it comes to alleged white racism—corrupt of all three branches. This helps explain what I will discuss further in Chapter 5, as the bought-and-paid-for compromised establishment politicized hacks on our federal bench and the High Court are beginning to realize that they will be taken first to the guillotines when all hell breaks loose, akin to the storming of the French Bastille on July 14, 1789, and its aftermath at Place de la Concorde in the center of Paris. This accounts for their arrogance and harsh and highly punitive approach to the peaceful protesters of January 6, 2021.

Third, the Biden-Harris regime also unleashed their attack dogs, through their pliant over-the-hill mouse—or perhaps more aptly put rat—of an attorney general, Merrick Garland, at DOJ and its FBI. Garland is not coincidentally formerly a judge on the U.S. Court of Appeals for the District of Columbia Circuit and then a failed Obama Supreme Court nominee. His threats to parents who attend school board meetings to protest antiwhite critical race theory curricula, the new minority-driven math, where two and two no longer equals four so as not to offend those who have not learned to add or subtract, and object to the teachings of radical homosexuals and transgenders, was beyond reprehensible but also unconstitutional and outright illegal. Like his allies on the Left, Garland showed his colors and propensity to further divide the races as well his desire to promote the rapid push toward "normalizing" abnormal and unfortunate gay, lesbian, transgender, and transsexual lifestyles.

And if that is not enough tyranny, Biden and Harris and their fellow third stooge Nancy Pelosi, were planning to sic the Internal Revenue Service on anyone with over $600.00 in his or her account—or should we now say gender-neutral accounts—so the impending socialist and communist state can presumably later confiscate one's hard-earned earnings, Soviet style.

Fourth, destroying capitalism and inserting socialism and eventual communism in its place, the Biden-Harris regime, singing to the tune of the anti-Semitic left, financed by admitted Nazi collaborator George Soros[2] and led by Bernie Sanders, also a card-carrying, self-hating Jew, Soros ally and member of the so-called progressive or should we rather say "regressive" movement, in addition to radical leftist ringleaders of the so-called squad, Congresswoman Alessandra Ocasio-Cortez and radical Muslim Representatives Rashida Tlaib and Ilhan Omar, to name just a few, have

2.   "Infamous George Soros 60 Minutes Interview," YouTube, https://www.youtube.com/watch?v=npvHhGZTSXo.

all worked together to dump trillions of dollars in free cash into the economy during the COVID-19 pandemic, destroying any real desire for the millions of recipients to return to the workplace. The result, small, medium and even large businesses are without workers, to the point even finding an Uber driver is a near miracle. Most acute is the shortage of workers at the nation's ports and railroads, where millions of containers cannot even be unloaded, causing product shortages and stoking supply-and-demand inflation, undercutting the purchasing power of the lower and middle classes. While our transportation system was breaking down last fall, our in-your-face "flamer" of a gay Secretary of Transportation had taken two months off with so-called "maternity leave," posing in bed with his "wife," holding two newborn babies they had somehow birthed through surrogates, saying it all about the state of the nation.

The result: to make the citizenry dependent on the largess of the new god, government, and to addict them to and thus make them dependent on handouts. Their apparent mantra: Vote leftist Democrat: it's easier than working!

Fifth, the welcoming of millions of illegal aliens into the United States, allowing them to run rampant across our southern border, many infected with COVID-19 and other infectious diseases. Also welcomed in our midst are drug and human traffickers, other varieties of criminals and likely terrorists, causing further threats to and destabilizing the country but more importantly significantly increasing the population of eventual Democrat leftist voters. The dual goal—to overload the capitalist economy, further causing it to eventually collapse in favor of socialism and eventual communism, with more free money being doled out to pay for the illegals and to help ensure that a conservative, libertarian person of faith or someone like Donald Trump never gets elected president again, much less shutting the door for an antileftist-dominated congressional makeup in the future.

Sixth, bankrupt the republic within yet more proposed and likely multitrillion-dollar spending legislation, with secret provisions embedded into them such as amnesty for illegal aliens.

Seventh, destroying law enforcement by defunding police departments and in some areas of the United States even abolishing them. The result: violent crime is now rampant and growing daily, especially in our major cities such as Chicago, Philadelphia, Los Angeles, Seattle, Portland, and Miami, which have become killing fields. It's so bad that one can no longer even sit in an outdoor café, a mandated "necessity" in the age of COVID-19, and not think about getting stabbed or shot in the back by some radicalized individual reacting to the race or some other social and ethnic war the Left has stoked effectively.

Eighth, destroying our national security, prestige, and standing as a beacon of freedom throughout the world. The debacle in Afghanistan is just one example, where the Biden-Harris regime surrendered to the Taliban, Al Qaeda, and ISIS terrorists, and sold out even our European allies in the process. And that is not to mention the thousands of Americans and Afghan allies left to rot there as hostages at the mercy of the Taliban and their Muslim terrorist friends. This has forsaken and dishonored all of our proud and heroic servicemen who died there, in Iraq and throughout the Middle East in particular. To top off all this outrage, Biden even ordered a drone strike on allied civilian Afghan aid workers to deflect from his negligent homicide of thirteen servicemen and hundreds of Afghans who were killed by terrorists at the Kabul airport—murdering seven young, innocent children in the process.

Biden and Harris have done the bidding of the Left, which has always hated the military. They have destroyed our brave servicemen's and women's morale and mocked their dedicated respect for our flag and the republic for which it stands, thereby showing disrespect for and endangering the rest of us. And, what about all of those Americans who were maimed and mutilated in battle, notwithstanding the tens of thousands who gave their lives to protect us, left behind by their wives and children and of course their Gold Star parents? Biden-Harris and their leftist allies just danced if not spit on their graves, trashing their sacrifice as the ultimate American patriots!

Ninth, trashing our Judeo-Christian values and beliefs, with more killings of unborn children, to add to the hundreds of millions already murdered in abortion clinics and godless doctors' offices. And, if that is not enough to cause the Father's and His Son's ire, akin to God's wrath inflicted on Egypt centuries ago which set Moses and his Jewish people free, this may explain the current downfall of this modern-day nation. Does anyone with a righteous and religious mind think that God will just sit idly by as the Left, as most in society just take a back seat and parties on, erases any concept of the sexes and promotes homosexuality with its gay marriage, transgenderism, and anything-goes culture, defiling the scriptures and any aspect of a "normal" God-fearing society?

To make matters even worse, our religious leaders generally have been scared to speak up, much more act, save for a few. American Catholic bishops at least wanted to deny communion to the pseudo-Catholic Biden and his cronies who push abortion, only then to have the Communist Pope Francis clip their wings and handcuff them. Other religions have also kowtowed to the Left, as have our sports leagues, corporations, labor unions, universities, and other institutions, and of course degenerate Hollywood, seeking to win favor for more government handouts and benefits. It reminds me of the Third Reich, when German industry and society put Hitler in power and then propped him up and the churches, including the Catholic Church, looked the other way, effectively giving the Führer a green light for the Holocaust. Indeed, we appear to be living through the Fourth Reich of the Biden-Harris regime, underscored by the Left's virulent strain of anti-Semitism.

Tenth, but hardly least, there is the total breakdown of our so-called system of justice, laid bare in the first and now even more so in this new version and sequel of my book, where hack and corrupted politicians in robes do the bidding of the establishment of both bankrupt major political parties and compromised government institutions. As Thomas Jefferson predicted, his prophecy now having come home to roost, federal judges, unelected, life-tenured and unaccountable to We the People, have become despots and tyrants, the yes men and women of the elite and corrupt ruling class—and, in fact, they consider themselves as judicial gods—which will cause us to again shed the blood of patriots and tyrants, adding what is a few thousand dead to refresh the tree of liberty.

Jefferson did not want to see bloodshed to renew the foundations of our republic, and neither do I. So, fellow patriots, read on carefully to digest and then act on my plan to wage what is now a counter-revolution of liberation to throw off the noose that Biden-Harris and their rabidly leftist allies have tightened around our necks.

It is time yet again to take back our legal system from our present rulers, to declare independence, not a new nation, to establish an ethical and real government with new political parties, to install an honest electoral system, to elect sincere and uncompromised patriotic judges and government leaders, and to resurrect the now all-but-dead vision and creation of our Founding Fathers. We must leave the current corrupt government behind and literally pull the plug, and not try to reform it, as it is irrevocably broken, terminally ill and on life support. As my Hebrew name is Lazar, for Lazarus who rose from the dead, please join me in our collective destiny by doing our part to breathe life back into our sacred land begun on July 4, 1776, and then furthered literally with blood, sweat, and tears of true Americans, that is until now!

Wake up, America! If you are a senior, get out of retirement and join our peaceful and legal fight for the good of your children and grandchildren; and if you are young and middle-aged, enlist in our citizens army so you will have a life free from the bondage of socialism, communism, and atheism and every other sick and perverted radical leftist ideology that has all but enslaved us under their evil despotism literally inspired by the devil!

And "take this to heart" as my grandmom Freda Klayman, who fled Communist Russia as a young woman, used to tell her grandson: God will only help us if we help ourselves!

Now is the time, as did our Founding Fathers in our first Declaration of Independence, to be unafraid, risk all, pay any price, and to rid the nation of the hateful and highly destructive scourge of the leftists who have already taken total hold over our lives! Give us liberty or give us death, in the brave words of Patrick Henry!

We are already at war, and one side must win and the other must lose. Let us hang together and unite as one to make sure that you and your loved ones are on the winning side, the side of God!

Read on fellow patriots and then be prepared to act! Mere talk, or feel good and weak cosmetic gestures, such as school board protests and boycotts, put timidly forth by other authors and commentators such as Mark Levin, will not solve our rapid slide to extinction. Low personal risk, politically correct and socially acceptable convenient half-measures and cop-outs are no longer an option!

As conservative icon Barry Goldwater, who ran for president and was falsely smeared as a danger by President Lyndon Johnson during the Vietnam War, famously declared: "I would remind you that extremism in defense of liberty is no vice! And let me remind you also that moderation in pursuit of justice is no virtue."[3]

---

3. "Extremism in the Defense of Liberty Is No Vice," https://en.wikisource.org/wiki/Extremism_in_the_Defense_of_Liberty_Is_No_Vice.

INTRODUCTION

IT TAKES A COUNTER-REVOLUTION: WAKE UP AMERICA!

"The spirit of resistance is so valuable on certain occasions, that I wish it always to be kept alive. It will often be exercised when wrong, but better so than not to be exercised at all."

"The tree of liberty must be refreshed from time to time with the blood of patriots and tyrants. It is the natural manure."

"No free man shall ever be debarred the use of arms."

"The beauty of the second amendment is that it will not be needed until they try to take it."

—Thomas Jefferson[4]

As I penned in my autobiography, *Whores: Why and How I Came to Fight the Establishment!*, which still can be purchased on Amazon.com, BarnesandNoble.com, and other booksellers, I founded Judicial Watch, Inc. on July 29, 1994—twenty-eight years ago—because I had come to see government and the legal system as growing increasingly corrupt. As a former federal prosecutor in the Antitrust Division of the U.S. Department of Justice, I found

4.   Thomas Jefferson. *Quotations of Thomas Jefferson.* (Applewood Books: Carlisle, Massachusetts, 2004), https://www.applewoodbooks.com/Quotations-of-Thomas-Jefferson-P1967.aspx.

many of my colleagues and the judges before whom I appeared to be highly politicized at best, acting and making decisions not on the merits but on their own personal and professional interests. This offended me greatly, and my experience before a federal judge in Los Angeles, the less-than-Honorable William D. Keller, in the early 1990s, was the final straw that broke this camel's back. I thus conceived and founded Judicial Watch.

In the ten years that followed at Judicial Watch, Inc., and thereafter at Freedom Watch, Inc., which I also founded, I experienced many "successes" fighting dishonesty and outright corruption in government and the legal system. But to be candid, I never scored a knockout punch. One federal judge in particular, the Honorable Royce C. Lamberth, of the U.S. District Court for the District of Columbia, the tribunal located in what has become known as "the swamp," had the power, for instance, given the cases I put before him, to relegate Bill and Hillary Clinton—the Bonnie and Clyde of American politics—to multiple years, if not life, in prison, which is where they certainly belong. But even Lamberth, an appointee of President Ronald Reagan, shied away from holding them accountable, merely ordering up depositions of persons in and around them to expose their illegalities. At one point, before Lamberth was the criminal contempt of the Clintons, where they had hidden or destroyed millions of incriminating emails that exposed their criminal acts in a number of the more than forty scandals during their reign of terror in the White House during the 1990s. The judge held an evidentiary hearing on this caper, which lasted weeks. But in the end, years after I left Judicial Watch to run for the U.S. Senate in my home state of Florida, having apparently lost interest he dismissed the case and took an exit stage left.

To the contrary and by contrast, Lamberth who has lately, decades later, been on a virtual jihad against the peaceful protesters who entered the Capitol Building on January 6, 2021, most being literally let in if not escorted by the generally sympathetic Capitol Police, sentenced the so-called QAnon Shaman, Jacob Chansley, who was not violent but made the "mistake" of wearing a fur hat with horns and face paint, to forty-one months, that is three and one-half years, in federal prison. His apparent judicial establishment rationale, as discussed in greater detail in Chapter Five; to set an example for persons in the future who may rise up and challenge, even peacefully, the legitimacy of our establishment-run government, which of course he can thank for putting on the federal bench. It appears that this once principled jurist found Hillary's make-up and Bill's style of dress, who once infamously posed in a female gown for the ex-president's pimp Jeffrey Epstein, more to his liking![5],[6]

Judge Lamberth hailed from Texas and had no stomach for truly holding the Clintons accountable after his native son George W. Bush won the presidency in 2000. In retrospect, it would appear that he allowed me to conduct what, for him, must have been mostly a dog-and-pony show simply to weaken the political standing of the Clintons. But while they were down, they certainly were not out. In the many years that followed, Bill and Hillary continued their felonious ways, using the Clinton Foundation and other subterfuges as a virtual racketeering enterprise, selling access and favors to the highest bidders—and reaping in hundreds of millions of dirty dollars in cold cash—after President Barack Hussein Obama picked Hillary as his secretary of state. Lamberth had let the Clintons go free, and they sped away from his clutches in a court-sanctioned getaway car, making the original Bonnie and Clyde envious as they lay in their graves.

---

5. Dan Mangan, "Qanon Shaman Jacob Chansely Sentenced to 41 Months in Prison for Jan. 6 Capitol Riot Case," CNBC (November 17, 2021), https://www.cnbc.com/2021/11/17/qanon-shaman-jacob-chansley-sentencing-in-trump-capitol-riot-case-.html.

6. Jon Blistein, "Jeffrey Epstein Owned a Portrait of Bill Clinton in a Blue Dress," *Rolling Stone* (August 15, 2019), https://www.rollingstone.com/culture/culture-news/epstein-portrait-bill-clinton-blue-dress-872203/.

I am, of course, thankful for the little that this federal jurist at one time did. But unfortunately, Lamberth is simply the best of the worst on the federal bench, which, as our great Founding Father and third American president predicted, eventually would morph into a bench full of despots, particularly since, for some reason, it has become the mistaken norm to believe that they were given life tenure on the bench—there is no such provision in the Constitution—and are not accountable to the electorate. The Clintons are just one of tens of thousands of examples of how the judicial branch has failed miserably, in the last decades in particular, to protect the American people from the tyranny of the other two branches of government—the executive and legislative branches—and the tyranny within its own judicial branch.

I have regrettably come to the conclusion, after toiling in the bowels of our legal system for going on forty-five years, appearing thousands of times before cowardly and outright corrupt federal judges, that the nation cannot be restored to that shining city on a hill envisioned by former President Ronald Reagan, nor to the faithful city described in the Old Testament Book of Isaiah, through the present-day federal courts or other conventional and so-called establishment means. This view has been reinforced in the extreme as a result of the despicable and lawless conduct of many federal judges who have become tyrants—both Democrat and Republican appointed—especially during the lead-up and during the first year of the Biden-Harris administration, as I will discuss later in this work.

And thus, I've titled this book, my book, *It Takes a Counter-Revolution: Wake Up America!*, which is an updated edition of and sequel to my former book published last year *It Takes a Revolution: Forget the Scandal Industry!* as much bad has happened since then.

I am sure you will recognize that the title is a cynical play on a book, not coincidentally, written by Hillary Clinton called *It*

Takes a Village. Yes, Mrs. Clinton, it does take a village, but not in the sense that you wrote about, which promoted a collective leftist and socialist approach to life and our body politic. My book focuses on "Village People" who take it upon themselves to enforce their God-given right to live free of government tyranny, as our Founding Fathers eloquently expressed in the greatest document ever written short of the Bible, the Declaration of Independence. Federal judges in particular have failed to protect us and have been one of the principal problems, not the solution. Figuratively speaking, it is they who should be first to the guillotines, the subtitle of Chapter Five on the tyranny of the judicial branch.

Read on, fellow patriots, and learn how we need to turn off cable television and the other purveyors of self-serving deception and profit that milk what has become the scandal industry. Then, if you want to protect and preserve the vision and conception of our great and enlightened Founding Fathers, roll up your sleeves and join me in getting to work. "Live Free or Die!", the battle cry of our first American revolution, rings true again today! I suggest peaceful means to wage what now is a counter-revolution, with the total leftist takeover of our nation. But if peaceful means do not prove successful, We the People will face the prospect of going the route prophesized by our greatest of Founding Fathers, Thomas Jefferson.

To the barricades, dear fellow Americans, and we will, with great resolve, win the counter-revolution, without a shot being fired if we peacefully and, without further, potentially terminal delay, act forcefully. If we do not act forcefully now, the nation will be enslaved in an evolving gulag, which all races, religions, sexes, and ethnicities fighting for the crumbs that are fed to us by the socialist; communist; atheist; radical black; radical Muslim; radical Jewish left; radical feminist; radical gay, lesbian, transgender and transexual despots. These radicals, with contested and suspect

President Joe Biden and Vice President Kamala Harris, much less House Speaker Nancy Pelosi, rubber-stamping their demands as their "three stooges," have tied a virtual noose around all of our collective necks, with little to no effective, much less real and honest opposition from the Republican Party.

This Republican establishment, floating the contrived and highly doubtful offering of a Trumpian return to power, mainly spends its time and resources raising boatloads of cash by suggesting that The Donald will again run for the presidency in 2024—an unlikely proposition given that were he to actually declare at some point, rabid leftist Democrat prosecutors will have him and many in his family criminally indicted on "Trumped-up" tax fraud and other charges, tying him down to try to keep him and his family out of prison, before what is likely to be Trump-hating juries in New York City and the District of Columbia.

And, then there is the so-called January 6 Committee, comprised of rabid leftist congressional Democrats and establishment anti-Trump hating Republicans like Representatives Liz Cheney and Adam Kinzinger, who are bent on sending a criminal referral to the Biden-Harris Justice Department to also indict the Donald for alleged obstruction of Congress and treason over the alleged insurrection carried out by mostly peaceful protesters who entered the Capitol Building that fateful day to advocate for delaying certification of the 2020 presidential election before a true auditing of votes could be performed as well at the current state of affairs in our corrupt government in general. All of this is designed to tie down and prevent the 45th president from running for and returning to the power in 2024.[7]

Sending out scores of fundraising emails each day but doing little to nothing to stem the tide of the ever-growing leftist

---

7.   Stephen Collinson, "Trump and the January 6 Committee Are Now Locked in a Full-On Confrontation," CNN (December 22, 2021), https://www.cnn.com/2021/12/27/politics/donald-trump-january-6-committee/index.html.

dictatorship, other than pontificating on Fox News and on the internet to raise more cash to get themselves reelected, Republican politicians consultants are enriching themselves but leaving We the People hung out to dry with what has literally become a RINO racketeering enterprise to shake down and rip off good-intentioned conservatives, libertarians, people of faith and those who believe in the vision and creation of our Founding Fathers.

In short, while the Democratic Party has become the vehicle of the devil, the Republican Party, infested with charlatans, conmen, and snake-oil salesmen, and fraudsters has become a Ponzi scheme and enterprise that would make Bernie Madoff proud. Accomplishing little to nothing when Republicans controlled all three branches of government; they could not even balance the budget or abolish, much less reform, Obamacare. And, in the last months during the lead-up to the Afghanistan debacle, where Republican senators and congressmen knew from national security briefings on Capitol Hill the consequences of pulling out all of our troops of the country but did not sound a clarion call, instead cynically wanting the Biden-Harris regime to fail for the RINO'S own political purposes, this poor excuse of party is much worse than a corrupt bad joke, providing no real opposition to the Democrats and their leftist allies as they march "goose step" toward socialism, communism, atheism, and nearly every other godless and destructive ideology.

It is the time, as it was in 1776, to take matters into our own legal hands!

CHAPTER ONE

"THE SEEDS OF REVOLT!"

*"You seem to consider the judges as the ultimate arbiters of all consti-
tutional questions; a very dangerous doctrine indeed, and one which
would place us under the despotism of an oligarchy. Our judges are as
honest as other men, and not more so. They have, with others, the same
passions for party, for power, and the privilege of their corps.... Their
power is more dangerous as they are in office for life, and not responsible, as the other functionaries are, to elective control. The Constitution
has erected no such single tribunal, knowing that to whatever hands
confided, with the corruptions of time and party, its members would
become despots. It has more wisely made all the departments co-equal
and co-sovereign within themselves."*

—Thomas Jefferson, Letter to William C. Jarvis, 1820.[8]

Thomas Jefferson understood that the constitutionally created
three branches of government were intended to serve as a
check, however futile, to despotism. He thus anticipated that, over

---

8.   Thomas Jefferson, 1743–1826. *The Thomas Jefferson Papers and Biographies Collections
     in Hathi Digital Library* (New York: Round Table Press, 1903), https://babel.hathitrust.
     org/cgi/mb?a=listis;c=648623310; William C. Jarvis was an American diplomat, finan-
     cier, and philanthropist.

time, the nation would face another revolution, as the corruption in government would grow in the natural course of human events.

So it was that many have attributed this quote to Jefferson, namely that "when the governments fear the people, there is liberty. When the people fear the government there is tyranny. The strongest reason for the people to retain the right to keep and bear arms is, as a last resort, to protect themselves against tyranny in government."[9]

Jefferson added:

> "When all government, domestic and foreign, in little as in great things, shall be drawn to Washington as the center of all power, it will render powerless the checks provided of one government on another, and will become as venal and oppressive as the government from which we separated."[10]

And, just two years before the Constitution was enacted by Congress, he also foretold:

> "The tree of liberty must be refreshed from time to time with the blood of patriots and tyrants. It is its natural manure."[11]

> "A little rebellion now and then is a good thing and as necessary in the political world as storms in the physical."[12]

Jefferson's wisdom and prophecy have finally come home to roost and have more than metastasized into a stage-four terminal cancer in our body politic. The executive branch of government is controlled by a Deep State that illegally and coercively spies on the masses and serves its own nefarious and greedy interests over

9.   Ibid.
10. Thomas Jefferson, "Letter to C. Hammond, July 1821," *Founders Archives*, https://founders.archives.gov/documents/Jefferson/98-01-02-2260.
11. Thomas Jefferson, "Letter to W.S. Smith, November 13, 1787," (son-in-law of John Adams), *Monticello.org*, https://www.monticello.org/site/research-and-collections/tree-liberty-quotation.
12. Thomas Jefferson, "Letter to James Madison, January 30, 1787," *Monticello.org*, https://www.monticello.org/site/research-and-collections/little-rebellionquotation.

the needs of We the People. The legislative branch has become a coopted, dishonest, and destructive clown show—a bunch of duplicitous court jesters and conmen in the general sense. And, most importantly, the federal bench has become an out-of-control, partisan coterie of political hacks, furthering the desires of those who got them their perpetual tenure—not dissimilar to the yes men on the Court of King James during the time of King George III. As Jefferson said, "[their] power is more dangerous as they are in office for life, and not responsible, as other [government] functionaries are, to elective control." [13]

This book, and its predecessor, which I feel compelled to write as a clarion call to educate the public and to hopefully help arrest the otherwise certain demise of our free republic—particularly given the leftist takeover of the nation under Biden and Harris—is the progeny to my previous autobiography, *Whores: Why and How I Came to Fight the Establishment!* That book was written after my attempt to infiltrate and become a "Trojan horse" inside the legislative branch of government when I ran for the U.S. Senate in Florida in 2003–2004, following my ten years as the founder, chairman, and general counsel of Judicial Watch, Inc. My concept then was to take Judicial Watch inside the bowels of legislative power and to clean up the swamp of our nation's capital from within. But today, things are too far gone to even attempt this.

Since the publication of *Whores*, and even the first version of this work, published in October 2019 before the presidential election, intellectual and rank corruption in all three branches of government has reached more than a fever pitch and burst into the public's consciousness like an open shotgun wound. If the downward slide continues much longer, the chances for the survival of the republic will become far worse—fatally worse if the citizenry does not NOW exercise its God-given rights. In my opinion, in

---

13. Thomas Jefferson, "Letter to William C. Jarvis, September 28, 1820," *Founders Archives*, https://founders.archives.gov/documents/Jefferson/98-01-02-1540.

just the first year of what has become known as the Biden-Harris regime, the Judeo-Christian and capitalist fabric of the nation is now about 90 percent trashed. It's as if the republic is akin to a body on its back gasping for ethical and honest air, in a death spiral before it finally succumbs to extinction.

Indeed, on or about July 4, 1776, just days before signing the Declaration of Independence in my birthplace of Philadelphia, another great former president and Founding Father, John Adams, predicted that it would not matter how many times the people change its rulers or forms of government, and that, without ethics, morality, and religion, there would be no lasting liberty. The answer is no longer at the current corrupt ballot box—now is not the time to put more intellectually bereft, dishonest, and greedy clownish despots in charge of the nation's fate. Instead, the preservation of our freedoms and liberties must be pursued in other more direct, if not forceful, ways.

We have come to that critical point, 247 years after the colonies declared independence. Given current life expectancies, this is a short three lifetimes. The downhill slide is now at its rock bottom as our country has been taken over by radical leftists and other anti-American forces!

We were, at one time, a free people but are no longer so. Both the executive and legislative branches have broken away from our constitutional underpinnings and have violated any norm of the rule of law, which embodies ethics, morality, and the Judeo-Christian concepts represented in the Ten Commandments. They have greedily stuffed money from lobbyists and other special interests into their pockets like the high priests and money changers chronicled in the Bible, all the while acquiring tremendous federal power. The nation is, therefore, already again in a counter-revolutionary state.

This is eerily reminiscent of the opening paragraphs of our Declaration of Independence, where Jefferson and our Founding Fathers proclaimed to the world the justification for their actions in breaking away from the British monarchy and its despot of a king. They wrote:

> ...Governments are instituted among Men, deriving their just powers from the consent of the governed, — That whenever any Form of Government becomes destructive of these ends, it is the Right of the People to alter or abolish it, and to institute new Government, laying its foundation on such principles and organizing its powers in such form, as to them shall seem most likely to affect their Safety and Happiness.

And, with the current Chinese coronavirus pandemic continuing to engulf the nation and the world—a condition that is likely to continue for several years if not ever in one manner, shape, or form, and the exercise of tyrannical power by the executive branches in both federal and state governments—where the citizenry is ordered to relinquish their liberties with mandates ordered to wear useless if not harmful masks and force unproven and potentially harmful vaccines shoved down our throats—it is evident that there is, again, post July 4, 1776, a rising tide of despotism at hand, and this time even worse. Couple this with the people's calculated dependency on multitrillions of dollars of handouts in welfare, payroll protection, disaster relief, and other massive perks, and the power and hold of the government over our lives has reached critical mass. In short order, we have been subjected to such government control and dependency that, ironically, would make Communist Chairman Mao of China proud. We the People now live in the equivalent of a communist gulag and are effectively enslaved to the power of government. Government has become god, and the people its peons and servants, reversing and turning on its head the conception and creation of our Founding

Fathers of a republican form of government by and for the people under the Divine guidance of our Judeo-Christian Creator.

In this ever-increasing cesspool of corruption and massive if not near total government control, now with the pretext of COVID-19 and other phony emergency measures, again equaling a noose around our collective necks, as the founder of both Judicial Watch and now Freedom Watch, and in my private legal practice, I have tried for decades to peacefully and legally use the courts—federal and state—to serve as a check on the tyranny of the other two branches of government. Along the way, since I founded Judicial Watch, which I no longer head, the reasons for which are explained in *Whores*, I have scored many successes.

As just a few examples, I am the only lawyer who has ever had a court of law rule that a sitting president, in this case Bill Clinton, committed a crime. I exposed perhaps the biggest scandal in American history, Chinagate, where the Chicoms lined the pockets of Bill and Hillary Clinton with cold cash for under-the-table favors, such as transferring missile technology to Beijing through Clinton donors such as Bernard Schwartz, then the CEO of Loral Corporation, stopping Clinton corruption, at least at that time, in its tracks. I sued President George W. Bush and his vice president, Dick Cheney, over their secretive energy task force, a prelude to their ill-advised and failed war in Iraq—the case went all the way to the U.S. Supreme Court. I have enjoined President Barack Obama's National Security Agency from conducting mass surveillance without probable cause on the American people. I also shut down Obama's illegal executive amnesty for over five million illegal aliens. Then, most recently, as I will elaborate in the following chapters, along with other experiences, there were the successful criminal defenses of Cliven Bundy, that Nevada rancher, and his family, as well as Dr. Jerome Corsi, when both were subjected to politically motivated, vile, and oppressive government prosecutorial abuse by the Obama Justice Department and Special Counsel Robert Mueller, respectively. I can go on and on.

But with all of my successes, this is not enough. Those successes just scratched the surface, and the hard reality is that the federal judiciary, as Jefferson predicted and warned, has grown so compromised and corrupt over the years that it no longer serves as any check on the tyranny of the other two branches of government, which have been left to run wild to the low and dangerous point we find ourselves in today. As Ronald Reagan would have said had he now been alive, it is not the solution but the primary problem. The American people have been left virtually defenseless when it comes to settling matters peacefully and legally in the courts or for that matter anywhere else in society.

Ironically, it was another Founding Father, Alexander Hamilton—a foe of the Anti-Federalist Jefferson—who naively championed the creation of a federal judiciary. Hamilton wrote:

> Whoever attentively considers the different departments of power must perceive, that in a government in which they are separated from each other, the judiciary, from the nature of its functions, will always be the least dangerous to the political rights of the Constitution; because it will be least in capacity to annoy or injure them. The Executive not only dispenses the honors, but holds the sword of the community. The legislature not only commands the purse, but prescribes the rules by which the duties and rights of every citizen are to be regulated. The judiciary, on the contrary, has no influence over either the sword or the purse; no direction either of the strength or of the wealth of the society; and can take no active resolution whatever. It may truly be said to have neither FORCE nor WILL, but merely judgment; and it must ultimately depend upon the aid of the executive arm even for the efficacy of its judgments.[14]

---

14. *Federalist Papers*, Number 78, The Judiciary Department (New York: McLean's Edition, Wednesday, May 28, 1788), https://founders.archives.gov/documents/Hamilton/01-04-02-024.

Hamilton's clueless push for a federal judiciary to effectively rule over state judiciaries in many respects, where these federal judges would be, in principle, learned and honest people beyond all reproach, and thus deserve lifetime appointment, would later prove to be complete folly if not outright stupidity. He thus wrote:

> And it proves, in the last place, that as liberty can have nothing to fear from the judiciary alone, but would have everything to fear from its union with either of the other departments; former or latter, notwithstanding a nominal and apparent separation; that as, from the natural feebleness of the judiciary, it is in continual jeopardy of being overpowered, awed, or influenced by its co-ordinate branches; and that as nothing can contribute so much to its firmness and independence a permanency in office, this quality may therefore be justly regarded as an indispensable ingredient in its constitution, and, in a great measure, as the citadel of the public justice and the public security.
>
> ....
>
> If, then, the courts of justice are to be considered as the bulwarks of a limited Constitution against the legislative encroachments, this consideration will afford a strong argument for the permanent tenure of judicial offices, since nothing will contribute so much to that independent spirit in the judges which must be essential to the faithful performance of so arduous a duty.[15]

In this regard, naively, if not ignorantly, believing that we would get the proverbial "best and brightest" on the federal bench, Hamilton added:

> According to the plan of the convention, all judges who may be appointed by the United States are to hold their offices during good behavior...[16]

---

15. Ibid.
16. Ibid.

As later came true with regard to the creation of a central bank, now embodied in the Federal Reserve Board, which Jefferson also opposed as creating too much federal power, Hamilton and his Federalist cronies ultimately got their way. Article III of the Constitution, enacted in 1789, provides in Section 1:

> The Judicial Power of the United States shall be vested in one supreme Court, and in such inferior Courts as Congress may from time to time ordain and establish. The Judges, both of the supreme and inferior Courts, shall hold their Offices during good Behavior, and shall, at stated Times, receive for their Services, a Compensation, which shall not be diminished during their Continuance in Office.

Interestingly, the Constitution does not specifically state that federal judges will have lifetime tenure—only that they "shall hold their Offices during good Behavior."

Given that historically only eight federal judges among the tens of thousands who have been appointed and confirmed have been impeached, convicted, and, thus, removed from the bench for "bad behavior"—about one every thirty-one years since our founding—or for high crimes and misdemeanors, this section has been interpreted to bestow lifetime tenure on unaccountable federal judges, bringing into reality, if not a national nightmare, all that Jefferson feared. Contrary to Hamilton's prophecy, federal judges have been left in power as the "king's yes men and women" and, thus, have also become the unbridled and unhinged despots Jefferson wisely knew they inevitably would become.

But Hamilton was not alone in his naivety if not folly. Alexis de Tocqueville, the famous French political philosopher and analyst, marveled at the American invention of federal judges. Post French Revolution, in his 1835 historic work, *Democracy in America*, he proclaimed:

Governments in general have only two ways of overcoming the resistance of the people they govern: the physical force they find in themselves and the moral force they derive from decisions by the courts.

A government has no choice but to resort to war to enforce its laws on the brink of ruin. One of two things is likely to happen. If weak and moderate, it will employ force only as an ultimate remedy and wink at countless instances in which the law is partially flouted. Little by little the state will thereby lapse into anarchy.

If bold and powerful, it will resort to violence constantly and soon degenerate into pure military despotism. To the governed, action and inaction are equally catastrophic.

The paramount aim of justice is to substitute the idea of right for the idea of violence, to place intermediaries between the government and the use of physical force.

The presumptive power that people are generally willing to grant to interventions of the courts is surprising. So great is that power that it attaches to judicial forms even when drained of all substance; it gives body to the mere shadow of justice.

The moral force vested in the courts makes the recourse to physical force infinitely more rare than it would otherwise be, for in most cases moral force takes its place. And if, in the end, physical force is necessary, it is backed by moral force and therefore twice as powerful.

A federal government needs the support of justice even more than other types of government because it is by nature weaker, and resistance to it can be organized more easily. If constrained always to use violence as its first resort, such a government would be inadequate to its task.

Hence the Union, in order to compel citizens to obey, and to repel attacks upon its laws, had particular need of courts.[17]

Ironically, what the revered and venerable Alexis de Tocqueville was actually saying was simple. If the federal courts of the Union do not do their job—that is, protecting the citizenry from the tyranny of the other two branches of government and from the citizenry itself—then the last resort would tragically be more revolutions, both in the United States and in his native France, among other newly created democracies.

And that is precisely why, based on political hackery and other forms of dishonesty, which have regrettably come to pass again, as Jefferson predicted, we stand on the brink of another violent revolution. In my forty-five years of legal practice, I have only encountered a few federal judges who had the intellect and integrity, on only some convenient occasions, to do what is right and just, without regard to cronyism, political payback, and other latent forms of dishonesty and self-serving prevarication.

Why is it then that the high moral and ethical character of federal judges to faithfully enforce the laws of the land and to protect its populace have, as will be chronicled in this book, failed so miserably? Could this stem from the hard fact that federal judges are appointed and confirmed based on their establishment credentials and connections, and the concomitant hard fact that they are put up for appointment to the president based largely on political campaign contributions, that is "legalized bribes," and other forms of frequently corrupting influence greased by slimy special interest lobbying groups, large mega-law firms, corporations, labor unions, and others who want their "yes men" on the federal bench?

After digesting this book, you will be able to "judge" for yourselves. You will be convinced that the slippery, compromised,

---

17. Alexis de Tocqueville, *Democracy in America* (University of Chicago Press, 1835), https://press.uchicago.edu/ucp/books/book/chicago/D/bo3612682.html.

selfish creatures that currently and largely occupy space in the federal courts, paid for with your tax dollars, are not the best and the
brightest but generally among the most despicable and dishonest patrons of our broken if not collapsing democratic republic.
And to make matters worse, they are effectively ensconced for life,
almost as figuratively indestructible as cockroaches, who will be
the only surviving species left after a nuclear exchange between
superpowers, or they are potentially as detrimentally infectious as
national and worldwide pandemics such as now remains underway
with the Chinese COVID-19.

Under these increasingly dire circumstances, in this book, I
feel duty bound to propose concrete ways that the doomsday scenario of another violent revolution can hopefully be prevented.
But not before I prove to you how We the People have gotten
ourselves into the current state of potentially fatal affairs. The past
is a prologue, and if we are to survive as a nation, the sleaze and
corruption in government and, most particularly, on the federal
bench, our so-called protectors, must be exorcized, cauterized, and
not subject to repetition. Americans—that is, true patriots—must
put their collective foot down and remedy this now at the twelfth
hour of our demise, as the country faces many ongoing and growing crises that are likely to have, internally and externally, an explo-
sive and fatal effect.

CHAPTER TWO

"FORGET THE SCANDAL INDUSTRY!"

AND GET TO WORK!

"We're all born ignorant, but one must work hard to remain stupid."
—Benjamin Franklin[18]

When I founded Judicial Watch, Inc. in 1994, after seventeen years of experiencing judicial deceit, dishonesty, prejudice, and tyranny on the federal bench in particular, I honestly believed that I could turn the legal system against itself. Thus, the name "Judicial Watch," which was conceived originally to watch judges and to help ensure that they acted and ruled in an honest and nonpolitical way, based on the law and not their own predilections, biases, and prejudices.

In Judicial Watch's office in San Marino, California, which I opened some years later, I instituted an innovative "Judicial Monitoring Program," where I would send volunteers downtown to the U.S. District Court for the Central District of California, to

18. Benjamin Franklin *Quotations of Benjamin Franklin*, Applewood Books, 2003

"watch," report on, and later grade federal judges. As I wrote in *Whores*, there was one federal judge on this court, the less-than-Honorable William D. Keller, that crystalized my thinking about federal judges. As disclosed in the *Los Angeles Times*, Stephen Yagman, a civil rights attorney who had practiced before Keller, claimed this federal judge was an alcoholic, bigot, and anti-Semitic.[19] My own experience with Keller finally pushed me over the edge and provoked me to start Judicial Watch. In particular, I assigned volunteers to monitor and report on him, among others.

Keller, incredibly, was a Ronald Reagan appointee—proving that presidents generally do not even know who or what they are nominating for the federal bench, as recommendations are fed to them, usually as payback for political campaign contributions. In this regard, Keller's appointment was put forth by then-counselor to the president and later Attorney General Ed Meese.

Keller presided over the trial of my client, Frank Su, a Taiwanese bathroom accessory manufacturer, and his Jewish and gay importer and retailer in Southern California.[20] And during the course of the trial, which took place as Los Angeles was literally on fire during the Rodney King riots, Keller proceeded to make a number of prejudicial remarks, disparaging and mocking people of Chinese and Jewish origin, and gay persons. As for yours truly, I was branded by Keller as "Mr. Schmuckler"—another lawyer Keller claimed to have had problems with. Schmuck in Yiddish—I am of Jewish origin and also a Christian—means the foreskin of one's male private part.

When I asked Keller politely to remove himself from the case and the ongoing trial, he shot back that I would be tried at the end

---

19.   Henry Weinstein, "Attorney Sanctioned for Criticizing Judges: Courts: Panel Finds That Civil Rights Lawyer Stephen Yagman Tried to Force Jurist to Take Himself Off Cases. He Could Face Reprimand, Suspension or Other Discipline," *Los Angeles Times* (May 20, 1994), https://www.latimes.com/archives/la-xpm-1994-05-20-me-60126-story.html.

20.   Baldwin Hardware Corp. v. Franksu Enterprise Corp., 93-cv-1185 (C.D. Cal.), https://casetext.com/case/baldwin-hardware-corp-v-franksu-enterprise.

of the proceeding. He ultimately fined me $20,000 and banned me from his courtroom for life as punishment for my having raised his bigotry and stood up to his unethical and outrageous judicial misconduct. Sarcastically, I later thanked him publicly for the lifetime ban, as having a reason to never set foot in his courtroom again was not unwelcome!

Out of principle and because of the fine—I was not financially well off during this period—I took an appeal of his ruling. But appellate federal judges on the U.S. Court of Appeals for the Federal Circuit, which had jurisdiction to hear the appeal since the case was patent- and trademark-based, predictably circled their judicial wagons for their "soul brother" and refused to address Keller's misconduct and the sanctions order against me, affirming his bigoted actions.

It's a longer story than this—and you can read more about it in *Whores*—but my experience with Keller exhausted what was left of my "tolerance" for judicial bad behavior, and I later founded Judicial Watch. Had I not done so, I would have quit the legal profession. During this period, I would quip to friends that my calling would have been better, and more productive, had it led to flipping hamburgers as an employee of McDonald's.

Needless to say, Judicial Watch quickly proved to be a great success. Uncovering and addressing ethical misconduct and corruption on the federal bench and, later, in the other two branches of government was as easy as shooting goldfish in a bowl. That is how rampant it had become—even twenty-eight years and almost three decades ago when things had not degenerated to the point they have today! I quickly learned that Judicial Watch could not only be effective by watching federal and state judges but also by using the courts to watch and seek redress over the wrongs of the executive and legislative branches of government. And my early cases in this latter respect, by the grace of God, were randomly assigned to one of the few federal judges who, at least at that time, had some courage to enforce the law against the establishment elite, including the Bonnie and Clyde of American politics, Bill and Hillary Clinton, then the president and first lady of the United States. His name is Royce C. Lamberth, a federal judge who still, as a senior judge, sits on the U.S. District Court for the District of Columbia.

Lamberth's rulings in cases concerning a myriad of Clinton scandals—and there were over forty during their reign of corrupt terror in the White House—coupled with video depositions of such lowlifes as James Carville, Harold Ickes, and George Stephanopoulos, related only in part to my representation of the women who Slick Willy had allegedly abused and raped, catapulted me and my organization into the stratosphere of cable news and other media coverage.

During the mid- to late 1990s, cable news was just getting its wings. Fox News was simply a start-up, as was MSNBC and, to some extent, CNBC. With every new discovery of a Clinton scandal—from Chinagate to Filegate to IRSgate, you name it, no crime was beneath the Clintons—and my video depositions of persons in and around them in the White House and Commerce Department in particular, I literally would appear tens of times each week on all of these networks, sometimes all four networks on the same night. At the time, even CNN and MSNBC, not as far left and hate-filled toward conservatives and persons of faith as they are today, would report the news. In fact, Geraldo Rivera, who had a show on CNBC named *Rivera Live* and who was rabidly pro-Clinton (Geraldo had little concern about extramarital affairs, of which he was rumored to have had several), would showcase my video depositions but, at the same time, take shots at what he would call my anti-Clinton crusade. I did not mind the attacks, which were usually good-natured. All news is good news. Plus, nothing is harmful about being called ugly by a frog, and Geraldo, who the conservative movement used to call "Whoreraldo," boosted my standing.

But the cable network that benefitted most from my anticorruption work at Judicial Watch was the newly created Fox News. The network launched on October 7, 1996, headed by the conservative Roger Ailes, with the financial backing of media mogul Rupert Murdoch—about two years after I conceived of and founded Judicial Watch. We were natural partners of sorts during these early days. Combined with appearances by conservative media pundits such as Ann Coulter, Matt Drudge (who then had his own show until he was fired for showing a photo of an aborted baby on screen), and others, we collectively were responsible for building what is Fox News's big market today.[21] Interestingly, during these early years, I ran ads for Judicial Watch on Bill O'Reilly's show, *The O'Reilly Factor*, for only $250 for a thirty-second spot. That was how small Bill's viewership was in those seminal years. The same was also true for another prime-time show on Fox News, *Hannity & Colmes*. *The O'Reilly Factor* then had only about 150,000 to 200,000 viewers per night, and *Hannity & Colmes* even less.

In short, Larry Klayman and Judicial Watch were primarily responsible, among other prominent conservatives, for jump-starting the growing viewership and success of Fox News. Put simply, my work triggered and largely helped Fox News build a market niche that over the next twenty-five years would go through the roof.

However, my relationship with Fox News did not last. During one of Bill O'Reilly's broadcasts during the Clinton impeachment, he interviewed my client Dolly Kyle Browning while sitting on a

---

21. Michael Shane, "Bye-Bye, Matt Drudge; Fox Cuts Him Loose From Contract After His Apology," *New York Post* (November 19, 1999), https://nypost.com/1999/11/19/bye-bye-matt-drudge-fox-cuts-him-loose-from-contract-after-his-apology/.

director's chair on Miami Beach in the lead-up to the Super Bowl in Miami on January 31, 1999. O'Reilly, who appeared inebriated, damaged the reputation of Dolly, who had been Slick Willy's girl-friend for over twenty-one years. O'Reilly and Fox News's interest in her was that she was a potential material witness in the impeach-ment hearings on Capitol Hill.

O'Reilly began the interview by saying that he had just spoken with Dolly's ex-husband (she had had more than one) and was told that she abused her children. Hearing this, Dolly ran off the set in an emotional meltdown. To try to lessen the damage, to make the long story short, I called Roger Ailes and demanded that she be reinterviewed by O'Reilly in person to set the record straight, par-ticularly since she was a material witness at the time in the House's impeachment proceedings. Dolly told me that her ex-husband was a drug addict and a vindictive liar. Ailes promised to reinterview Dolly but never carried through.

As a result, in a letter she sent to Ailes without my knowing, an incensed Dolly threatened to smear Ailes and the network in her new upcoming tell-all book, a sequel to her previous one, a semi-fictional account of her long personal and tortured relationship with "Billy," as she called him, titled *Passions of the Heart.*

You can read about my travails with Fox News, which con-tinue to this day, in *Whores.* But for now, let it be reiterated that, although the network continues to pass itself off as conservative, under the new leadership of Rupert Murdoch's liberal son Lachlan Murdoch it has been increasingly left-leaning and during the 2020 presidential election it showed its slimy hand, infamously under-cutting President Trump with premature predictions of his defeat before all the ballots, however cooked by leftist Democrat polls, were counted.

Their reputation was further damaged with the disgusting and vile story of Ailes himself, a sexual predator just short of Jeffrey

Epstein, and the numerous other sexual harassment scandals involving Fox News. In this regard, I represented Laurie Luhn, the woman at Fox News, and Ailes' head booker, who was so destroyed that she attempted suicide on at least two occasions and continues to have severe bouts of suicidal depression daily.[22]

To make matters worse, when Ailes was forced out of Fox News because of his, and his other network hosts like O'Reilly's, previously covered-up sexual scandals, the Murdochs "cleverly" elevated Roger's personal assistant, Suzanne Scott, to take his place as CEO of the network. Scott was actually one of Ailes's primary facilitators and enablers, even procuring hotel rooms for him to work his sexual blackmail and extortion on Laurie Luhn by forcing her to give him oral sex among other sexual acts, lest she be fired and hung out to dry. This was depicted in the recent Showtime miniseries *Loudest Voice*, which featured Ailes's extreme sexual abuse of Laurie, even showing her throwing up after one of Ailes's many piggish outrages, with her head being thrust between his legs as if he were a real-life version of Jabba the Hutt.

Scott was made the operational head of Fox News after Ailes left. Cleverly placing a woman in charge seems to be a way to help cover other allegations and distract from the headlines, such as Gretchen Carlson's lawsuit against Ailes and Fox News. Scott was inserted as top management to obviously help ensure that the numerous female bodies who had been abused and sexually harassed by Ailes (whose sordid stories had been covered up with numerous settlements containing nondisclosure clauses) and others at the network stayed buried.

More about this later, when you will read about the lawsuit I filed for Laurie against Scott and Fox News and the compromised and intellectually dishonest female federal judge, a recent Trump appointee, who dismissed the case. I had been confident that this

---

22. Luhn v. Scott and Fox News, 1:19-cv-1180 (D.D.C), https://www.scribd.com/document/434035983/Luhn-v-Scott-Opinion.

ruling by this federal judge, showing favoritism for Scott and Fox News—who perhaps appear to her to be helpful to a then-president who gave her a seat on the bench—would be reversed by a leftist and anti-Fox News/Trump U.S. Court of Appeals for the District of Columbia Circuit. But regrettably, this very politicized court failed to mete out justice and simply circled the wagons to protect the establishment media, which not coincidentally covers their conduct on the federal bench.

Since the early years of Fox News during the Clinton era, Fox News and other unruly and rogue cable networks have been on a literal "jihad," making use of every new scandal emanating from both sides of the political spectrum. Virtually the same guests appear each night on their prime-time shows, expressing distaste for the other side and evoking a visceral response from the audience to boost viewership and increase advertising revenue.

But even Fox News, supposedly the cable network of conservatives, consistently holds back in order to appease advertisers. What the audience receives is only partial truth, so as not to offend. As just a few examples, Fox News would never allow its hosts to seriously discuss the mysterious death of Vince Foster during the Clinton years, even though most thought that the Clintons had played some role. Foster was Ms. Hillary's close confidante, a former partner and likely extramarital paramour of hers in the Rose Law Firm in Little Rock, and a deputy White House counsel. He thus intimately knew the details of the crimes the Clintons had committed, but he was reportedly in love with the first lady and was charged with covering her tracks on allegations of tax fraud, real estate and bank fraud in the Whitewater scandal, and her procurement of over 900 FBI files on the Clinton's adversaries, among myriad other ethical and legal "indiscretions."

Linda Tripp, who sadly died during the early stages of the coronavirus pandemic and later lockdown, although the cause was not reported, testified that Foster was the only person who she considered to have some moral decency in the Clinton White House.[23] Shortly before giving a speech at Harvard, days before his death, he stressed that honesty and ethics are everything, and when one loses a reputation for these virtues, all is lost. How did Linda know this? She had worked closely with him in the White House Counsel's Office. And how did I learn of this? Because I had deposed Linda on two occasions at Judicial Watch!

Thus, there was a motive for Foster to either take his own life or be killed that was wholly relevant to understanding much with regard to the Clinton scandals and attempted cover-up. But Fox News was hesitant to broadcast the full truth, for fear of appearing too anti-Clintonesque.

During the Obama years, despite the president's intense dislike of Israeli Prime Minister Benjamin Netanyahu and Israel proper, his many laudatory representations extolling the peaceful virtues of the "Holy Quran," his holding Ramadan feasts at the White House while forgoing National Day of Prayer celebrations favored by Christians and Jews, the ordered removal of references to Islamic or even radical Islamic terrorism in government manuals on fighting terrorism, Fox News discouraged its hosts, contributors, or guests from referring to Obama as even half Muslim descent and heritage. Not coincidentally, at the time, Saudi investors owned substantial shares in Newscorp, Fox News's parent company, largely owned by the Murdochs.[24] Avoiding this important conversation robbed viewers of their educated understanding of the reasons why Obama appeared pro-Muslim and, on many occasions, anti-Semitic and anti-Christian in his words and deeds.

---

23 . Alexander v. FBI, 96-cv-2123 (D.D.C.), https://www.govinfo.gov/app/details/US-COURTS-dcd-1_96-cv-02123/USCOURTS-dcd-1_96-cv-02123-0.

24 . David Folkenflik, "The Saudi Prince, the Mosque and Fox News," *NPR.com* (September 1, 2010), https://www.npr.org/templates/story/story.php?storyId=129584557.

In addition, during the Obama years, hosts, contributors, and guests were also forbidden to discuss what later forensic analysis by one of my clients, Sheriff Joe Arpaio, and his Cold Case Posse uncovered was the president's fraudulent Hawaiian birth certificate, leading to speculation that he was born outside of the United States and that he was not a natural-born citizen eligible to be president. But Arpaio and his Cold Case Posse never speculated on where Obama was born; just that the birth certificate was doctored. One of my other clients, Dr. Jerome Corsi, wrote a *New York Times* bestselling book, *Where's the Birth Certificate?* making similar verifiable claims, but he too was never allowed to speak about the birth certificate on Fox News. Obviously, Obama's birthplace was relevant! If he was not a natural-born citizen, he would have pulled off perhaps the biggest fraud in American history.

Now, during this age of the coronavirus, a.k.a. COVID-19, pandemic, Fox News, going lock-step with its sister leftist cable news networks, early on obediently dismissed out of hand the likelihood that this deadly disease was manufactured in a laboratory in Wuhan, China (but has now had to backtrack with proof that it was)—one that is known to also carry out bioweapon experiments and research. On a related note, I have instituted suit as a class action in Texas and Jerusalem, Israel, with Jewish legal colleagues for the trillions of dollars of damage the Communist Chinese have caused as a result of the intentional or accidental release of this bioweapon.[25] I have two prominent experts who will testify to it being a bioweapon: Professor Francis Boyle, a bioweapons expert at the University of Illinois, and Dr. Judy Mikovits, who has a PhD in biochemistry and is steeped in retro-virology. She worked with Dr. Anthony Fauci at the nation's premier virology lab at Fort Detrick, Maryland. Fort Detrick is the hub of the U.S. Army Medical Research and Material Command, the Army Medical Research

25. Buzz Photo et. al v. People's Republic of China, 3:20-cv-656 (N.D. Tx.), https://law.justia.com/cases/federal/district-courts/texas/txndce/3:2020cv00656/329969/38/.

Institute of Infectious Diseases, and the National Cancer Institute. Thus, Dr. Mikovits has firsthand knowledge that this military facility, which does research on bioweapons, actually exchanged samples of the virus with its "sister lab" in Wuhan. The reason? Research on the precursor to COVID-19, which emanates from the deadly SARS virus, could not ethically and legally be done in the United States.

It has been reported and recently confirmed that during the Obama administration, Fauci arranged for a multimillion-dollar U.S. grant for the Chinese lab at Wuhan, suggesting that it was to further this illicit research. Thus, our own Deep State government likely has, along with its Communist Chinese counterparts, sowed the seeds of the COVID-19 worldwide pandemic, much like this same lab at Fort Detrick, Maryland, did with the anthrax that escaped after September 11, 2001, killing eight postal workers at the main Brentwood Post Office that serves Washington, D.C., whose families later became my clients in wrongful death suits.[26]

Importantly, about 30 percent of the putative plaintiffs who have signed up for this class-action are patriotic Chinese and Asian Americans, as it is not the good Chinese and Asian people that are at issue.

I also have filed a criminal complaint before the International Criminal Court in The Hague, Netherlands, to hold the Communist Chinese accountable. In response, the Communist Chinese press publicly attacked me and Freedom Watch through

---

26. Glen Owen, "REVEALED: U.S. Government Gave $3.7 Million Grant to Wuhan Lab at Center of Coronavirus Leak Scrutiny That Was Performing Experiments on Bats from the Caves Where the Disease Is Believed to Have Originated," *Daily Mail* (April 12, 2020), https://www.dailymail.co.uk/news/article-8211291/U-S-government-gave-3-7million-grant-Wuhan-lab-experimented-coronavirus-source-bats.html; Jack Dolan and Dave Altimari, "Anthrax, Other Pathogens Lost at Fort Detrick in 90's," *Baltimore Sun* (January 21, 2002), https://www.baltimoresun.com/news/bs-xpm-2002-01-21-0201210015-story.html; Tim Wyatt, "Research Into Deadly Viruses and Biological Weapons at US Army Lab Shut Down Over Fears They Could Escape," *Independent* (August 6, 2019), https://www.independent.co.uk/news/world/americas/virus-biological-us-army-weapons-fort-detrick-leak-ebola-anthrax-smallpox-ricin-a9042641.html.

its national propaganda media, notwithstanding their ongoing attempts to dishonestly evade service of process of our complaint. Obviously, they see and fear the merit and strength of our legal actions. But Fox News has yet to report anything about our cases, which leads me to believe the network will not report any news associated with me or my clients. For the CEO Lachlan Murdoch and his obedient hosts on the network, it's no longer even a semblance of "fair and balanced"; instead, it's more akin to what the clownish former Senator Al Franken once correctly termed "unfair and imbalanced." But the sad part is that the viewers are not getting the truth, all for the sake of political correctness and vindictive retaliation against me.

But to the contrary, Fox News was the first to showcase death charts on the left-hand television screen, showing Americans and infected persons around the world dying on a second-by-second basis. This reminded me of the billboards on highways alarmingly showing the national debt increasing in real time. And the other left-leaning cable networks, so as not to be "left" totally behind financially and otherwise, quickly followed suit, keeping the citizenry glued to their television sets waiting for the world to end. And, now with the Delta and Omicron variants, all of the cable news networks are again sowing panic to boost ratings with worried viewers, as their viewership fell in 2021 after Biden and Harris took office and the newsworthy and controversial Trump was largely gone from the public's consciousness.[27]

Two other relatively small cable networks also followed suit: Newsmax and One America Network. Newsmax, founded and run by Christopher Ruddy, tries to pass itself off as conservative but, in fact, is just a façade for Ruddy's marketing. The opportunist and unprincipled Ruddy even contributed one million dollars

---

27.   Joseph Choi, "News Networks See Major Viewership Drop in 2021," *The Hill* (December 27, 2021), https://thehill.com/homenews/media/587401-news-networks-see-major-viewership-drop-in-2021.

to the Clinton Foundation in years past when it appeared Ms. Hillary might be elected president and could "return the favor."[28] Ruddy, who is a member of Mar-a-Lago, at other great expense, also tries to trade off of his alleged close relationship with President Trump, a claim that is more than suspect. At one time, I had a blog on Newsmax's website called "Klayman's Court," a play on the inscription of "Coach K's Court" proudly inscribed on the basketball floor of the Cameron Indoor Stadium at my alma mater, Duke University. Ruddy and his pliant staff would censor my writings when they appeared too conservative, and I later decided not to waste my time and deal with them further. As for Newsmax's television transmission, the viewership is small—much like the audience of One America Network, although the latter does try to be a conservative voice and its owners, the Harding family, are sincere in their conservative beliefs and advocacy. They are good people, while Ruddy and his minions at Newsmax are not, with few exceptions such as host Grant Stinchfield. Most of its truly conservative hosts, such as Miranda Khan and Wayne Allen Root, have left the network, some after having sued it for sexual discrimination, as is the case with Khan.

Sure enough, during and as a result of the coronavirus pandemic, the cable networks and other media are having a record year in terms of revenues and profits as the rest of the country suffers.

This also helps explain Fox News's push by the Sunday anchors, who were, that is until their ratings dropped precipitously after the 2020 elections, on an anti-Trump campaign to help remove the president from office at the ballot box. Couple this with the anti-Trump dialogue of former leftist Sunday anchor Chris Wallace

---

28. Erik Wemple, "Newsmax Boss Chris Ruddy Explains Why He Gave to the Clinton Foundation," *Washington Post* (February 23, 2015), https://www.washingtonpost.com/blogs/erik-wemple/wp/2015/02/23/newsmax-boss-chris-ruddy-explains-why-he-gave-to-the-clinton-foundation/.

(who eventually defected to CNN), Judge Andrew Napolitano, Juan Williams, and the not-too-subtle jabs by newsman Bret Baier, and you had a network talking out of both sides of its mouth, trying to serve up anti-Trump leftist rhetoric with its news anchors and raking in the viewers and dollars on its nightly prime-time shows with the right-wing likes of Sean Hannity, Laura Ingraham, and Tucker Carlson. But for the hard fact and cold cash these hosts bring to the network, Lachlan Murdoch would have them relegated to the "Siberia Room" of Fox News. If the money stops flowing, they ultimately will be let go, just as a few years ago with Trish Regan, a very conservative host on Fox Business, Fox News's sister network. Trish's offense? She accused Democrats of exploiting and profiting from the coronavirus pandemic.

And as for Hannity in particular, with the undying gratitude of his guests, virtually the same do-nothing ones each night, who fawn over and kiss his derriere for the chance to also sell their wares on prime time, this hack journalist with not even a junior college diploma but a good but canned delivery, serves up false hope to his couch potato fans, proclaiming "major breaking news" each evening during his rote, canned, and monotonous monologues lasting up to twenty minutes, that justice for the criminals who cooked up and furthered the Russian and Ukrainian collision/impeachment is just around the corner. He frequently ends his monologues trashing leftists, however deservingly, with the now all-too-familiar refrain that they even accuse conservatives of "throwing Granny over the cliff." Memorized and canned rote commentary but good for ratings and advertising dollars. Hannity avoids telling the hard truth to the American people for fear that they won't tune in to hear that our justice system is more than damaged and misguided. Instead it is nonexistent!

Interestingly, Hannity, who plays the role of a super-righteous conservative, reportedly profited from tens of millions of dollars of federal government subsidies to purchase low-income housing units in and around Atlanta. He then proceeded to evict a large number of low-income tenants and, in particular, blacks, who had difficulty paying his rents. So much for the free enterprise independence from government largesse and handouts that Hannity promotes to the conservative community each evening.[29]

And, Hannity's well-cultivated persona of being a good Christian family man was dashed when it was disclosed that he had been secretly divorced for a year and has had an "understanding" with his wife dating back five years, while attempting to secretly date another Fox News host Ainsley Earhardt of the morning show *Fox & Friends*, which she unconvincingly denies.[30]

Hannity shies away from putting the "real deal" on the air, such as my brave clients, freedom fighters such as Sheriff Joe Arpaio, Chief Justice Roy Moore, Cliven and Ryan Bundy, Laura Loomer, Dr. Jerome Corsi, and many more when they become too "hot to handle." Notwithstanding Hannity hypocritically playing it safe with the advertisers that effectively pay his salary, my courageous

29. Aaron C. Davis and Shawn Boburg, "Sean Hannity's Properties In Low-Income Areas Take an Aggressive Approach to Rent Collection," *Chicago Tribune* and *Washington Post* (May 11, 2018), https://www.chicagotribune.com/business/ct-biz-sean-hann-ity-rental-properties-eviction-20180511-story.html; "Sean Hannity Bought $90M in Properties Using Government Assistance," *Atlanta Black Star* (April 25, 2018), https://atlantablackstar.com/2018/04/25/sean-hannity-bought-90m-properties-us-ing-government-assistance-report-reveals/; Matt Pierce and Stephen Battaglio, "Fox News Host Sean Hannity Real Estate Holdings Draw Scrutiny," *Los Angeles Times* (April 23, 2018), https://www.latimes.com/nation/la-fi-ct-hannity-real-estate-20180423-story.html.

30. Cheyenne Roundtree, "EXCLUSIVE: Fox News Anchor Sean Hannity 'Has Been Divorced from His Wife for Years and Separated for Nearly Five' As Friend Reveals Workaholic TV Host 'Couldn't Slow It Down and It Broke His Marriage,'" *Daily Mail* (June 3, 2020). https://www.dailymail.co.uk/news/article-8384795/Fox-News-an-chor-Sean-Hannity-divorced-wife-years.html; Karen Ruiz and Cheyenne Roundtree, "Fox News Anchor Sean Hannity Has Been 'Dating Ainsley Earhardt for Months' After It Was Revealed He and Wife Jill Quietly Separated Five Years Ago," *Daily Mail* (June 12, 2020), https://www.dailymail.co.uk/news/article-8412193/Sean-Hanni-ty-Ainsley-Earhardt-dating-quite-time.html; Charlotte Triggs, Adam Carlson, Clau-dia Harmata, "Fox News' Sean Hannity & Ainsley Earhardt Have Been Dating 'Very Secretively for Years': Source," *People* (June 11, 2020), https://celebrityinsider.org/sean-hannity-has-been-secretly-dating-this-fox-news-host-for-years-claim-multiple-insiders-405422/.

clients are obviously too hot for him to handle, under the watchful eye of Fox News's CEO Lachlan Murdoch. These clients and many others in my fold have actually done something to try to right our sinking ship of state, as opposed to the likes of the ever-smiling and mostly unaccomplished Hannity guests such as Sara Carter, a nice lady with a photogenic smile, and a more showcased cleavage, but really very limited in terms of real achievement or even intellect. I would also put do little to nothing blowhards like Congressman Jim "Rolled Up Sleeves" Jordan, Senators Tom "Giraffe Neck" Cotton and Lindsey "Closet" Graham, former congressman Jason Chaffetz, Greg Jarrett, Dan Bongino, and Tom Fitton in this category, the latter offering up only new and never-ending documents obtained through the Freedom of Information Act but not hard-hitting legal actions to seek justice and return the rule of law to the republic.

It is no wonder that Roger Ailes once told me during one of my early visits to his office when we were on good terms, and as I first revealed in *Whores*, that he would televise two dogs having sex if it would boost ratings. Roger's legacy lives on past his death. He is laughing in his grave.

And this, fellow patriots, is why you need to forget the scandal industry. Get your news each day but "basta," Italian-style. While enriching themselves through cynical reports and empty promises, the major cable news networks used the coronavirus pandemic to scare viewers with death charts in real time. They play on the emotions of the viewers, discouraging anyone who can see through it and who has a real desire to right the wrongs in our nation rather than just be entertained!

So, to those of you who are addicted to cable news, get up off the couch; put down the popcorn, cheese, and crackers; stow away your diet soda, beer, wine, or martini and perhaps even marijuana; turn off cable television and their comrades; and get to work with real action. One way to not be a do-nothing summer soldier or a sunshine patriot, in the words of Thomas Paine, is to join Freedom Watch's Justice League or take up some other bona fide cause. You are the superheroes, not the two-faced, dishonest, and greedy scandal industry snake-oil salespersons comprised of all political persuasions who make a handsome living at your expense!

CHAPTER THREE

EXECUTIVE BRANCH TYRANNY!

A DEEP STATE AND ROGUE BUREAUCRACY MORE POWERFUL THAN THE PRESIDENT!

"When you reach the end of your rope, tie a knot in it and hang on."
—Thomas Jefferson[31]

What is the Deep State? It's a term that is bandied about without definition. But I have fought against it for the majority of my adult life, particularly at Judicial Watch and now Freedom Watch. Regrettably, I understand all too well who, what, and how sinister it is! And it grows "deeper" and more dangerous minute by minute, hour by hour, month by month, year by year, and decade by decade! It is not exclusively Democrat or Republican but instead largely unto its own nefarious self!

In essence, the Deep State is comprised of those in the executive branch and in other congressionally mandated agencies who

---

31. Thomas Jefferson. *Quotations of Thomas Jefferson* (Applewood Books: Carlisle, Massachusetts, 2004), https://www.applewoodbooks.com/Quotations-of-Thomas-Jefferson-P1967.aspx.

have their own generally leftist, rightest, or even fascist authoritarian dictatorial agendas. They do not follow or think they owe allegiance even to the president of the United States, specifically in the executive branch departments such as the U.S. Department of Justice (DOJ), the Federal Bureau of Investigation (FBI), the Central Intelligence Agency (CIA), the National Security Agency (NSA), the Defense Intelligence Agency (DIA), the U.S. Department of Defense, and all other such agencies.

Those who are part of the Deep State are effectively employed for life. It is harder to remove government functionaries, including politically appointed ones, from their jobs than it is to remove a cancerous growth in one's anal canal, to use an apt analogy under the dire circumstances in which we now find ourselves. Government employment laws and the reality of the swamp in Washington, D.C., mean that the worst that can generally happen to an individual caught cheating, lying, or stealing—or, for that matter, committing a traitorous act—is that he or she is put out to pasture in another government office; it is virtually impossible to fire him or her. And if the offender is a political appointee, he or she has ways to retaliate, which, in turn, dissuades supervisors from disciplining the person.

Often miscreant federal functionaries and political appointees are given raises by their supervisors as an incentive to keep their mouths shut about what they know. So, there is no real consequence to committing illegal or unethical acts, particularly since, again, that person frequently has acquired lots of dirt, accumulated over time, on his or her supervisors or the politically appointed head of the department or agency. Once someone becomes a member of the government bureaucracy, in one manner, shape, or form, that person is there for life, much like our federal judges—practically as indestructible as cockroaches. Indeed, the two have much in common, as they collectively form a renegade shadow government more powerful than the president of the United States and certainly not loyal to We the People and our constitutional government. They are generally loyal only to themselves and those who grease their existence!

So it was, using a recent example, that when Obama's politically appointed intelligence czars John Brennan and James Clapper were, as a matter of course, removed from office after the election of Donald J. Trump to the presidency in 2016, they left behind a Deep State loyal not just to Obama and these former spook masters—minions as I will call them—to illegally carry out their own frequently nefarious agendas. How else, other than Brennan's and Clapper's minions intercepting the president's communications with foreign leaders, made on so-called secure White House lines, such as occurred with the president of Ukraine, would these communications come to be intercepted and then leaked to smear Trump and trigger the second leftist witch hunt? The intercepted and leaked presidential communications concerned Joe Biden's and his son Hunter's lucrative quid pro quo shakedown in that country, which led to Hunter's shady and allegedly criminal enrichment by the Ukrainian company Burisma.

I came to know a lot about the illegal mass surveillance of the intel departments and federal law enforcement agencies. This was the result of my filing complaints against the Obama intelligence agencies, most particularly the NSA and CIA, after Edward Snowden revealed their illegal mass surveillance on millions of American citizens. In what may be the biggest legal victory of my career, I obtained two preliminary injunctions against them in 2014 and 2015 enjoining their mass surveillance, in violation of the Fourth Amendment prohibition against unreasonable searches and seizures.[32] This unconstitutional mass surveil-

---

32. *Klayman v. Obama et. al,* 13-cv-851 (D.D.C.); *Klayman v. Obama et. al,* 13-cv-881 (D.D.C.),   https://www.cadc.uscourts.gov/internet/opinions.nsf/ED64DC482F-286F1785257EAF004F71E8/$file/14-5004-1570210.pdf.

lance was also trained on U.S. Supreme Court justices, hundreds of federal judges, prominent businessmen such as The Donald, and, yes, activists such as yours truly. And that explains how I was able to predict from the get-go, with near absolute certainty, that they would use their spying powers to try to take down the newly elected forty-fifth president of the United States.

It was not just Trump's antiestablishment campaign and his threats to drain the swamp that led me to predict the Deep State would rear its ugly head. I also thought his perceived desire to be friendly with Putin and Russia could provoke illegal actions against the forty-fifth president.

In this vein, many prominent investigators, such as now deceased New Orleans District Attorney James Garrison, have concluded, after an investigation challenging the likely manufactured findings of the Warren Commission, that President John F. Kennedy was assassinated by the CIA over his widely known desire not to get involved in a major war in Vietnam and his failure to remove Fidel Castro and, thus, to overthrow the Communist Cuban government as a result of the failed Bay of Pigs invasion. There, Kennedy left anti-Castro and exiled Cubans from Miami to die on the beaches of this once-treasured island. Later, Kennedy's peace deal with Soviet Premier Nikita Khrushchev was not, contrary to the Kennedy administration's claims, totally successful in ending the Cuban Missile Crisis. In exchange for removing nuclear-tipped missiles from Cuba, Kennedy had agreed to remove our nuclear missiles from Turkey as well as to never attempt an assassination of Fidel Castro and his clan, leaving Communism in place—perhaps not a "bestseller" with the hardliners at the CIA.

In an article in the *New York Times* following the release of thousands of documents by The National Archives during the Trump administration about the Kennedy assassination, the Garrison investigation was discussed:

Over the years, the Warren Commission findings remained in doubt in some circles. In 1988, David W. Belin, a lawyer who had advised the commission, wrote: "Yet 25 years ago after the event, A majority of the American public does not believe the truth. Rather, polls have shown that most Americans believe President Kennedy was assassinated as an outgrowth of a conspiracy."[33]

The article further opined:

In 1991, the conspiracy reignited in the form of a major Hollywood movie.... The Oliver Stone movie "J.F.K." ... reimagined...the extensive investigation by Garrison, the New Orleans district attorney. As the Times wrote in Garrison's 1992 obituary: "Announcing that he had 'solved the assassination,' Mr. Garrison accused Anti-Communist and anti-Castro extremists in the Central Intelligence Agency of plotting the President's death to thwart an easing of tension With the Soviet Union and Cuba, and to prevent a retreat from Vietnam."[34]

In short, it appeared to me that the Deep State intel agencies could have similar "feelings" about Trump, whom they perceived was soft on Vladimir Putin and Russia. Later, at the early stage of the Russian witch hunt, Trump held a press conference with Vladimir in Moscow, and questioned so-called intelligence agency conclusions that Russia had interfered in the 2016 presidential election. He also said he believed the Russian president's denials. These aggravating circumstances, given that the Deep State remained highly partisan in favor of the Obamas and the Clintons—with the likes of the minions of CIA Director John Brennan and DNI James Clapper left in place—helps explain their later attempts to remove Trump from office.

---

33. Lori Moore, "The J.F.K. Files: Decades of Doubts and Conspiracy Theories," *New York Times* (October 25, 2017), https://www.nytimes.com/2017/10/25/us/jfk-assas-sination-files-questions.html.
34. Ibid.

Predictably, the Deep State did strike with a vengeance against Trump, even if the blows were as fatal as those President Kennedy suffered, as manifested in the Fusion GPS and related Steele dossier scandals. These were used by the FBI and its mother, the Department of Justice, to issue phony and fraudulent warrants, impose wiretaps at Trump Tower and elsewhere, and illegally gather alleged dirt to politically destroy Trump, his associates, family, and close friends. This attempted coup was carried further by another Deep State establishment operative, Special Counsel Robert Mueller—a former FBI director no less—in his Russian collusion witch hunt, after—you guessed it—the president's handpicked attorney general, one Jefferson Beauregard Sessions and Sessions' handpicked "bitch," Deputy Attorney General Rod Rosenstein, previously an Obama-appointed United States Attorney for the District of Maryland, named former FBI Director Mueller to investigate after Sessions recused himself from the Russian collusion investigation.

And why did Sessions recuse himself? Likely because, as part of Trump's presidential campaign and later transition team, Sessions was also wiretapped, and he likely knew or had reason to know that potentially illegally obtained dirt on him would be used to smear him. Couple that with Sessions' unnecessary and stupid lying, under oath, to Congress during his confirmation hearing to be attorney general, namely that he had not met with the Russian ambassador during the presidential campaign and discussed a possible Trump presidency, and this cowardly excuse for our then-chief law enforcement officer exited stage left in rapid order. It does not take a rocket scientist to figure out that Sessions did not want to take further heat in the proverbial kitchen of the Democrat leftists in Congress, who had caught him lying under oath, and he did not want to also risk retaliation by the Deep State embedded in the FBI, and the intel departments and agencies, who metaphorically knew the size of his private part.

Indeed, I had spoken with Sessions by phone—I had my process server get his cell number—shortly after he was confirmed as attorney general and advised him that I had a whistleblower client who claimed to have evidence, computer hard drives with over 600,000,000 pages of information, much of it classified, showing that the intel agencies and the FBI were illegally surveilling the populace, as well as influencing election rolls to have their candidates such as Obama, those loyal to their cause, elected. I added that this whistleblower had data showing that even President Trump had been illegally surveilled when he was a businessman. Putting two and two together, I told Sessions that I believed that Trump and all who had been and were still associated with him were illegally spied on and wiretapped in the days leading up to and after the president's election.

The attorney general seemed concerned and said he would assign Rod Rosenstein, once he was confirmed as deputy attorney general, to be in touch with me, but that since he had recused himself from anything involving Russia and the Trump presidential campaign or transition, he would not be able to play a part. Needless to say, despite my repeated efforts to have Sessions make good on his commitment, I never heard from Rosenstein or anyone else at DOJ. This later squared with Sessions also taking an exit stage left when I asked him during the same telephone conversation to simply review what I argued to him was a political prosecution under the Obama DOJ of my Nevada ranching client Cliven Bundy, his sons, and peaceful protesters after their successful standoff against hostile federal agents at Bunkerville. Again, he promised that he would but later did nothing, despite my repeated polite requests. More on this later.

The intelligence capabilities of the Deep State, embodied in the NSA, CIA, DNI, and FBI, were also likely used to harm President Trump with regard to the ongoing coronavirus, a.k.a.

COVID-19, pandemic, which has severely damaged the people of the United States and the world. With their mass surveillance and spying capabilities, which they have freely trained on the American people as a whole, on Trump, and even on my clients and me, can anyone with an IQ over fifty believe that they did not know early on of the virus's release from what many experts believe was a laboratory in Wuhan, China, that has worked on biological weapons and is the only such lab in this communist country?

This helps explain why the chairman of the Senate Intelligence Committee, Senator Richard Burr, a Republican from North Carolina, and his Democrat colleague on the committee, Senator Diane Feinstein from California, previously the chairman herself, sold—that is, dumped—millions of dollars in stock, reaping huge profits shortly before the nation and the world fully understood the magnitude of the pandemic, which harmed the health of American people and, at last count, killed hundreds of thousands of people in this country alone, sending the American and world economy into a tailspin, with the U.S. stock market losing over 30 percent of its value and counting.[35] It is likely that they got early wind of the virus outbreak in Communist China by these intel agencies, while President Trump and the White House were left in the dark. And, even if Trump was informed, he was so preoccupied with the ongoing impeachment proceedings, that it caused him and his administration to take their eyes off the ball, much as occurred with Bill Clinton and Osama bin Laden when Slick Willy was being impeached, resulting in our nation's having been caught with its pants down on September 11, 2001, and I do not mean this just metaphorically when it comes to Clinton.

Thus, by most likely withholding early intelligence from Trump, the Deep State likely tried to set him up for defeat in the

---

35. Staff, "Burr, Other Senators Dumped Stocks Before Coronavirus Market Crash," *Associated Press* (March 19, 2020), https://www.nbcdfw.com/news/politics/senator-sold-off-stocks-before-market-losses-from-virus-began/2334971/.

2020 presidential election, having him take the blame for not acting quick enough to combat COVID-19. Indeed, this would later cost The Donald dearly, notwithstanding the election irregularities if not outright fraud that occurred during the November 2020 presidential elections resulting in his alleged defeat.

If this was not enough, as previously discussed, in April, 2021, it was leaked that both the Obama and Trump administrations had sent a total of 3.7 million USD to the Wuhan laboratory, which yours truly and many experts believe also performed bioweapon research for the Communist Chinese government, as a grant from the National Institutes of Health—outrageously all at U.S. taxpayer expense. Again, Trump had likely taken his eye off the ball, with $700,000 of this grant, first approved under Obama, going to the Wuhan lab during his administration. Ask yourself this question as well: Why should We the People be subsidizing what could be our own death warrant, particularly since Communist China is even more solvent than the good old USA?

And again, evidence has since emerged that it may even be that our own military virus research laboratory at Fort Detrick, Maryland, gave the Communist Chinese the seeds of COVID-19, along with Obama's grant money for research, which they then engineered into a bioweapon that is lighter than air so that it can spread rapidly and, having been injected with HIV, is highly deadly. Expert Judy Mikovits, having worked with Dr. Anthony Fauci of the National Institutes of Health, has come forward to blow the whistle on both the "bad doctor" and our own government Deep State's complicity in the pandemic, in her bestselling book *Plague of Corruption*, co-authored with Kent Heckenlively.

Put simply, there are many ways that the Deep State can pursue its agenda as a shadow second government, not accountable to anything or anyone other than itself, and in particular, not accountable to We the People.

As a further example, did the Deep State in the intel agencies also set up President George W. Bush by giving him phony intelligence after September 11, 2001, that Iraq's Saddam Hussein possessed weapons of mass destruction? Was this payback for Daddy Bush, former President George Herbert Walker Bush, not finishing the job in the prior Persian Gulf War by taking Saddam and his regime out then? Did the Deep State see President George W. Bush and his hawkish veep, Dick Cheney, as rabid stooges who would take their phony intelligence hook, line, and sinker and then do what W's father did not have the guts to do? The rest is sordid and tragic history, as the ill-conceived Iraq War resulted in the needless deaths of thousands of American servicemen, and tens of thousands maimed, and for what? Today, Iraq has become greater Iran, an even more fanatical and evil Islamic foe that exports terrorism throughout the Middle East and the world. And today, as a result of post-traumatic stress disorders (PTSD) and other severe emotional scars left by this needless and stupid war, about twenty servicemen who served in Iraq and, later, in Afghanistan, in another foolish and never-ending war, commit suicide each day![36]

But is there a way to remove or even cut the Deep State down to size and bring it to justice? As I will discuss in depth in Chapter Five, one federal judge in particular, Richard J. Leon, had the power and means to at least rein in the Deep State with regard to its criminal illegal surveillance and traitorous actions during the Obama administration. After the judge initially had the courage to preliminarily enjoin Obama's NSA and CIA from what he termed "almost Orwellian" spying on the American people in two cases that I brought after the revelations of whistleblower Edward Snowden, Leon got cold feet and took an exit stage left from allowing my cases to go forward into even the discovery phase.

---

36.   Leon Shane III and Patricia Kime, "New VA Study Finds 20 Veterans Commit Suicide Each Day," *Military Times* (July 7, 2016), https://www.militarytimes.com/veterans/2016/07/07/new-va-study-finds-20-veterans-commit-suicide-each-day/.

Around this time, I had been advised by another whistleblower client that Leon himself had been illegally surveilled by the spy agencies. And, when I offered to bring this whistleblower before Leon to testify, he did not respond but instead strangely dismissed my cases.

Because this seemed more than strange, albeit not coincidental, I asked the judge if he had been contacted *ex parte*—that is, behind closed doors—and thus leaned on or even threatened by the Deep State intel agency and FBI defendants. Rather than answering my legitimate inquiry, he mocked me by simply branding my question as part and parcel to one of my conspiracy theories. Here is what he disrespectfully wrote and how he sarcastically mocked my clients, hardly the tenor to be admired in a federal judge.

> The general theme of this action is similar to the previous three and is a veritable anthology of conspiracy theorists' complaints. According to plaintiffs, "each and every" defendant has engaged in "ongoing illegal, unconstitutional surveillance of millions of Americans…such as the [C]hief [J]ustice of the U.S. Supreme Court, other justices, 156 judges, prominent businessmen and others such as Donald Trump, as well as Plaintiffs themselves."[37]

Sorry, Judge Leon, you too were surveilled! Just a coincidence that you bailed out?

By the way, Leon was not an appointee of either Presidents Clinton or Obama, but instead of President George W. Bush, an intellectually limited and ill-prepared commander in chief who himself used the spy agencies to conduct illegal surveillance after September 11, 2001. I have often said that W's biggest "achievement" as president was when he dodged the shoe an Iraqi journalist threw his way at a press conference in Baghdad. But W's

---

37. Montgomery v. Comey et. al., Civil Action No. 17-1074 (RJL) Memorandum Opinion of March 5, 2018, https://casetext.com/case/montgomery-v-comey.

amateurish foibles and unconstitutional excesses notwithstanding, the rank dishonesty, lawlessness, and even criminality in the Deep State and government extend to all political persuasions and pose a threat to all presidents and the citizenry in general.

But even the intel- and FBI-driven Deep State does not have a monopoly on executive branch tyranny. Here are just a few other examples of the tyranny the populace has been subjected to over the last few decades.

During the Lyndon B. Johnson administration, the Department of Defense went along with a phony and staged Gulf of Tonkin attack that served as a fraudulent justification for Johnson to do what President Kennedy would not do: get the nation mired in a major war in Vietnam. This resulted in the deaths of over 55,000 American servicemen and maimed well over several hundred thousand more. To make matters even worse, this divided the nation like never before and, along with the later Watergate scandal, its cover-up, and President Richard Nixon's resignation—the first in U.S. history—it marked the beginning of destroyed trust in our government, which became much more pronounced over the ensuing decades. The later administrations of Presidents Gerald Ford and Jimmy Carter did little to arrest this, as both were perceived, in my opinion, to be bumbling idiots. Ford, for instance, gave Nixon an undeserved executive pardon, and Carter was humiliated by Ayatollah Ruhollah Khomeini with his felonious lack of effective executive action during the Iranian hostage crisis, where he ordered a poorly planned and failed hostage rescue that resulted in our military's helicopters crashing into each other.

Then there was Ronald Reagan's presidency, generally a success, but for the illegal use of executive authority, put into effect largely by Colonel Oliver North. This resulted in the Iran-Contra scandal, where arms were sold to Iran in exchange for Iran funneling aid to the contras in Nicaragua—a not-so-clever scam that illegally skirted Congress's Boland Amendment. While perhaps well intentioned in Reagan's effort to thwart the spread of Communism in Central America, the plot was clearly illegal, and he was lucky he wasn't impeached.

During the next administration of President George Herbert Walker Bush, this first Bush, along with Department of Defense Secretary and later W's Vice President Dick Cheney, misused so-called executive authority to supply Saddam Hussein with chemical and biological weapons to train against Iran. One of these weapons of mass destruction, much like Communist China's coronavirus, later somehow leaked, not coincidentally having been manufactured at Fort Detrick, the same military virus lab that sent the seeds of COVID-19 to the Communist Chinese. This deadly anthrax was then used to attack us after September 11, 2001. To try to deflect criticism for its incompetence, if not malevolence, in not preventing these anthrax attacks, the FBI later falsely accused Steven Hatfill, a former biodefense researcher for the United States Army Medical Research Institute of Infectious Diseases (USAMRIID), and Army biodefense researcher, Bruce Ivins, when they could not solve the crime. As for Ivins, he was so emotionally devastated that he soon committed suicide. The FBI's "cover-its-incompetent-derriere's" framing of these two suspects underscores the treachery of the Deep State and elements of the unaccountable executive branch of government.

Under the Bonnie and Clyde of American politics, Bill and Hillary Clinton, it was not just the Monica Lewinsky scandal that mired this felonious but less-than-dynamic duo in stench. Let us not forget the Clintons taking money for the president's reelection from Communist China and the ensuing Chinagate-campaign finance scandal, which I was instrumental in uncovering at Judicial Watch. This gave rise to congressional investigations and hearings. In exchange, President Clinton provided national security information to the Communist Chinese concerning Taiwan. One of his big donors, Bernie Schwartz, the CEO of Loral Corporation, transferred high-tech missile technology to China. There was much more, but predictably, those congressional hearings ended abruptly when the Democrats "cleverly" dug up dirt on Republican ties to Communist China, and in the end, no prosecutions of the Clintons were initiated. Further, the bogus campaign finance reform enacted by Congress—akin to telling O.J. not to kill again—was later largely ruled unconstitutional by the U.S. Supreme Court, no beacon of justice in its own politicized right.

And when talking about the Clinton administration's DOJ, how can we forget its unfettered heavy handedness and use of excessive force at Waco and Ruby Ridge, under the corrupt reign of Attorney General Janet Reno, where scores of persons were needlessly killed in cold blood by federal law enforcement agents. On top of this, there was the outrage involving Elian Gonzalez, a young Cuban boy who miraculously survived—while his brave mother did not—a raft journey to the shores of Miami, as they both fled Castro's hellhole. Reno and her federal henchmen snatched the young boy from his uncle's home in Little Havana, Miami, at gunpoint, without due process to litigate his right to remain in the United States and sent him back to Cuba. Then brainwashed, today Elian is a mindless communist propaganda tool for the Cuban government. The Clinton DOJ's tyrannical acts broke the minds and hearts of the American Cuban community, and to this day, they have never recovered, largely forfeiting any further activism and attempts to remove Fidel and his successor, Raul Castro, the former of whom is thankfully dead, and the latter retired, with their handpicked henchmen still in control of the communist island. The courts in Miami had failed to step in to protect Elian, and thus Cuban Americans have also lost faith in our federal courts.

Then there were over forty other Clinton scandals, ranging from Filegate to Travelgate to IRSgate—you name it—that went unprosecuted, despite the Clintons and their henchmen using executive power to coerce their adversaries into submission. In addition to their illegal procurement of FBI files on the Clintons' adversaries, was their ordering Deep State audits by the Internal Revenue Service (IRS) on other perceived foes and "problem persons," such as the women Slick Willy has harassed, abused, or had affairs with. The IRS was sicced on the likes of my client Gennifer Flowers, who dared to tell the truth about Slick Willy's female abuse and sexual appetite. One other such woman, Kathleen Willey, who Bill had sexually harassed in the Oval Office pantry shortly after the poor woman's husband had died, even had her Privacy Act-protected White House employee file released to smear her. Kathleen, also one of my clients, had spilled the beans to the media. In effect, Bonnie and Clyde used whatever illegal means they could to beat their perceived adversaries into submission. Even yours truly and Judicial Watch were recipients, with bar complaints and political audits that illegally asked about the political party affiliations of our Board of Directors, an improper inquiry. The audit ended favorably, but only after six years of litigation and after George W. Bush won the presidency.

And at the end of the Clinton administration in 2000, with the election of the intellectually challenged and limited president George W. Bush, who later got us into never-ending wars in the Middle East, Hillary Clinton was caught leaving the White House with the people's furniture, which she had to return.[38] This caused me to proclaim that there was no crime, however small, beneath Hillary, a pathologically addicted felon. This was a fitting end to their presidency. But predictably, Hillary would rear her ugly head

---

38.   "Clintons Began Taking White House Property a Year Ago," *Los Angeles Times* (February 10, 2001), https://www.latimes.com/archives/la-xpm-2001-feb-10-mn-23723-story.html.

again with later scandals over bribery at the Clinton Foundation, with hers, her hubby's and daughter Chelsea's pay-to-play schemes profiting off her appointment as secretary of state during the first four years of the Obama administration, not to mention Benghazi and her use of an unsecure private email server while she was Obama's secretary of state. This likely allowed terrorists to pinpoint the location of and then assassinate U.S. Ambassador Christopher Stevens, several of his staff, and two fallen heroes, sons of my clients, Charles Woods and Pat Smith. I can go on and on, but I think you get the point. Indeed, even former FBI director James Comey, himself an unprosecuted felon, confirmed that foreign adversaries of the United States had easily hacked and infiltrated Hillary's "private" email accounts.

For good measure, one should also not forget how Slick Willy used his executive authority to "wag the dog," attempting to divert the public's attention away from his impeachment proceedings, by ordering attacks in the Sudan and Afghanistan that killed innocent civilians. The phony pretext: Clinton's half-hearted and feigned attempt to take out Osama bin Laden, who Clinton claimed was hiding at the bombed sites and who would later rear his ugly terrorist head on September 11, 2001. Later after the infamous debacle in Afghanistan during the Biden-Harris regime, where thirteen American servicemen were killed by Muslim terrorists at the Kabul airport, and hundreds of Afghans also killed or seriously wounded, Joe Biden likewise would order drone strikes on the terrorists who allegedly carried out the massacre, only for the American people and the world later to learn that he had killed tens of civilians including seven children, in this latest phony if not murderous attempt to wag the dog.

And again, what did our executive branch's so-called DOJ do about all of this under successive administrations? Nothing, nada, zilch! DOJ was and remains the "lackey" of the president and his executive authority and is not independent by any means under any administration, save for President Trump, who, given his "illegitimate status" among the entrenched establishment elites in and out of government, was unable to exercise any real authority over either the Deep State or the rest of the executive branch.

The corrupt beat thus goes on and gets worse with each successive president. Elites in the nation's capital are the protected species of the executive branch, no matter which major political party occupies the White House. It's an unwritten rule: you protect my derriere, and I will protect yours, and we all can go to the bank and cash in at the people's expense with little or no worry.

The Clinton scandals were, of course, followed by the reign of President George W. Bush and his veep, "Uncle Dick" Cheney, who he had ceded power to, given his limitations and perhaps general lack of interest, spending much of his time reportedly in the White House gym. Cheney, taking charge, pushed for the Iraq War, refusing to divulge what I had uncovered at Judicial Watch, a plan to have American oil interests divide up the oil fields in this Sunni-run nation once we conquered it. And after "mission accomplished," Bush and Cheney did not even have the Iraqis pay for their own "liberation" with their oil proceeds.

In addition, there was the illegal mass surveillance, ordered by W at Cheney's authoritarian urging, on millions of Americans who had not committed any crime or had any connection to terrorists or terrorism. There was also the equally unconstitutional denial of right of counsel to Americans who, post September 11, 2001, were imprisoned at Guantanamo, Cuba—which was later ended by the U.S. Supreme Court. Executive branch tyranny was in full swing.

While I am obviously no fan of the Muslim terrorists, I have many filed legal actions against them—including Saddam Hussein, Osama bin Laden, and the Taliban—and have even played a major role in stopping the construction of a mosque at Ground

Zero in New York City, an American citizen cannot be denied the right of legal counsel under the Constitution's Sixth Amendment.

The arrogance and lawlessness of Bush and Cheney knew no bounds, and tongue in cheek challenged the Clintons for the world indoor title, at least until President Barack Hussein Obama won and acceded to the presidency with his lovely bride, First Lady Michelle, in 2008. Now Joe Biden has "inherited" the mantle of the Clintons, Bushes, Cheney, Obamas of a near complete disrespect for the rule of law.

As for Cheney, he even stonewalled the public knowing what he and energy-industry lobbyists were doing with their secret energy task force. While the case went all the way to the U.S. Supreme Court, the justices ultimately bailed out, and Cheney continued to rule as "Darth Vader," a nickname he deservedly earned.

The Obama years from 2008 to 2016 were also a real piece of tyrannical work. In addition to his even more massive use of unconstitutional surveillance over the populace and his unilateral decisions to use drones in the Middle East to kill Americans who were thought to be terrorists—making President George W. Bush's abuses look like a warm-up act—was his despicable improper intervention in cases that had a phony racial component, such as the Trayvon Martin debacle. Obama's DOJ was a disgrace. Attorneys General Eric Holder and then Loretta Lynch, two other anti-white race baiters, left a trail of destruction at the DOJ, further eroding its prestige and trust among We the People. These white haters sowed the seeds for the race war that rages today, not just in government, corporate America, universities, and the media, but now also our public elementary and middle schools, with white children being taught that they are racist from birth, and privileged, as part of the now infamous critical race theory mandated in several blue states.

Among the early Obama/Holder executive outrages was a caper that came to be known as Fast and Furious. *The Washington Times* accurately described what was at issue:

> The House Oversight Committee let loose with a scathing assessment of Eric Holder in a recent report, accusing the Barack Obama-era attorney general of outright misleading Congress on its investigation of the "Fast and Furious" gun running scandal.
>
> And get this: Among the report's 300 pages is the committee's finding that Holder regarded the family of murdered Border Patrol Agent Brian Terry as a "nuisance."
>
> ...
>
> Terry, of course, was killed in December 2010 by a firearm believed to be part of the Bureau of Alcohol, Tobacco, Firearms and Explosives' Operation Fast and Furious program.
>
> ...
>
> Terry's death was supposedly the incident that led to revelation of Fast and Furious—the program that saw the feds [that is Obama's executive power] turn blind eyes to 2,000 or so firearms illegally purchased by drug smugglers, in hopes of tracing them to cartel big-wigs. Sadly, the feds then lost track of 1,400 or so of these weapons—two of which turned up at Terry's crime scene.
>
> Holder told investigators he didn't know of this program before Terry's murder. But report authors say that's just not true.
>
> "The new report states that the Justice Department knew before Terry's death in 2010 that the ATF was 'walking' firearms to Mexico and knew the day after the agent's death that weapons from Fast and Furious were involved in the shootout, despite denying these facts to the media," Fox News said.

The report also claims Holder's Justice officials purposely stonewalled Sen. Chuck Grassley with his requests to learn more of the program.[39]

Holder was found in contempt of Congress for his lying and deceit, if not obstruction, but this was obviously for show, not for dough, which was the norm with the clowns in our legislative branch. Good to get on Fox News and raise funds for one's next election, but no real action to hold the attorney general legally accountable with real punishment. Thus, characteristically, no prosecution of him ever took place. And the Republican establishment in Congress, which like the Dems, use scandals just to feather their own nest in the media, let it drop. Par for the course in our corrupt ship of state. No justice for either agent Terry or the American people, only smoke and mirrors!

Then there was the Obama-era political prosecution, or shall we say persecution, of the Bundys and the peaceful supporters who had flocked to their Nevada ranch when they saw the tyranny of the federal government in real time on Fox News and on the internet. Here, yet again, the Obama DOJ, then run by race-centric Attorney General Loretta Lynch, had her U.S. Attorney Daniel Bogden and his pliant and corrupt Assistant U.S. Attorneys Steven Myhre and Daniel Schiess, along with Bureau of Land Management (a.k.a. the government's BLM) and FBI agents, illegally entrap Cliven, his sons, and his supporters in a fraudulent sting operation, replete with government sharpshooters and snipers surrounding the Bundy home and training high-powered rifles on them at the Bundy Ranch. In the ensuing criminal trial,[40] which will be discussed more in Chapter Five, it came out

---

39. Cheryl K. Chumbley, "Eric Holder Slammed for 'Fast and Furious' Obstruction," *Washington Times* (June 7, 2017), https://www.washingtontimes.com/news/2017/jun/7/eric-holder-slammed-fast-and-furious-obstruction/.

40. United States of America v. Bundy et. al, 2:16-cr-46 (D. Nev.), https://casetext.com/case/united-states-v-bundy-45.

that after the Obama DOJ prosecutors were caught hiding exculpatory evidence, suborning perjury, and lying themselves to the presiding judge, even the Obama-appointed and recently deceased Senator Harry Reid-recommended Honorable Gloria Navarro was forced to declare a mistrial. At the same time, it was also revealed that these prosecutors had threatened a BLM whistleblower, Larry Wooten, to keep his mouth shut when Wooten, out of conscience, disclosed that there was a kill list that included the heads of the Bundys, largely as a result of their Mormon faith. Wooten is also a Mormon.

Ultimately, Judge Navarro was forced to throw the entire criminal prosecution out, so bad was the Obama DOJ's prosecutorial conduct, even though she had slavishly and systematically violated the defendants' constitutional rights in the earlier stages of the three trials that ensued after the Bundys and tens of peaceful protesters who waged the successful standoff with the feds were indicted. Her prior conduct had been so despicable that even the local newspaper, no bastion of conservatism or friend of the Bundys, wrote in an editorial that the prosecutors had a friend in Gloria Navarro. For more on this case, go to www.clivenbundydefensefund.com.

Incredibly, if one does not get the drift and now understand the corruption inherent in the executive branch and its law enforcement agencies, this same U.S. Attorney's Office, under the Trump DOJ, was permitted to appeal Judge Navarro's dismissal of the Bundys' and the peaceful protesters' indictments, underscoring the inherent Deep State executive branch rot embedded in the DOJ. And, while I filed complaints with the Office of Professional Responsibility and the Inspector General of DOJ to seek redress for the crimes Department lawyers had committed, my complaint, to this day, has been ignored and thus covered up, despite a court case that attempted to force compliance but that landed with an Obama-appointed federal judge, Rudolph Contreras, an apt family name for this political hack of a jurist. And my pleas to Trump's former attorney general, Jeff Sessions, and later to Attorney General William Barr to order a dismissal of the appeal went unheeded. Birds of a feather do indeed stick together, as apparently, there is honor among thieves.

Executive branch prosecutorial abuse and criminality is one thing, but the failure to also take legal action can be just as tyrannical. The best example of this during the Obama years was the refusal of his DOJ to prosecute Secretary of State Hillary Clinton for her illegal use of an unsecure private email server, where she routinely sent classified information in the course of her professional endeavors. As previously mentioned, one such example occurred with regard to Benghazi, Libya, where Al Qaeda terrorists obviously learned of the whereabouts of Ambassador Chris Stevens and his staff as a result. The rest is sad and tragic history as concerns those who died there, but Hillary shrugged it off as "what difference does it make?" As usual, she skirted any legal accountability at the hands of DOJ, even when I at Freedom Watch sued her for wrongful death on behalf of the parents of Ty Woods and Sean Smith, both of whom died with the ambassador.[41] And then, by now you have guessed it, an Obama-appointed federal judge, Amy Berman Jackson, now even more infamous for presiding over several prosecutions brought by Special Counsel Robert Mueller in furtherance of his Russian collusion witch hunt, dismissed the case. To add insult to injury for the still-grieving parents, Judge Jackson dismissed the complaint on the eve of Memorial Day, cruelly driving a stake through the hearts of parents Charles Woods and Pat Smith, two Gold Star parents, as they grieved for their unnecessary loss.

---

41. Smith et. al v. Hillary Clinton, 1:16-cv-1606 (D.D.C.), https://casetext.com/case/united-states-v-bundy-45.

And talk about how Obama and his executive Department of
Defense (DOD) treated other Gold Star parents, the survivors of
special ops forces who were killed by the Taliban in the largest loss
of life in one attack during the never-ending Afghan War. Here,
thirty special ops forces on a mission code-named Extortion 17
went down in an old 1982 vintage Chinook military helicopter
under more than mysterious circumstances, perhaps not coincidentally just three months after Osama bin Laden was allegedly
killed. Despite repeated pleas by the families of the brave servicemen, several of whom I represent, to learn of the cause of the crash
and to seek justice, Obama's DOD refused to fully explain the
circumstances of this tragedy and covered it up!

At issue were the indisputable facts: The thirty special ops
servicemen, some of whom were from Navy Seal Team VI, were
loaded onto an old copter on short notice for a raid on a terrorist
hideout. Several joint command Afghan troops were mysteriously
substituted out at the last minute and several inserted into the mission. The black box that could have disclosed the exact cause of the
crash went missing—which crash was the alleged result of what the
DOD described as a lucky shot by Muslim terrorists firing a rocket
propelled grenade, commonly referred to as an RPG. Those and
a host of other irregularities went unanswered. The DOD's lame
excuse for not finding the black box was that a flood had washed
it away. Hearing this, I quipped that there has not been a flood in
this arid part of the Middle East since Noah's Ark.

If this was not enough to make one's blood boil, a Muslim
cleric damned the dead servicemen as infidels to be relegated to
Islamic hell on a ramp ceremony as the heroes' bodies were being
loaded onto a plane to take them to Dover Air Force base in
Delaware. How did this cleric come to give his "sermon?" One
can only surmise that this policy, to reach out to Muslim clergy,
was ordered by the "Muslim in Chief" himself, President Barack

Hussein Obama, as part of his widely publicized campaign to "win the hearts and minds" of his fellow Muslims. Also, an Obama policy: Our troops were never permitted to shoot first, which effectively valued Muslim terrorist lives over our own. This also contributed to the shooting down of Extortion 17 and thousands of other deaths at the hands of terrorists in the recent Middle East wars and operations.

And, once the bodies of the fallen were returned to U.S. soil, some of them were cremated without the consent of the families. Could this also have been to cover up the real cause for the crash? Indeed, one of the bodies cremated, that of Michael Strange, an NSA cryptologist assigned to Seal Team VI, was originally found totally intact. If the crash had been caused by the substituted Afghan commandos as part of a "green on blue" suicide attack, for instance, there may have been bullets and their fragments lodged in Strange's body.[42]

In short, Obama and his political appointees in the executive branch at DOD had limited respect for and devalued the lives and emotional well-being of our military heroes and their families, particularly the ones who had served in the Middle Eastern theatre after September 11, 2001. Biden, Obama's vice president and now president himself, would later one-up Obama, with the debacle in Afghanistan, trashing the military in the process and costing the lives of thirteen brave servicemen with his negligence and stupidity.

And last but hardly least, since I can go on and on when it comes to the misuse of executive power under Obama, he likely committed two major frauds against the citizenry.

First, there was the so-called "Birther" birth certificate issue. As previously discussed, whether or not Obama was born in another country and was thus not eligible to be president, the

---

42. Strange v. Islamic Republic of Iran et. al, 14-cv-435 (D.D.C.), https://www.govinfo.gov/app/details/USCOURTS-dcd-1_14-cv-00435.

birth certificate that he was forced into displaying on the White House website, primarily under pressure from Donald Trump, is fraudulent. As just one example, it refers to "Baby Barack" as an African American, a term that was coined by Jesse Jackson in the early 1970s. Obama was born on August 4, 1961. Moreover, various forensic analyses of the certificate, and no one has ever seen the original, assuming there is one at this point, shows that it was photoshopped. But most importantly, Obama is, by all accounts, not a natural-born citizen as required by the Constitution, which provides: "No person except a natural born Citizen, or a Citizen of the United States, at the time of the Adoption of this Constitution, shall be eligible to the Office of President…"

The Framers looked to a treatise, *The Law of Nations*, compiled by Emmerich de Vattel and published in 1758, thirty-one years before our Constitution was enacted, to define terms that were not defined in our founding document. "Natural born citizen" was so defined as a person who was born to two citizen parents. Obama's father was from Kenya, which also raised the possibility that he was born on foreign soil. Again, more on this in Chapter Five, but suffice it to say for now that Obama may have pulled off the biggest fraud in American history.

Then, there was his Obamacare fraud, where he falsely used his "bully pulpit" to muster support for and trick Congress into passing his disastrous healthcare legislation, the Affordable Care Act. Telling We the People that we could keep our own doctor even under his socialist-style plan, where persons had to pay a penalty if they did not purchase "his" health insurance, his lies gave rise to its passage primarily by exclusively Democrat votes. The fraud inherent to Obamacare's passage was furthered by the now infamous quote of House Speaker Nancy Pelosi that "we have to pass the bill to find out what is in it."[43] This insipid if not venomous

---

43.　Jonathan Capehart, "Pelosi Defends Her Infamous Health Care Remark," *Washington Post* (June 20, 2012), https://www.washingtonpost.com/blogs/post-partisan/post/pelosi-defends-her-infamous-health-care-remark/2012/06/20/gJQAqch6qV_blog.html.

snake-oil saleslady of the lower chamber was obviously complicit in this executive fraud on the populace and, in retrospect, given the damage to the economy and people's lives that Obamacare caused and continues to cause, Pelosi's off-the-cuff quip cannot be considered to be a laughing matter but rather a calculated attempt, along with her dishonest president, to deceive the American people.

And speaking of healthcare, Obama readily agreed to allow Africans and physicians infected with the deadly Ebola virus into the country, a risk that was unforgivable. One has to wonder, if Ebola had run rampant in white parts of the planet, would he have been so generous and caring? In any event, by the grace of God, Ebola never metastasized into a never-ending pandemic as COVID-19 has.

But with Barack and Michelle, and their leftist cronies in the executive branch and elsewhere throughout government, nearly everything was seen through the prism of race, color, and ethnicity, sex, and sexual persuasion—pitting black against white, Muslim against Christian and Jew, woman against man, and gay against straight, dividing the nation like never before, post-Civil War. In short, the Obamas, in my opinion, used all of the executive tools at their disposal to profit from reliving and reviving prejudices and backlash, however unjustified, that had long since lessened. The president and his first lady were, in effect, Manchurian candidates to take down the vision and creation of our Founding Fathers and to make the white male in particular pay dearly by relegating him to the back of their socialist bus as revenge for past discrimination.

It is no wonder that a "serious discussion" on having the Treasury, another executive department, pay reparations to African Americans over slavery was born during the Obama years. The discourse continues today, with other groups also wanting their piece of the reparation pie—namely, radical gays, lesbians, transgenders, and other like-minded leftist minorities. It is no wonder that major

Democratic presidential candidates in the 2020 presidential election primaries, socialists such as Bernie Sanders, Elizabeth Warren, Pete Buttigieg, and Kamala Harris, played the race card to the hilt, many even backing the call for reparations. The Obamas had made "payback" vogue among the progressive movement in particular. And the Biden-Harris regime later upped the ante and used race to define nearly every issue, dividing the nation further.

Indeed, Van Jones, a so-called civil rights advocate in the lesser mold of Al Sharpton and Jesse Jackson, whom President Obama had appointed as advisor for green jobs, whatever that was, and who had been forced to resign when his communist past was exposed, correctly attributed the defeat of Hillary Clinton to Donald Trump in the next presidential election as being the result of white backlash over Obama. Jones was right, and Trump has Obama's misuse, if not criminal perversion of his executive authority, to, in part, thank for his victory in November 2016.

And let's not forget about Obama's then-Vice President Joe Biden and regrettably now president, who was credibly alleged to have used his office to extort millions of dollars from interests in the Ukraine, Russia, and Communist China to "lovingly" benefit his son Hunter, a former drug addict, now artist and general loser who lacked any experience to become hired by the Ukrainian company Burisma to line his pockets with cold cash.[44]

Beginning on January 20, 2016, with the incoming administration of newly elected President Donald J. Trump, ironically there ensued little opportunity for The Donald to abuse and misuse executive authority, so preoccupied was he with saving his own skin. His executive orders and policies attempting to limit immigration from certain Muslim nations in the Middle East that carried a high terrorist risk, as well as his asylum policies,

---

44. Mark Moore, "Giuliani Claims Ukrainian Company Paid Joe Biden $900,000 in Lobbying Fees," *New York Post* (October 10, 2019), https://nypost.com/2019/10/10/giuliani-claims-ukrainian-company-paid-joe-biden-900000-in-lobbying-fees/.

primarily over the influx of illegal immigrants on the U.S.-Mexican border, were well within his presidential authority, even if rabid leftist federal judges struck them down in the lower courts. They were ultimately reversed by the conservative majority on the U.S. Supreme Court.

To the contrary, and as previously detailed in this chapter, the Deep State embedded primarily in the executive branch was trained on him, with unconstitutional wiretaps, fraudulent warrants at the Foreign Intelligence Surveillance Court, and an endless series of other criminal acts—which even today go unpunished, much less prosecuted, by the corrupt DOJ. The FBI, in particular, under former Director James Comey and Deputy Director Andrew McCabe, along with the so-called "love bird" special agents, Peter Strzok and Lisa Page, and Special Counsel Robert Mueller, waged a war against the forty-fifth president and his colleagues and family, hoping to have them removed from office. Two witch hunts and two impeachments later, and The Donald was still standing, thanks in large part to the lack of resolve of the establishment of both parties to either have him deep-sixed or kept in office. Instead, he was likely cheated of reelection at the ballot box in November 2020.

The swamp rarely plays for keeps with its own but instead plays the politics of personal destruction. In Trump's case, the plan of the forces pitted against him was always to weaken his chances for reelection in November 2020, and it ultimately succeeded. No one in his or her right mind would have ever surmised that a Republican-controlled Senate would vote to convict the president of high crimes and misdemeanors, which in the end it did not.

But along the way to saving Trump's presidency prior to the 2020 presidential election, many persons were seriously hurt by the minions Obama and the Clintons had left embedded in the Deep State. Notwithstanding self-proclaimed and proud "dirty trickster" Roger Stone; Paul Manafort, Stone's equally felonious partner; Rick Gates, a former employee of both Stone and right-hand man to Manafort during the 2016 presidential campaign; and equally sleazy Michael Cohen, Trump's former fixer and half-wit lawyer, who got what they deserved for serious crimes of perjury, obstruction of justice, witness tampering, tax and other fraud, and who had been caught in the web of Mueller's Russian collusion investigation. Then there were others like General Mike Flynn, George Papadopoulos, Carter Page, and myriad others who fell victim to the witch hunts. They are targets of the Deep State embedded "deep" into the executive branch, and they hardly will be the last.

Under the leftist Biden-Harris regime, following the uprising of January 6, 2021, the Deep State contained within the Justice Department and it's FBI has been used as a "Gestapo," to round up, arrest, indict, and try virtually all persons who were in the nation's capital that day near or in the Capitol building, mostly conservative, libertarian, people of faith, and those who believe in the vision and creation of our Founding Fathers, to quell dissent to the near total socialist, communist, atheist radical leftist takeover that has occurred. And, as will be discussed and documented later, federal judges, particularly those in the district court in Washington, D.C., have served as the yes men and women of this "Gestapo," denying bail to even peaceful protesters, throwing several in solitary confinement as they await trial, meting out multi-month or multi-year sentences for mere alleged trespasses, and using as a false and dishonest pretext that Trump continues to spew the "Big Lie" that he won the presidency, absent Democrat and leftist fraud during the last election. This "Big Lie," the federal judge lackeys claim—both Democrat- and Republican-appointed—will incite more so-called violence from the criminally charged peaceful protesters, justifying their unconstitutional prison confinement even prior to their trial. And then to try to lessen their sentences with these dishonest federal judges, many peaceful protesters have been compelled to make what are in effect forced confessions of guilt. Shades of the former Soviet Union, Communist China, North Korea, Castro's Cuba, the Supreme Leader's Islamic Republic of Iran, and Hugo Chavez's and later Nicolas Maduro's Venezuela, to name just a few dictatorships with corrupt legal systems. This Marxian, leftist and even establishment Republican treachery finally has come home to roost in Biden's and Harris's AMERIKA.

All Americans must fear for their loved ones and themselves. They must be prepared for what now appears to be inevitable counter-revolution, as executive power and criminality over the last many decades has increased to the level predicted by Jefferson when he wrote in 1787 as American foreign minister to France, two years before our Constitution was enacted, to the son-in-law of another great Founding Father, John Adams:

> I do not know whether it is to yourself, or Mr. Adams I am to give my thanks for the copy of the new constitution. I beg leave through you to place them where due. It will be yet three weeks before I shall receive them from America (Jefferson was then in Paris, France). They are good articles in it: and very bad. I do not preponderate. What we have lately read in the history of Holland, in the chapter on the Stadtholder, would have sufficed to set me against a Chief magistrate eligible for a long duration (meaning federal judges), if I had ever been disposed towards one: and what we have always read of the elections of Polish kings should have forever excluded the idea of one continuable for life. Wonderful is the effect of impudent and persevering lying. The British ministry have so long hired their gazetteers to repeat and model into every form lies about our being an anarchy that the world has at length believed them, the English nation has believed them, the ministers themselves have come to believe them, and what is more wonderful, we have believed them ourselves. Yet

where does this anarchy exist, except in the single instance of Massachusetts? And can history produce an instance of rebellion so honorably conducted? I say nothing of its motives. They were founded in ignorance, not wickedness.[45]

And then Jefferson wisely and with prophetic vision drove his point home:

God forbid that we should ever be 20 years without such a rebellion. The people cannot be all, and always, well informed. The part which is wrong will be discontented in proportion of the facts they misconceive. If they remain quiet under such misconceptions it is a lethargy, the forerunner to death to the public liberty. We have had 13 states independent in 11 years. There has been one rebellion. That comes to one rebellion in a century and a half for each state. What country ever before existed for a century and half without rebellion? And what country can preserve its liberties if their rulers are not warned from time to time that their people preserve the spirit of resistance? Let them take arms. The remedy is to set them right as to the facts, pardon and pacify them. What signify a few lives lost in a century or two?[46]

And then, as well, Jefferson pronounced his inevitable conclusion based on his own experience and that of the colonies:

The tree of liberty must be refreshed from time to time with the blood of patriots and tyrants. It is the natural manure. Our (constitutional) Convention has been too much impressed by the insurrection in Massachusetts: and in the spur of the moment, they are setting up a kite to keep the hen yard in order. I hope in God this article will be rectified before the new constitution is accepted.[47]

---

45.   Thomas Jefferson, "Letter to William Stephens Smith, 1787," *Founders Archive,* https://founders.archives.gov/documents/Jefferson/01-12-02-0348.
46.   Ibid.
47.   Ibid.

While I, like Jefferson, hope to avoid having to refresh the tree of liberty with the blood of patriots and tyrants, it may become in even the near term inevitable if the intellectual and other forms of executive branch corruption and congressional confusion, dishonest games and deceit continue and worsen, as has been the case over the last several decades. Under the Biden-Harris regime it has already reached critical mass and the caldron of dissent may be ready to explode, as occurred on July 14, 1789, with the storming of the Bastille in Paris, France. Ironically, Jefferson was also an architect of the French revolution. And the federal judges appointed for life in the third judicial branch, as Jefferson alludes to, and as I chronicle in Chapter Five, will be the first taken to the guillotines.

On to tyranny in the legislative branch of our presently totally corrupt government, essentially a bunch of court jesters, con men and "money-changers" and in some cases even sexual perverts who largely represent their own interests and let those of We the People be damned.

CHAPTER FOUR

LEGISLATIVE BRANCH TYRANNY!

SHIP OF FOOLS AND NOT SHIP OF STATE!

"Someone once said that politics is the second-oldest profession. I'm beginning to think it bears resemblance to the first."

—Ronald Reagan[48]

President Reagan was talking primarily about his dealings with Congress. Originally created and patterned by our Founders after primitive early democracies in Greece and ancient Rome, the American Congress was intended to provide a republican branch of government, with representatives elected by and for the people of the United States, and thus owing only their allegiance to them. But this noble design has sadly failed—and worsened over time, again as Thomas Jefferson predicted it would.

Today, our senators and congressmen seem more akin to the character played by Woody Allen in his comedy *Everything You Always Wanted to Know About Sex* (*But Were Afraid to Ask)*, where

---

48. Ronald Reagan, *BrainyQuote*, brainyquote.com, https://www.brainyquote.com/quotes/ronald_reagan_147698.

the king calls for his security guards to bring him the fool! The fool, played by Allen, has been sleeping with the Queen—having given her a magic lovemaking potion provided by a sorcerer—hardly the province of this court jester.

Instead of sleeping with the queen, our present-day court jesters, the nation's senators and congressmen, have been feeding We the People their dishonest potion—whoring it up with special interest lobbyists and other slimy characters, mostly feathering their own nest, greedily stuffing money into their pockets and acquiring more power to further their own improper interests. Frequently they even sleep with themselves, as the incidence of homosexuality is significant, with I would estimate about twenty percent nominally married to the opposite sex only for appearance purposes. Gay, straight, or transgender, our so-called representatives prance about Capitol Hill, frequently with similarly dyed chocolate brown hair, donned in three-to-five-thousand-dollar tailored Italian blue suits or dresses, adorned with congressional pins, expensive silk ties or Gucci shoes, and fancy solid gold cuff links and watches, or bracelets, doing their own business—that is, their "monkey business"—but not the people's business! To further their ends and to raise money for their next election, they are the frequent media guests who get their dyed and coifed dos and faces on Fox News, CNN, or MSNBC—take your pick depending on party affiliation. And, given the perks of being incumbents and the war chests they acquire with fundraising gambits and sometimes outright frauds—where they attempt to sell access to government officials and agencies for political campaign contributions—generally they are entrenched for life, much like the federal judges we will dissect and put on the chopping block in the next chapter.

As a general matter, what we have in our legislative branch of government is not a ship of state but a ship of fools, very intellectually corrupt and deceitful clowns, who are sleeping not with

the queen—but again often secretly with mistresses and significant others of their own gender and those in particular who want
favors and are willing to pay for them. They are akin to the new
American nobility, not unlike the hedonistic irreligious courts of
King George III in Great Britain and the minions of King Louis
XVI and his queen Marie Antoinette at Versailles, France. Of
course, we have long since learned of the fate of these beautiful
people and despots.

An example of the fundraising corruption, fraud, and criminality endemic to Capitol Hill, as I discussed in *Whores*, was the
wholesale selling of access to IRS officials by former Republican
Speaker of the House Tom DeLay. Not to be outdone by the
Clintons during this sad period in American history—when I
caught Bonnie and Clyde selling seats on Commerce Department trade missions under corrupt Secretary of Commerce Ron
Brown—DeLay, on behalf of the fundraising arms of his political party, the Republican National Senatorial Committee and
National Republican Congressional Committee, offered and
then greased access to Bush administration IRS officials to solve
tax issues with a hefty political contribution. This prompted me,
while chairman and general counsel for Judicial Watch, to file
ethics complaints against DeLay and other establishment party
members complicit in these fundraising scams. This obviously
did not win me any new friends in the Republican Party and
among its lackeys in the establishment media, such as Byron
York, now with the establishment-skewed *Washington Examiner*
and Fox News, who then slavishly, at DeLay's obvious urging,
penned a hit piece against me.

To name another notable caper on the other side of the
congressional aisle, there was former African American Democratic congressman William Jefferson, who was arrested and
later convicted of hiding $90,000 in cash—in his freezer no

less—in exchange for favors to the briber. As reported by the Associated Press:

> William Jefferson, a Democrat who had represented parts of New Orleans for almost 20 years, was stoic as the verdict was read and had little to say afterward. Asked how he was doing, he said "I'm holding up."
>
> Prosecutors contended Jefferson accepted more than $400,000 in bribes and sought millions more in exchange for brokering business deals in Africa. After a two-month trial, jurors took five days to convict him on 11 of 16 counts that also included racketeering and money laundering. He was acquitted on the other five.[49]

Typically, while Jefferson was sentenced to thirteen years in federal prison, DeLay and his Republican establishment hacks were not held legally accountable by the DOJ or even the Congressional Ethics Office. The elite in the swamp almost never are!

I can go on and on, but the corruption among members of Congress is rampant, and only a few ever get caught or are ultimately held accountable. Ironically, if you want to watch an accurate comedy produced, written, and acted by Eddie Murphy, titled *The Distinguished Gentleman*, it will tell the tale of what goes on in Congress. And the name of the main character in this comedy is named Thomas Jefferson Johnson!

These are just a few examples among thousands of deceitful scams. On the lighter side, I have never seen a congressman take money out of his or her pocket over lunch or any other event. They "honestly" believe that they are the privileged new American nobility and that all is coming to them. Well, there certainly is something eventually coming to them, again as Thomas Jefferson

---

49. Staff, "Former Congressman William Jefferson Who Hid $90,000 in His Freezer Could Face 20 Years in Jail," *Associated Press* (August 5, 2009), https://www.nydailynews.com/news/world/congressman-william-jefferson-hid-90-000-freezer-face-20-years-jail-article-1.395138.

predicted. And, when it does, it will not be pretty, and we saw the early stages of their likely fate on January 6, 2021, which was not an insurrection as the Left tries to paint it, but a Jeffersonian uprising. Indeed, I believe that if Jefferson had been alive on that day, he would have been the first into the Capitol building.

But apart from this rank profiteering, often illegal, at the people's expense, are the lies and deceit that permeate the congressional body politic. Perhaps the most historic recent gambit, as previously alluded to in Chapter Three, was House Speaker Nancy Pelosi's entreaty to her members to pass Obama's concocted and tortured creation Obamacare, because only then could we know what was in it. Later, and last year, she would spew the same bullshit with regard to the proposed 3.5 trillion-dollar welfare boondoggle bill, calculated to put millions on the public dole, reducing the incentive to work for a living, and further bankrupting our previously capitalist economy. Apparently confusing her myriad face lifts with "lifting" Americans out of poverty, this insipid witch of a House speaker couldn't tell the truth if her life depended on it. Indeed, there is no limit to what these court jesters will dishonestly spew in the Senate and House chambers and on cable news networks, not to mention their favorite and pliant agenda-driven print and internet media. It's no wonder that Congress has granted itself immunity for false and defamatory statements made on the floors of the House and Senate. These dishonest clowns gave themselves a license to lie!

And, these purveyors of deceit and deception have even granted themselves immunity from insider stock trading, which explains how many of them become millionaires by using insider classified and confidential information given to them by special corporate interests to enrich themselves.[50]

---

50. Glenn Greenwald, "Nancy and Paul Pelosi Making Millions in Stock Trades in Companies She Actively Regulates," Substack.com (July 15, 2021), https://greenwald.substack.com/p/nancy-and-paul-pelosi-making-millions; Sarah Jones, "Nan-

But while prolific at otherwise illegal insider trading, giving Pelosi some minor slack, as she is hardly the sole worst example of the malevolent clowns in Congress, is the troika of Representatives Adam Schiff, Jerrold Nadler, and Eliot Engel, who waged a dishonest jhihad against Trump over alleged Russian collusion and then, when the first clown show failed, Ukrainian collusion, making false claims that they had the goods on President Trump, when all they had was lie upon lie.

And how can we dismiss from our collective memories the ridiculous antics of the socialist, Muslim, anti-Semitic, and anti-white-male congresswoman Alexandria Ocasio-Cortez (a.k.a. AOC), Rashida Tlaib, and Ilhan Omar. I was forced to bring suit for my client, female Jewish activist Laura Loomer against Tlaib for her assault on Laura at a joint fundraising event in Minnesota,[51] and as for Omar, a complaint to have her investigated and later deported over immigration fraud, as it is now uncontroverted that she married her brother to gain citizenship for him, among other illegalities. Of course, true to form, even the Trump immigration authorities laid off of Omar. And cynically, why not? Omar, AOC, and Tlaib were, in effect, The Donald's BFFs, as with their hateful and stupid rhetoric, coupled with their outrageous behavior, they have become the poster girls of the now dominant largely anti-Semitic communist-oriented progressive wing of the Democrat establishment, with even Speaker Pelosi kissing their hateful derrieres. And the anti-Israeli left-wing media sucks it all up, increasing their influence over the Democratic Party establishment.

But now, let's turn to the other side of the House aisle and relive the outrage that occurred over the Extortion 17 tragedy with now retired congressman and newly minted ever sick smiling—even

---

cy Pelosi Wrong About Trading Stocks in Congress," *Intelligencer* (December 15, 2021), https://nymag.com/intelligencer/2021/12/nancy-pelosi-is-wrong-about-trading-stocks-in-congress.html.

51   . Loomer v. Tlaib, 19-cv-2322 (D. Minn.), https://casetext.com/case/loomer-v-tlaib.

when he is commented on a tragedy such as Biden's Afghanistan debacle—third-rate Fox News commentator Jason Chaffetz, as well as other members of the Republican establishment and the House Government Oversight and Reform Committee.

Extortion 17 was the largest loss of life in the Afghan war, as previously discussed. Our fallen heroes, special ops forces, were shot down by the Taliban while on a hastily convened raid to take out terrorists in the Tangi Valley in the south of Wardak Province. The cause of the shoot-down by terrorists only three months after Bin Laden was allegedly killed (many think he died much earlier of natural causes), never having been fully explained, was a source of great emotional distress to my Gold Star parent clients. Obama's DOD, and Obama himself, who had personally promised to look into the tragedy, turned a blind eye on the parents' hopes to learn the truth.

Completely frustrated, my clients instructed my staff and me to contact Congress to try to commence an investigation into the crash. The logical place to turn was the House Committee on Oversight and Government Reform, which is generally the investigative arm of the House. Chairing the committee at that time was Representative Darrell Issa from California. We ultimately succeeded in arranging a meeting with him and his subcommittee chairman, Representative Jason Chaffetz from Utah.

Some of the families of the fallen victims attended the meeting, and Issa, feigning to feel my clients' pain, assigned Chaffetz and his subcommittee to conduct the investigation. Obviously, this was to their political advantage. As establishment Republicans, they knew the importance of generally conservative military family support and thus their votes in future elections.

Later, Chaffetz assigned a former CIA case officer, who was on his staff in charge of military and national security matters, to the case. His name was Jim Lewis.

Working with Lewis over many months in the lead-up to an eventual congressional hearing, my chief of staff and I also visited the offices of other committee members to gin up support for a thorough and honest investigation and hearing. One of these representatives was Trey Gowdy, who later chaired the subcommittee that investigated Benghazi. Despite our going to his office when his staff did not respond to our requests for a meeting, Gowdy never even appeared and did not show up to the later hearing. From my experience with Gowdy, he is a complete charlatan: a lot of great, seemingly authoritative talk but no real action. He has, over the years, become a favorite of Fox News, as he later, like Chaffetz, left his theatrical perch on the committee to rake in more cash in private legal practice. And while he was part of the committee supposedly investigating Benghazi, he took a dive and let Hillary Clinton off the hook, much to the surprise of others but not yours truly. I had to ask again and again, what did the executive Deep State intel and FBI have on him?

But now let's get back to Chaffetz and his cloak-and-dagger spook investigator Lewis. The two of them created the appearance of conducting a bona fide investigation but never really did. To the contrary, Lewis tried to co-opt my chief of staff by secretly offering her a job, which she revealed to me. And when it came time to hold the hearing, none of our Gold Star clients were permitted to testify. The only witnesses who appeared were the military personnel who had made arrangements to dispose of the bodies and one Obama DOD political appointee, Gary Reed, who simply declared that a series of unfortunate events, à la Hollywood film *Lemony Snicket's A Series of Unfortunate Events*, had caused the crash. Put another way, very sad, but "shit happens!"

As for Chaffetz and his clown show, a Jew who had converted to The Church of Jesus Christ of Latter-day Saints, with newly minted phony Mormon tears (I respect Mormons but not him), he feigned remorse for the tragedy but offered up no substance. And when the hearing concluded and he approached my clients in the House hearing committee gallery to routinely express his sadness, I asked him when we were going to have a real hearing to get to the bottom of why my clients' sons had died. He looked at me in fascination with a dumb expression and simply walked off.

It was clear to me and my chief of staff, who had attended the hearing with the families, that Chaffetz and his CIA stooge Lewis had simply covered it all up. One of the parents of the victims, Charley Strange, the dad of an NSA-assigned SEAL Team Six cryptologist, speculated that the death of his son had been furthered by someone in our military who tipped the Taliban off to the raid and profited from it. Thus, this may have been the reason to cover up what actually happened to our brave heroes.

After seeing the charade put on by Chaffetz and his lackey spook Lewis, I would have to agree that this was a real possibility.

And, it was not long thereafter that Chaffetz, who had ascended, not like Jesus but as an establishment Republican hack, to replace Issa, whose last name means Jesus in both Farsi and Arabic, as chairman of the full House Committee on Oversight and Government Reform, decided "unexpectedly" to retire and relinquish his considerable so-called power in Congress. His next destination was Fox News and his fairly regular beat on *Hannity*, where he could assist Sean in spreading more empty promises of justice to the public, boosting viewership, ratings, and ad dollars for Fox.

In light of all this, I have to wonder what caused Chaffetz to quit what is the most powerful committee in the House, short of the Committee on Ways and Means, which controls the public's purse. What might the Deep Intel executive establishment have on him? Perhaps his ex-CIA case officer and later congressional investigator Jim Lewis might know? He is now third-rate substitute host on, you guessed it, Fox News, appearing in every interview with the same Republican establishment smirk, even when reporting on tragedies such as occurred under the Biden-Harris regime in Afghanistan. His rivals in this genre are only other Republican hacks like Senator Tom Cotton, who talks a good game with regard to the Communist Chinese threat, but does nothing, and of course "Mr. rolled up sleeves" Representative Jim Jordan, another clown with a sick smile who spews about Democrat corruption but then does not produce.

Now let's take a walk through the other destructive clown show known as the Senate. In the early 1990s, this committee under the leadership of then Senator Joe Biden, conducted, in the words of now Justice Clarence Thomas, a "high-tech lynching." At the time, Thomas was a U.S. Supreme Court nominee during the first Bush administration and the lynching to which Thomas referred was over the Anita Hill sexual harassment scam. Senators Chuck Grassley from Iowa and Lindsey Graham from South Carolina continue to sit on this same committee, with Graham being the chairman who succeeded Grassley following the election of Donald Trump as president.[52]

In later years, during the Trump administration, the Senate Judiciary Committee attempted to conduct another "high-tech lynching," using equally false, salacious allegations that federal judge Brett Kavanaugh had sexually assaulted a woman by the name of Christine Blasey Ford. True to leftist Democrat form, Senator Richard Blumenthal of Connecticut, Senator Kamala Harris from California—later, not coincidentally, a presidential candidate in the 2020 primary and now regrettably our cackling witch of a vice president —and Senator Sheldon Whitehouse of

---

52   . Michael S. Rosenwald, "A High-Tech Lynching': How Kavanaugh Took a Page from the Thomas Playbook," *The Seattle Times* (September 27, 2018), https://www.seattletimes.com/nation-world/a-high-tech-lynching-how-kavanaugh-took-a-page-from-the-thomas-playbook/.

the Mafia-infested State of Rhode Island led the dishonest charge, completely destroying the poor man's reputation on the way to his eventual tortured confirmation as a justice. Watching this vicious and unhinged attack on Kavanaugh was disgusting. Nevertheless, the irony is that, in my heart, I did not want to see the judge confirmed but for another fundamental reason.

Kavanaugh is not a strong defender of the Fourth Amendment, which protects We the People from unreasonable searches and seizures. He had previously ruled, with gratuitous dicta—meaning, it was not the actual holding of the case—that Obama's mass surveillance through the executive Deep State intel agencies and the FBI was "peachy keen." So, in reality, I wanted to see him go down, but not for the hateful, conjured-up, phony reasons manufactured and furthered by the likes of "Do it to Me Sheldon" Whitehouse (the humorous quip uttered by Meg Ryan in the restaurant scene of the Hollywood comedy *When Harry Met Sally*). In effect, with the eventual confirmation of Kavanaugh to the High Court, it was the American people who were getting screwed, not Christine Blasey Ford!

Since his confirmation, Kavanaugh has gone on the defensive, shedding much of his so-called conservative leanings. He is, in truth, an establishment Republican regardless of the promotional hype spewed when he was nominated by President Trump. And he apparently fears that some later false sexual allegations will lead to an impeachment proceeding. I believe that this is why he now conveniently votes frequently with the leftist wing of the court. So, in the end, the rabid Democrats on the Senate Judiciary Committee largely won!

As for Senator Grassley, I ran him down on the Capitol steps a few years ago when I wanted to have his Judiciary Committee open an investigation of the mass illegal surveillance on the American people by the Deep State executive intel agencies and FBI.

Grassley, looking a bit bewildered and perhaps showing his octogenarian credentials, promised me that he would order an investigation, as my whistleblower client had claimed that the chief justice of the Supreme Court, John Roberts, and other justices, such as Ruth Bader Ginsburg, had been illegally spied upon, along with at least 156 others, mostly federal judges. This clearly was within the purview of the Senate Judiciary Committee.

Later, I would be in contact with members of his staff to plan the investigation as the whistleblower, a former NSA/CIA and FBI contractor, had in his possession forty-seven hard drives and 600,000-plus pages of data, much of it he claimed was classified, showing this alleged criminality.

Incredibly, the committee staff, who I wanted to turn the data over to for analysis, would not accept it, ridiculously claiming that they did not have the computers or the resources to open and review it. Instead, they suggested I go with the forty-seven hard drives to the inspector general of Obama's DOD, which would be the last place anyone with an IQ over fifty would take his client's information, given that the illegal surveillance largely occurred during the Obama administration.

To make this long story short, Senator Grassley and his staff punted and did nothing.

The same was also true of the establishment Republican chairman of the Senate Intelligence Committee, Richard Burr, whom I also approached to investigate. He and his staff also brushed me off, suggesting to me that, as it likely happened with Judge Leon, they were afraid to take on these spy agencies for fear of retaliation by being smeared with dirt that had been acquired on them and their families.

And when the Senate Intelligence Committee also abdicated its public responsibility to investigate and took an exit stage left, I then approached the chairman of the House Intelligence

Committee, Devin Nunes of California, also a favorite clown-ish guest on *Hannity* of Fox News. Over the years, it has become clear to me that Nunes and Fox News are linked through their disappointing promises of justice, aimed at benefiting their own interests—such as what occurred during the efforts to oust Trump. Again, the scandal industry marches on as the nation continues its downward slide.

The serious matter of mass executive Deep State Orwellian spying on the American people is no small matter, but these small men hid in their compromised cave and never came out.

Another small man in stature, but characteristically big in talk, was the prior blowhard chairman of the Senate Judiciary Committee, Lindsey Graham, before the last 2020 congressional elections—also a favorite of Fox News and of Sean Hannity, in particular. Graham had been promising to investigate the anti-Trump Democrat and Deep State criminal witch hunts of Presi-dent Trump, his family, and staff for going on two years. But the only thing that he repeatedly is "going on" is *Hannity*, to again, like the majority of visitors to this show who are perpetuating mislead-ing ideas, make empty promises that justice will be done. Given rumors that Senator Graham is closeted, could that be what he fears the Deep State will expose him for? In today's world, no one really cares, and there is no shame in being gay, so long as one does not push this lifestyle on others. But for Graham, it may be a matter of his old-style Southern thinking and ways. One can only speculate, but what is not mere speculation is that Graham, like most of his congressional colleagues, is a study in prevarica-tion and deception for personal gain, putting his own self-centered interests ahead of those of the American people. While he pretends to be a Trump ally, his two-faced self gave an interview to famed *Washington Post* Watergate investigative reporter Bod Woodward, in Woodward's new book *Peril* and trashed the Donald. When it comes to Graham, perhaps like his sex life, he likes it both ways.

But apart from the endemic corruption in the legislative branch, there is its general cowardice to address important issues that it legitimately is supposed to address and remedy. The abdication of responsibility by the House Judiciary Committee to police the federal judiciary it presides over is just one example. In the nation's entire 133-year history since the Constitution was enacted, it has impeached only eight federal judges for high crimes and misdemeanors or "bad behavior." That is one judge about every thirty years. And one of the last federal judges it had the "displeasure" to show the door to was Alcee Hastings of the U.S. District Court for the Southern District of Florida, in 1989, thirty-one years ago. It was one of those rare instances where the FBI made a real effort to catch a federal judge taking a bribe—although one has to assume it is not that uncommon. Ironically, and it tells you a lot about our current state of affairs, what was Hastings's next stop in the federal government? He was elected to the House in a majority black district in and around Fort Lauderdale and West Palm Beach, proving that crime does indeed pay. And Hastings has been happily a "Distinguished Gentleman" in Congress ever since, making Eddie Murphy's comedy film by the same name even more relevant.

I, for one, have made numerous attempts, as the head of Judicial Watch and now Freedom Watch, to simply have the House Judiciary Committee initiate investigations of allegedly corrupt federal judges. This will be laid out more in the next chapter. In doing so, I went to the then two highest members of the committee, then Republican Chairman Bob Goodlatte of Virginia and Steve King of Iowa. When no investigation was ever undertaken of these corrupt federal judges, at least King was candid with me, saying that Chairman Goodlatte lacked the stomach to do so. And it again comes as no surprise that while Goodlatte occupied this perch during the Obama administration and until 2018 when he left Congress, he was a guest on Fox News, complaining but doing nothing about the witch hunts against his president waged by the DOJ's Special Counsel Robert Mueller and his complicit ex-cronies at the FBI. Goodlatte and the rest of the worthless court jesters of the House Judiciary Committee contributed greatly to the scandal industry but not to an honest legal system of justice for all.

And, to bring all of this even more current, who again can forget President Reagan's analogy to prostitutes having more ethics than politicians, the whoreish conduct of our current alleged President Joe Biden when he presided over as the head of the Senate Judiciary Committee what now Justice Clarence Thomas called was a "high-tech lynching" over the phony sexual harassment allegations of Anita Hill, calculated by the Left to try to derail the confirmation of this now most conservative of the SCOTUS justices. Biden's whoredom with Thomas should have been a clarion call as to what was to follow decades later when he occupied the White House.[53]

Then, of course, there are other vital areas of national importance where the legislative branch has gone AWOL—be it a dangerous open-borders immigration policy, running up the national debt, price-fixing in the inflated pharmaceutical drug industry, the discriminatory power of social media, bankrupting the republic with free money and handouts such that people do not want to work, such that even Uber drivers are now scarce, and so many more that there are too many words to pack into this book.

Congress, notwithstanding the severe harm that it has done to the body politic of the nation, has become the weakest branch of government, far surpassed by the executive branch and the most

---

53. Staff, "FLASHBACK—Clarence Thomas: "It's a High-Tech Lynching for Uppity Blacks," CNSNews (September 17, 2018), https://www.cnsnews.com/news/article/cnsnewscom-staff/flashback-clarence-thomas-denies-anita-hill-allegations-calls-senate.

powerful unelected federal judicial branch. In effect, the American people no longer have a representative form of government but instead a generally cowardly, incestuous, and evil sideshow on Capitol Hill, occupying space and time and emptying out the public's purse but providing nothing of value. It is no wonder that the majority of our so-called representatives in Congress are lawyers. Paraphrasing the satiric words of Mark Twain, at least prostitutes, as opposed to lawyers, provide something of value to their clients! Of course, our politicians in the legislative branch have these "virtues" both ways; they are largely lawyers and also whores!

Now on to the worst and most malevolent, powerful, harmful, and traitorous branch of government, the branch that is supposed to protect us from tyranny at the hands of the other two branches: the federal judiciary. Enough said about the executive and legislative branches! By now, you get the point! No need to belabor things when the leaders of the U.S. Senate are Democrat Majority Leader Chuck Schumer and Republican Minority Leader Mitch McConnell, and of the House of Representatives Democrat Speaker Nancy Pelosi and Republican Minority Leader Kevin McCarthy, whose sleazy and cynical fun and games at the expense of we peasants speak for themselves!

CHAPTER FIVE

TYRANNY ON THE FEDERAL BENCH

"FIRST TO THE GUILLOTINES!"

"A good lawyer knows the law, a clever one takes the judge to lunch."
—Mark Twain[54]

It has come to pass, as Jefferson predicted, that federal judges have evolved into the biggest threat not just to our justice system but, just short of the coronavirus and nuclear holocaust, the biggest threat to the nation's well-being as a whole. In this chapter, I will provide concrete examples of how and why, particularly in cases that touch on political or highly charged but important social issues, federal judges more often than not twist if not pervert the law to suit their own biases and ends or to feather the nest of those who helped put them on the bench. It's called "you scratched my back and now I will repay the favor." In effect, they leave us defenseless from the tyranny of the other two branches of government and other well-connected nefarious actors.

---

54. Mark Twain. *Mark Twain Quote,* https://quotefancy.com/mark-twain-quotes.

In my nearly forty-five years as a trial lawyer, I have encountered no more than a few federal judges who would do the right thing and enforce the law as written in these types of high-profile cases. One for whom I still have a lot of respect is deceased federal judge Stanley Sporkin[55], a strong and unafraid champion of the "little guy" and ordinary Americans, who did what he thought was right, with a goodness to his heart and with adherence to the law, while serving the nation honorably. But another federal judge whom I also had once upon a time held in high regard, as I previously mentioned, was the Honorable Royce C. Lamberth of the U.S. District Court for the District of Columbia. But unlike Sporkin who always held true to his principles,[56] Lamberth, in recent years, seems to have sold out or kowtowed to the establishment that put him on the federal bench. So before I get into the "judicial chamber of horrors," which I will coin the Federal Judicial Hall of Shame of the top sixteen (and counting) worst federal judges (originally the top ten, but the list keeps growing since I first penned and published the precursor to this book) that I have regrettably come to experience in my career—and these are just a sampling of the rank dishonesty on the bench—let's deal with Lamberth first, since he is currently the "best of the worst." But regrettably, he has most recently also proven to be exemplary of the endemic problem with our ever-comprised and continually degenerating system of justice.

And so it was that a few years ago my previously "favorite" federal judge Royce Lamberth took a dive and sold out, this time to the leftist media comprised of CNN, *Huffington Post*, and

---

55. Sam Roberts, "Stanley Sporkin, Bane of Corporate Corruption, Dies at 88," *New York Times* (Mar. 24, 2020), https://www.nytimes.com/2020/03/24/business/stanley-sporkin-dead.html.

56. Matt Schudel, "Stanley Sporkin, Crusading SEC Enforcer and Tough-minded U.S. Judge, Dies at 88," *Washington Post* (Mar. 24, 2020), https://www.washingtonpost.com/local/obituaries/stanley-sporkin-crusading-sec-enforcer-and-tough-minded-us-judge-dies-at-88/2020/03/24/c51a1db8-6ddc-11ea-a3ec-70d7479d83f0_story.html.

Rolling Stone.[57] All three of these publications, to stick it further to President Trump, defamed his now-pardoned greatest immigration-policy supporter, America's Sheriff, Joe Arpaio, by maliciously publishing that he is a "convicted felon." By defaming Arpaio, of course, the leftist media was really seeking to further tar, feather, and harm President Trump.

Feeling that it was time for someone to take the leftist media to the woodshed, the sheriff and I brought suit. By the grace of God, we thought, after we filed suit, the case was randomly assigned to the Honorable Royce C. Lamberth. Finally, we thought, a jurist who would have the will to put the leftist media in their proper place and to set an example for all media, no matter what its political persuasion, by allowing the case to go before a jury with the opportunity to have these rabidly hate-filled news outlets pay huge damages.

But, to make the long and sordid story short, Judge Lamberth, for whatever improper reason, would not allow the case to go forward, even into discovery. He summarily dismissed Arpaio's complaint, claiming that we did not plead that the leftist media had acted with actual malice, which means that they knew that Arpaio was not a convicted felon or that they acted with reckless disregard for the truth. This was simply false and completely dishonest.

Indeed, during oral arguments on the defendant's motion to dismiss, I reminded Judge Lamberth that these leftist media publications closely covered Arpaio's conviction for a misdemeanor—for which he had been pardoned by the president. The conviction resulted from his allegedly violating a court order preventing ethnic profiling at day-worker sites, the scene where illegal immigrants hang out. I argued that this showed that the defendants knew he was not a convicted felon. But if the judge wanted more specificity, Sheriff Arpaio and I could easily amend the complaint.

---

57. Arpaio v. Robillard et. al, 1:19-cv-3366 (D.D.C.), https://www.jassyvick.com/pdfs/ OpinionreMotiontoDismissandSanctionsDkt38042920.pdf.

After inordinate delay in issuing his ruling, Lamberth issued a dismissal with prejudice. The case was over, and Arpaio would not be allowed to routinely plead with more specificity. It is textbook law that leave to amend a complaint is to be freely granted—meaning that it is almost automatic. To add serious insult to injury, by the time Judge Lamberth ruled, given all of his delay, the one-year statute of limitations on Arpaio's defamation claims had run out.

In the course of the various court pleadings that followed, I asked Judge Lamberth to vacate this dismissal and allow my client to plead actual malice with more specificity, even though what had already been alleged was more than legally sufficient. In rapid fire, the judge refused.

Here are a few excerpts from my last legal filing to Judge Lamberth, which express not just my disappointment in him but also speak candidly to his intellectual dishonesty:

> (The court), showing its desire to get rid of Arpaio's claims by whatever means, ignoring Plaintiff Arpaio's alternative request...to properly allow Plaintiff Arpaio to amend with greater specificity, to avoid statute of limitations issues," created a "heads I win, tails you lose analysis, (and) Plaintiff Arpaio is now out of luck because the statute of limitations has run on defamation.

> In this regard, Plaintiff Arpaio and his counsel were hopeful that this Court would correct this error, intentional or otherwise.... Indeed, another court recently allowed a defamation lawsuit to proceed at least to discovery... ruling that actual malice has been properly pled when the defendants had published and then defamed the plaintiff as a felon, when he was only convicted of a misdemeanor. Blankenship v. Napolitano et. al, 2:19 -cv-00236 (S.D. Va.). While this court ruled properly, this Court has conjured up factually and legally unsupportable excuses to deny Plaintiff his due process rights.

I filed a copy of this other federal judge's decision with Lamberth, hopeful that he would then do the right thing and allow the sheriff's case to go forward. I went on:

> In short, while this Court has on occasion been critical of Plaintiff's counsel in the past, the shoe must now candidly be worn on the other foot. Plaintiff and his counsel thus respectfully request that this injustice be expeditiously corrected, as this Court has seriously erred in denying due process to Plaintiff Arpaio, for whatever apparently improper reason.

My brave client is now out of court, and while only Judge Lamberth knows for sure why he allowed these media outlets to get off scot-free, I have my own thoughts. Knowing Judge Lamberth as I do and having considered him a friend with whom I have interacted over the years when I did not have a case before him, I can surmise that he bailed out for one or more of these reasons.

First, Sheriff Arpaio's misdemeanor conviction for contempt was over his alleged violation of another federal judge's order enjoining ethnic profiling at alien day-worker sites. As a result, perhaps Judge Lamberth felt he could not side with someone who was found to have violated a court order; it was not part of the judicial creed of loyalty, so to speak. Never mind that this other federal judge, G. Murray Snow of the U.S. District Court for the District of Arizona, had threatened to destroy Arpaio and his career in law enforcement at all costs.[58] Federal judges who do not stick together can't dine together, so to speak.

Second, to rule in favor of Arpaio that I had properly pleaded actual malice and that my client had been defamed would have allowed the case to proceed to discovery. And I did plead actual malice, which frankly was a "chip shot" to prove before a jury, since these defendants had covered the sheriff closely over the years

---

58. Melendres et.al v. Arpaio et. al, 989 F. Supp. 2d 822 (2013), https://casetext.com/case/manuel-de-jesus-ortega-melendres-v-arpaio-6.

and knew that he had not been convicted of a felony. One can only imagine the treasure trove of bile, invective, and hatred toward the sheriff that is in the files of CNN, *Huffington Post*, and *Rolling Stone* concerning America's Toughest Sheriff, a supporter of President Trump. Judge Lamberth may not have wanted to open this Pandora's box, exposing the hatred and deceit that obviously lies beneath the surface of this leftist media.

And why not? Because this leftist media would then retaliate against Lamberth and viciously smear him as well! Judge Lamberth likely had already had his fill of this venom during the Clinton administration, when he had made a number of good rulings in my favor. In fact, since Lamberth is a Reagan appointee, the leftist media has always tried to tie us both into one conservative bow, and sometimes he would even unfairly criticize me to show his independence. I would go along with this and did not push back, knowing that he wanted some cover for taking (at the time but no longer) strong actions. Perhaps in this case for Arpaio, the judge did not want to open this can of leftist slimy worms again, and maybe, as a jurist of senior status, he decided he no longer wanted to take the heat in the leftist kitchen.

Third, Sheriff Arpaio had been made so "radioactive" by the leftist media that for Lamberth to have him in his courtroom would compromise the judge's desire to be seen as part of the "judicial club." It would not be good for one's image with fellow federal judges, in particular in the most leftist and most politicized courthouse in the land short of the U.S. District Court for the North District of California, based in San Francisco and Oakland.

Fourth, not long after Judge Lamberth made his initial ruling dismissing the sheriff's defamation lawsuit, he made a strong ruling, many years late given intervening investigations in Congress—not coincidentally led by two-faced phony former congressman Trey Gowdy who, as chairman of a subcommittee of the

House Government Oversight and Reform Committee, dishonestly exonerated Hillary Clinton of wrongdoing that led to the terrorist massacre at Benghazi. Judge Lamberth ruled that Hillary could be deposed in a Freedom of Information Act case over this avoidable tragedy. The lawsuit had been filed by my former group Judicial Watch. Thus, knowing that most people still associate me with Judicial Watch—particularly since its current head Tom Fitton is not a lawyer but mostly just a spokesman for the group—it could also be that he did not want to look like he was bending over backward on my behalf with my client Arpaio.

Fifth, sixth, and seventh is anyone's guess. But whatever the reason, Judge Lamberth's oath of office requires him to adhere to and obey the law without regard to the person before him, not to concoct phony reasons to skirt it. And the bottom line is that my previously favorite federal judge, the one I used to cite as one of the few shining examples of federal judicial integrity and as a model of impartiality, finally succumbed and sold out. His newly minted application for membership in the "backroom judicial club" of hypocrites and compromised hacks—that is, the incestuous coterie of the "politicians in robes" who infest the federal bench—was accepted.

If the now less-than-Honorable Royce C. Lamberth could throw in the towel of judicial impartiality and respect for the letter of the law, then what trust can yours truly, or anyone else for that matter, have moving forward in pursuing legitimate attempts to resolve major politically and socially tinged disputes peacefully and legally. Jefferson, again, proved to be omniscient, and the "blood of patriots" appeared to inevitably be on the horizon, and the federal judges, seeing the reaction of the citizenry on January 6, 2021, realize that they are next on the people's "hit list." This helps explain why federal judges, particularly on the D.C. federal court, have been harsh on even the overwhelmingly peaceful protesters who entered the Capitol Building on January 6, 2021, and were later rounded up en masse by Biden's Gestapo of an FBI, and then criminally charged by Biden's Department of Justice. The January 6, 2021, uprising was, as an increasingly final straw to the stage-four cancerous government corruption in general, provoked after President Trump's own hand-picked jurists, including Supreme Court Justices Kavanaugh, Gorsuch and Coney Barrett, threw him under the bus by refusing to even hear The Donald's and the state of Texas's election challenges. Many of these peaceful protesters have been denied bail, kept in the slammer, and thrown into solitary confinement, until their scheduled trial, forcing them to confess to their alleged crimes and plead guilty to lessen perceived punishment, to months and years in prison, on the phony pretext that since Trump continues to spew the so-called "Big Lie" that he won the presidential election, they will again (sic) resort to violent protest—a falsity in the extreme. In my opinion, these federal judges fear for their own lives, as the public is increasingly learning of their own crimes against the republic and the Constitution.

But all of this notwithstanding, the sellout by Judge Lamberth was the proverbial final straw for me, underscoring why we need to radically change how we select and police federal judges and why we need a viable means to remove them from the bench when they intentionally ignore and stray from the law.

And, to make matters worse, with regard to January 6, 2021, Lamberth has followed the lead of his other judicial brothers and sisters in the venomous federal court in the District of Columbia also seeing fit to do a number on the peaceful protesters, save for one ruling where he held prison officials in civil contempt for denying medical care, but then referred the matter to the Biden Gestapo for investigation, yet another cop out. If he had chosen not to protect the legal and prison establishment, he could have taken action that was not couched for public perception and held the prison officials in criminal contempt, throwing them in the slammer, rather than referring them to the Department of Injustice, which will bury the charges.[59]

Now let's take a walk down my memory lane of the top twenty and counting worst federal judges I have experienced in my over four decades of legal practice, ones who are but a small representative sample of the legal hacks that sit atop our federal courts—but, sadly, are not that much different from the rest. Rather than serving as the protectors of the citizenry who our Founding Fathers envisioned they would be, federal judges arrogantly have become our worst adversaries and, in many respects, enemies of the state— unaccountable to anyone and anything! They are a clear and present danger to the survival of our democratic republic as the despots Jefferson foresaw they would become as unelected officials, chosen on the basis of political patronage, bestowed with life tenure at taxpayer expense, and shielded by contrived claims of immunity from liability—which they gave to themselves—and no practical or presently viable means to remove them.

In the 246 years since the founding of our republic on July 4, 1776, only eight federal judges, among tens of thousands, have been shown the door through impeachment by an inept and equally compromised legislative branch that mostly feathers its own nest at the expense of We the People. As just one horrific example among many, one of the few federal judges to be impeached in recent history for taking bribes, Alcee Hastings, thankfully formerly of the U.S. District Court for the Southern District of Florida, later ran for Congress, won a seat in Florida's Twentieth Congressional District, and has since lived happily ever after as a "Distinguished Gentleman" on Capitol Hill. But Hastings's "resurrection" was not

---

59. Harper Neidig, "Judge Holds DC Corrections Officials in Contempt Over Treatment of Jan. 6 Defendant," *The Hill* (October 13, 2021), https://thehill.com/regulation/court-battles/576561-judge-holds-dc-corrections-officials-in-contempt-over-treatment-of.

funny, as could have been included as part of the same theme by actor and producer Eddie Murphy in his classic comedy film *The Distinguished Gentlemen*, which is sadly an accurate depiction of the swamp. How did this African American ex-federal judge convince voters in this predominantly black district to elect him? You guessed it. Years ahead of the current times—where many blacks and other minorities hide behind charges of racism and thus in practice enjoy more rights than the majority by virtue of "minority privilege"—Hastings predictably and cynically played the race card, claiming that he was impeached by white senators because he is black! This former federal judge is a poster boy for what still lurks on the federal bench even today.

MY TOP TWENTY WORST "DESPOTS" ON THE FEDERAL BENCH AND COUNTING!
The Federal Judicial Hall of Shame

Number One and Winner—Honorable Colleen Kollar-Kotelly (Clinton Appointee)

Appointed by President Bill Clinton to the federal bench and taking an oath to obey the law and the Constitution before assuming her office on March 26, 1997, Judge Colleen Kollar-Kotelly ironically also succeeded Judge Lamberth as the Chief Judge of the U.S. Foreign Intelligence Surveillance Court (FISC) and served in that capacity between May 19, 2002, and May 18, 2009. As far as her nomination to the U.S. District Court for the District of Columbia, she was strenuously opposed for confirmation by dozens of conservative public interest groups under the umbrella of the Free Congress Foundation, then run by conservative icon Paul Weyrich. Kotelly was seen as far too leftist by this coalition and as someone who would not enforce the dictates of the

Constitution as an "originalist"—someone who would maintain a strict interpretation of the Founders' original words and intent, rather than view the Constitution as a "living document" that is subject to reinterpretation over time. A federal judge like Kotelly, who was predicted to stray from the law, is commonly called a judicial activist. Judicial activism is a staple of left-leaning judges appointed mostly by Democrat presidents.

During the Clinton impeachment saga, Judge Kotelly's husband, also a lawyer, represented a U.S. Secret Service agent in the president's detail who had been subpoenaed by independent counsel Ken Starr. The purpose of this legal representation was to try to prevent the Secret Service agent from testifying about what he knew of President Clinton's sexual dalliance with the White House intern Monica Lewinsky. Regrettably, Kotelly's lawyer husband succeeded.

Thus, Judge Kotelly and her hubby possess a leftist Democrat establishment bent if not radical bias. This comes as no surprise to anyone who follows the federal courts. Yours truly and my clients are, to put it bluntly, not their "cup of tea," as you will see later.

And someone who has been forced to endure the dishonest politics of the federal courts had been our forty-fifth president, Donald J. Trump. One by one, his attempts to enforce the rule of law with regard to limiting illegal immigrants flowing across the nation's southern border and from Middle Eastern nations that harbor Islamic terrorists in particular, thereby enhancing the security of the republic by preventing drug cartels, terrorists, and other dangerous individuals and groups from gaining entry, had been thwarted by federal judges of Kotelly's ilk.

After one such federal judge, Jon Tigar of the U.S. District Court for the Northern District of California, a tribunal not coincidentally located in the radically left-wing Bay area in Oakland, California, preliminarily enjoined Trump's new policy on granting political asylum to illegal immigrants, the then-president rightly reacted by declaring this was par for the course by an Obama-appointed federal judge. And this was mild criticism, given that Judge Tigar, a graduate of the ultra-leftist law school of the University of California at Berkeley (Boalt Hall), is also the son of radical leftist activist lawyer Michael Tigar, also a graduate of Berkeley's law school and an avowed communist—long ago photographed with Ramon Castro proudly sporting a Cuba tee shirt and the recipient of effusive thank you letters from his co-revolutionary big brother Fidel.

Michael Tigar was thus fired as a young law clerk to Justice Brennan of the U.S. Supreme Court at the request of then FBI Director J. Edgar Hoover and Chief Justice Earl Warren over his subversive communist ties. This firing was confirmed by none other than famed *Washington Post* investigative journalist Bob Woodward in his landmark book on the High Court, *The Brethren*.

The leftist inclinations of Judge Jon Tigar are obviously a chip off his father's old Communist block. More about Michael Tigar later, as he somehow crept into a quasijudicial hearing committee of the District of Columbia Board of Professional Responsibility that recently and outrageously recommended that I be suspended from the practice of law in the swamp for thirty-three months, not coincidentally on a case that involved Judge Kotelly, his leftist "soul sister." This recommendation is on appeal. True to his Marxist ideology, Michael Tigar, along with scores of leftist law professors, also filed a bar complaint against Trump White House Counselor Kellyanne Conway for simple remarks she made on MSNBC, so I am not his only intended conservative victim, to say the least.

Coming to the defense of Michael Tigar's son, Judge Jon Tigar, was none other than Chief Justice John Roberts, an appointee of President George H.W. Bush and a classic establishment

Republican swamp creature. Here is what National Republic Radio (NPR), also leftist, reported about an exchange with President Trump:

> In a rare moment of direct criticism, Supreme Court Chief Justice John Roberts rebuked President Trump on Wednesday for the president's description of a federal judge who ruled against his asylum policy as "an Obama judge." Within hours, the president fired back on Twitter, launching an unusual conflict between the executive and judicial branches.

> "We do not have Obama judges or Trump judges. Bush judges or Clinton judges," Roberts said in a statement. "What we have is an extraordinary group of dedicated judges doing their level best to do equal right to those appearing before them. That independent judiciary is something we should all be thankful for," Roberts said. Roberts has never responded to any president so directly and publicly before.[60]

Taken aback by this public tongue-lashing by Republican-establishment Roberts, the then-president replied in a patented Trumpian tweet, again as reported by NPR:

> Sorry Chief Justice John Roberts, but you do indeed have "Obama judges," and they have a very much different point of view than the people who are charged with the safety of our country.[61]

NPR then elaborated and emphasized further:

> Trump's initial response was to a ruling by U.S. District Judge Jon Tigar, who issued a temporary restraining order against Trump's asylum policy Monday, saying it violated a provision of the asylum law. Trump called the decision a "disgrace,"

---

60. Brian Naylor and Nina Totenberg, "Chief Justice Roberts Issues Rare Rebuke to Trump; Trump Fires Back," National Public Radio (November 21, 2018), https://www.npr.org/2018/11/21/670079601/chief-justice-roberts-issues-rare-rebuke-to-trump.

61. Ibid.

adding, "this was an Obama judge and I'll tell you what, it's not going to happen again like this anymore."

Trump went on the excoriate the 9th Circuit Court of Appeals which he wrongly blamed for the ruling, saying, "Every case that gets filed in the Ninth Circuit, we get beaten. And then we end up having to go to the Supreme Court, like the travel ban, and we won," Trump said.[62]

Ironically, Chief Justice Roberts is, as was "innocently" revealed to me by Judge Lamberth when I visited with him years ago in his chambers, a card-playing buddy of my now-compromised friend, as birds of a feather do indeed play poker together, even if Lamberth is more conservative in political ideology than Roberts, who has moved left in recent years. But the point here is that President Trump was right! Tragically, we do have Obama and Clinton judges!

Chief Justice Roberts, the "Supreme Leader" sitting atop the federal judiciary, simply lied, just as he did years ago over a matter involving the alleged Obama-appointed fellow Justice Elena Kagan, whom I asked to recuse herself from a seminal case involving the constitutional validity of Obamacare. Kagan had been a legal architect and advocate for Obamacare when she served as solicitor general in the Obama DOJ.

It was widely reported by *Business Insider* and throughout the media that "before taking the bench, Kagan served as solicitor general for the Obama administration. In that role, she helped create arguments defending the constitutionality of Obamacare. And when the act came under fire in Florida vs. HHS, she helped craft a legal defense for the Affordable Care Act…. During her time working for the Obama administration, Kagan called the act 'simply amazing,' in an email to Democrats. She also lauded the

---

62.   Ibid.

fact that Democrats had the votes to pass the Affordable Care Act, according to The Week."[63]

Despite Justice Kagan's obvious conflict of interest in ruling on the constitutionality of Obamacare—other justices were also claimed to have conflicts—in his 2012 year-end annual report on the federal judiciary, Chief Justice Roberts deceitfully dismissed calls for recusal, claiming that since the impeccable judicial ethics of the justices have been in effect "certified" by virtue of their having been confirmed by the U.S. Senate, and incredibly claiming that they are not bound by the Judicial Code of Conduct, which in his convenient view might be unconstitutional, he would do nothing about this more-than-appearance of bias in favor of Obamacare.

And indeed, Roberts did more than nothing! In a twelfth-hour "switcharoo," Roberts joined Kagan and four other leftist justices in upholding its constitutionality, despite having initially been against it—as was also widely reported.[64] One has to wonder if the executive Deep State intel community—a whistleblower I represented claimed that Roberts was surveilled by the NSA—had gotten to him and threatened to expose his personal secrets, causing his "inexplicable" reversal. Indeed, there have been strong rumors in the swamp for years that the chief justice, like many of the high and mighty in our nation's present capital, is a closet gay. While most people do not care about one's sexual persuasion, a person such as Roberts, then nearing sixty—he is currently sixty-seven—and a married man with adopted children, may feel differently.

---

63. Abby Rogers, "The Supreme Court Justices' Shocking Conflicts Could Determine the Fate of Obamacare," *Business Insider* (June 2, 2012), https://www.businessinsider.com/supreme-court-conflicts-with-obamacare-2012-5.

64. "The Inside Story on How Roberts Changed His Supreme Court Vote on Obamacare," *Forbes.com* (July 1, 2012), https://www.forbes.com/sites/theapothecary/2012/07/01/the-supreme-courts-john-roberts-changed-his-obamacare-vote-in-may/?sh=394f91fbd701.

In short, Chief Justice Roberts admitted that political biases and prejudices are welcome on the federal bench and then decided to nail shut the coffin on legitimate challenges to this unconstitutional legislation.

Sadly, tragically, we do have Clinton and Obama federal jurists and Bush, Reagan, Trump, and now Biden jurists, and contrary to the ridiculous and dishonest phony rationales and protestations of even Chief Justice Roberts—himself proven to be a "politician in robes" and judicial hack—Judge Kotelly has shown herself to be one of the worst offenders, among other "indiscretions." Kotelly, as a dyed-in-the-wool Clinton judge, has been paying back her lofty perch on the federal bench, which she owes to Slick Willy, for years, and my clients and I, among others, have been the victims of her bias and prejudice. Let me explain further, and you will see what I mean.

I first encountered Judge Kotelly in a lawsuit I brought after my unsuccessful Senate candidacy in Florida for an individual named Scott Tooley, who was an IT maven to then Republican Representative Chris Cox of California. Shortly after September 11, 2001, Scott was at the check-in counter of Southwest Airlines on his way home from Washington, D.C. The check-in stewardess routinely asked my client if he had any suggestions for the chairman of Southwest, in line with the airline's policy of being customer friendly. In response, still suffering from the shock of the tragedy at the World Trade Center in downtown Manhattan, Scott earnestly told her that the airline should do a better job of searching for bombs in the cargo hold. At the time, it was widely reported that airlines had inadequate security measures in place in this regard.

Shortly thereafter, Scott observed persons following him and heard strange clicks on his phone. He contacted me to find out if he had somehow been placed on a terrorist watch list and put under government surveillance.

Around this time, the *New York Times* had broken the story about illegal and unconstitutional surveillance by the George W. Bush administration which, like waterboarding and other forms of torture, were seen by W and his vice president, Cheney, as a necessity to aid in the capture of terrorists post September 11. The reporters who published these revelations were James Risen and Eric Lichtblau.

In order to better understand whether Scott's concerns were valid, I called Lichtblau, who I had come to know on other matters and asked him if he thought that my client, given what he told the stewardess at Southwest, would then be placed on a government terrorist watch list and surveilled. Eric, based what he had learned as one of the top national security reporters, told me yes.

Scott and I then decided to sue President George W. Bush and his intelligence agencies over what would be, if proven, a violation of the Fourth Amendment, which prohibits unreasonable searches and seizures, that is spying without probable cause that a crime is being committed or that the subject is communicating with terrorists.[65] The complaint, filed in federal court in the nation's capital, was supposedly randomly assigned to Judge Kotelly. At the time, Kotelly was also the chief judge of the FISC, which was largely created by Congress to administer Section 702 of the Foreign Intelligence Surveillance Act and other intel laws.

The story by the *New York Times* put Judge Kotelly and her FISC court under media scrutiny, since questions were now being asked about how she could let W's spy agencies have such free rein to violate constitutional rights, as the FISC court has supervisory authority. And during this period, Bush entered into an agreement with the FISC that his administration would provide greater transparency on their spying initiatives to the court post September 11. Indeed, this massive surveillance was the precursor to what was

---

65. Tooley v. Bush, 06-cv-306 (D.D.C.), https://www.govinfo.gov/app/details/US-COURTS-dcd-1_06-cv-00306.

later revealed in even greater detail by Edward Snowden during the Obama years.

To make the long story shorter, after Kotelly reached a deal with President Bush for his administration to be more transparent with the FISC, she conjured up a false reason to dismiss Scott's lawsuit, incredibly suggesting that she could discern through newspaper accounts that my client was not surveilled, as the spying was limited to Al Qaeda. This was patently false. I have always suspected that Kotelly's dismissal of Scott's complaint against President Bush over his illegal spying on my client and millions of other American citizens who had done no wrong, was a quid pro quo of W agreeing to advise Kotelly's FISC court of its clandestine, post September 11 surveillance activities. Kotelly's dismissal, which was later reversed by the U.S. Court of Appeals for the District of Columbia Circuit, as are many of her contrived rulings, was an attempted sell-out of the American people and their Bill of Rights.

Later, a whistleblower by the name of Diane Roark, years subsequently my client as well, approached Kotelly about what she had learned as a Republican staffer on the House Intelligence Committee charged with oversight over the NSA. Roark wanted to inform Kotelly about illegal spying by the NSA. Rather than listen to her, the judge turned her in to the FBI in order for this compromised law enforcement agency to investigate her over allegations that she had leaked this as well to the *New York Times*. As a result, the FBI raided her home and seized her computer, causing massive emotional distress.

During this time, Roark was suffering from severe breast cancer, and Kotelly's callous, insensitive, heartless, and frankly outrageous treatment caused severe anxiety, which worsened the cancer. After all, Kotelly was then the chief judge of FISC and had a duty and responsibility to hear Roark out, not just because that was her duty but for the good of the nation. In addition to her judicial hackery, the judge thus had shown that she was heartless.

As if this cruelty and judicial dishonesty was not enough, there is the case of the Persian Voice of America (VOA) female broadcaster who was allegedly sexually harassed by her co-anchor and then retaliated against by her managers.[66] The Persian broadcaster, an attractive female who, with her co-anchor who allegedly sexually harassed her, broadcast a message of freedom into the Islamic Republic of Iran during a period when it looked like the radical regime might fall at the hands of the Iranian people, asked me to bring suit.

The alleged sexual harassment and retaliation had driven my client to the point of possible suicide, she claimed, and rather than remaining at work in VOA's headquarters in Washington, D.C., she offered to be relocated to the network's offices in Los Angeles, away from the harasser and her retaliating managers, while her case wound its way through internal review by the agency's civil rights division. When VOA arbitrarily would not allow her to be stationed in LA, I filed suit in federal court to force the issue. The case was, again, assigned randomly to Judge Kotelly.

Despite a mountain of evidence that the female broadcaster could continue to do her job at VOA's Persian News Network's office in LA—and Tinseltown is the home to over one million Iranian-Americans, so much so that the city has been nicknamed Tehrangeles—Kotelly ruled against her. Her decision contained over seventeen single-spaced pages of factual misstatements and errors, so much so that its inaccuracy had to be intentional.

Not coincidentally, this Persian broadcaster was of a conservative bent, and her views were the polar opposite of President Obama and his administration, who wanted to establish closer ties with the radical Islamic regime in Tehran and used the propaganda

---

66. Sataki v. BBG et. al, 10-cv-534, (D.D.C.), https://www.govinfo.gov/content/pkg/USCOURTS-dcd-1_10-cv-00534/pdf/USCOURTS-dcd-1_10-cv-00534-2.pdf.

of the Persian News Network to try to do so. In addition, to put pressure on VOA to settle, before Kotelly issued her ruling, I had also sued its Board of Governors, which necessarily included as its titular head Secretary of State Hillary Clinton. Kotelly was also assigned to this related case.

It is my reasoned opinion that Judge Kotelly threw my client's cases out not just because I was her lawyer and had sued the wife of Bill Clinton, the president who "graciously" had put her on the federal bench, but also because the Persian broadcaster was a conservative, pro-Shah of Iran loyalist and anti-Islamic regime activist who despised the policies of Obama to appease the ayatollahs and mullahs in Tehran rather than to aid in the fall of the regime. These views obviously did not square with Judge Kotelly's Democrat-leftist bent, which generally has sought to appease the regime—the latest effort being Obama's previous dangerous nuclear deal with the mullahs.

The decision not to put my client back to work caused her severe emotional distress, which sent her over the edge, as well as cost her a career at VOA, which she said was her professional dream. To this day, my client has not recovered. And instead of blaming the right person, Judge Kotelly, confused and broken, she, as the victim see had come to see herself as on all fronts, struck back at me by filing a bar complaint with the Disciplinary Counsel of the District of Columbia Bar, a group of Trump and conservative-hating leftists who have tried to drag me through the mud for going on eleven years. Ironically, this is the proceeding where the father of federal judge Jon Tigar, Michael Tigar, an avowed and proud communist, sat on a hearing committee that recommended my suspension for thirty-three months from the practice of law, which I am challenging as I write. More on this later.

Kotelly's cruel ruling, which belied common sense, decency, and, yes, the law, was another reminder of the rank dishonesty, much more lack of humanity, of this federal judge. It affected me as well, and the evening after her ruling I nearly got into a fatal car accident, so upset I was when traveling on the dangerous 101 Freeway in Los Angeles, after having had a few glasses of wine to drown my sorrows with a friend at a local watering hole.

A few days thereafter, God's son came and spoke to me. Jesus told me not to despair and to press on, as he would be by my side. This was the biggest moment in my life.... Perhaps I do owe Kotelly something, much like I owe, to a much lesser extent, the controversial Judge William D. Keller, a Reagan appointee I write about in *Whores*, whose behavior was the final straw that caused me to found Judicial Watch and go rogue!

Then there was another case involving Iran that somehow wound up in front of Judge Kotelly. This involved the unexplained shoot-down of a Chinook Helicopter carrying thirty special ops forces, including some SEAL Team VI members, just three months after President Obama claimed to have killed Osama bin Laden. Ironically, another leftist hack judge in Kotelly's federal courthouse, the Honorable James Boasberg, an Obama appointee, blocked the release of photos of Bin Laden's claimed corpse in a Freedom of Information Act case, despite the law that no right of privacy exists for the dead, particularly for the world's numero-uno terrorist. Boasberg, appointed to the federal bench by the half-Muslim forty-fourth president, refused to order the release of the photo after Obama claimed this would be an affront to the Muslim world. Or was Boasberg also covering for Obama, as many terrorist experts believe that Bin Laden actually died earlier of natural causes, and that the Muslim-in-Chief staged the assassination to boost his political standing. This line of thinking may be the case, as the claimed assassin, former Navy Seal Rob O'Neill, violating his oath of confidentiality as a Navy Seal to claim credit, have never seemed credible to me.

That aside, I represent some of the families of the servicemen of Extortion 17 who were killed by these Taliban forces, as previously discussed in Chapter Three.

The suit was filed not just against Iranian defendants, as the Islamic state had a bounty of five thousand dollars on the heads of our brave servicemen in Afghanistan, but also the Taliban itself, which actually is a rogue government, and for good measure, the former president of Afghanistan, Hamid Karzai, a world-recognized thief and criminal.[67] My clients believed that Karzai had cut a deal with the Taliban where he would disclose the coordinates of the mission, Extortion 17, in exchange for cold cash—which is Karzai's modus operandi. This was believed to also be meant to be an "offering" to the terrorists to make amends for the death of Bin Laden.

The case is now going on nine years, and Karzai has continuously evaded service of process of the original complaint, having the current, equally corrupt Afghan government serve as his shield. But even more egregious, as my Gold Star parents grieved over the dishonesty of our own government in covering up the reasons for the deaths of their sons, Judge Kotelly refused to allow service of the complaint on Karzai by alternative means—that is, by sending it to him over Karzai's Twitter account, which would surely put him on additional notice of our clients' claims.

Other judges have ordered that alternative means of service of process—such as by Twitter—are proper and legal in cases involving evaders like Karzai, an alleged terrorist collaborator. But of course, not Kotelly! Now that Biden has surrendered Afghanistan to the Taliban, stranding thousands of Americans and Afghan allies to these terrorists, there is no point attempting to serve Karzai by other means, as he reportedly in hiding, like his successor president, Ashraf Ghani, with boatloads of cash, comprised mostly of

---

67. Strange v. Islamic Republic of Iran et. al, 14-cv-435 (D.D.C.), https://www.govinfo. gov/app/details/USCOURTS-dcd-1_14-cv-00435.

American aid, and is living underground in some God-forsaken place. In Karzai's case, he is being protected by the Taliban, having been bribed to the hilt by them during his years as president apparently not to personally order drone strikes against them. That said, Freedom Watch has asked Kotelly to finally get the case moving, after nearly nine years of delay, but do not hold your breath with this dishonest hack jurist.

Her callousness and deceit, as the vindictive witch she has proven to be, will undoubtedly continue on, and this heartless federal judge soldiers on—pun intended. Based on past experience, Kotelly will find a way to put the screws to my clients, ostensibly because I, a perceived anti-Clinton public interest lawyer, am counsel to Gold Star parents for whom she also has little respect, much less concern. In this regard, it is telling that when Judge Kotelly describes me in court orders, she disrespectfully refers to me as a "self-styled" public interest conservative advocate. I think the nation knows what I do for a profession, but apparently it does not equate for her that conservative activism is in the public interest!

But wait, my experience with Judge Kotelly does not end here. In the course of the prosecution of Cliven Bundy, his sons, and the peaceful but armed supporters who came to Bunkerville when they learned of and witnessed on television the gross government overreach and brutality by BLM and FBI agents who invaded the Bundy Ranch to destroy them and their family business, I filed a Freedom of Information Act request to obtain all of the documents and other records in these agencies' files for use in the Bundys' criminal defense.[68]

These documents and records had to be readily available to BLM and the FBI, as they must have been compiled to work up

---

68.   Freedom Watch, Inc. v. Bureau of Land Management et. al, 16-cv-2320 (D.D.C.), https://www.govinfo.gov/content/pkg/USCOURTS-dcd-1_16-cv-02320/pdf/US-COURTS-dcd-1_16-cv-02320-0.pdf.

the Obama DOJ's indictments in furtherance of the prosecution of my client. But rather than producing the documents and records, BLM and the FBI predictably stonewalled—the Deep State at its "best"—and told Judge Kotelly, after I was forced to file suit and the case was mysteriously reassigned to her from the docket of the original Judge Ketanji Brown Jackson— an Obama appointee and now under Biden an appellate judge who looks like the twin of Michelle Obama— that it would take them a whopping forty years to produce them.

Unbelievable as this representation was, Kotelly was happy to readily agree and refused to accelerate production, which she had the judicial authority to order. In court pleadings prior to her decision affirming the forty-year production, I told the judge that by the time all the documents and records were produced, not only would Cliven Bundy, who was then in his mid-seventies, be long since dead, but so would she and yours truly. And the young DOJ lawyer handing the defense of the suit for the BLM and FBI would be near death.

In issuing her order, Kotelly showed no concern and could not have cared less. After all, before her were the conservative "state sovereign" Bundys. They had resisted illegal federal power, which was used to tyrannically seize their cattle and destroy their livelihood. Also before her was their conservative lawyer, Larry Klayman, the man who was also her ideological and political polar opposite, perceived foe, and who, at Judicial Watch, later at Freedom Watch, and as a private practitioner, had sued her sponsors and benefactors, the Bonnie and Clyde of American politics, Bill and Hillary Clinton and their corrupt administration, over one hundred times. Among the numerous complaints I had filed against the Clintons was a very provocative one dealing with the racketeering and shakedown nonprofit known as the Clinton Foundation. Last, but hardly least, is my own personal litigation, now almost an unprecedented seventeen years old, against the current Judicial Watch leadership.[69] After I stepped down as chairman and general counsel in 2003 to run for the U.S. Senate in Florida, Tom Fitton seized control of the organization, which as a result—since Fitton is not a lawyer—now mostly just sells smoke and mirrors to rake in fundraising monies to enrich its coffers.

At the time that I left Judicial Watch to run for the U.S. Senate, I had learned that Fitton had not even graduated from George Washington University, despite him having represented on his resume that he had an undergraduate degree.

I originally founded Judicial Watch on July 29, 1994, to investigate and prosecute abuse and corruption in government and the legal profession—and, of course, to "watch" judges. But now it has, twenty-eight years later, morphed into little more than a document collection service and repository. Fox News even uses the documents Fitton and his staff obtain under the Freedom of Information Act to further its highly profitable concept of broadcasting, as we discussed in Chapter Two. But unlike when I conceived of, founded, and ran Judicial Watch, my baby no longer brings many, if any, real hard-hitting cases to attempt to mete out justice. Rather, non-lawyer Fitton and his "yes men" on the current board of directors mostly just file Freedom of Information Act requests and then bring complaints to obtain documents when the government predictably stonewalls. I do not think that they even have a real trial lawyer on their staff. That is fine and dandy, but then Fitton and company merely pleads with the government to take corrective action—the same government that stonewalled Judicial Watch's Freedom of Information Act requests in the first place. Thus, the smoke and mirrors of which I speak. Clever and lucrative as Judicial Watch's cases are "low budget," but no cigar! As of

---

69. Klayman v. Judicial Watch, Inc. et. al, 06-cv-670 (D.D.C.); Klayman v. Judicial Watch, Inc. et. al, 13-cv-20610 (S.D. Fl.), https://casetext.com/case/klayman-v-judicial-watch-inc-2021.

only 2019 this writing, according to its 990 tax return, my former organization has over $172 million in total assets but uses little of it to try to mete out real justice.[70] As of 2022—three years later—Judicial Watch's total assets are likely approaching $300 million, its 990 tax return not as yet having been filed and published on the organization's website!

When I voluntarily left Judicial Watch as its chairman and general counsel on September 19, 2003, to run for the U.S. Senate in my home state of Florida, Fitton and his co-opted directors, Paul Orfanedes and Chris Farrell, not only violated my severance agreement but also tried every trick in the book to try to harm my family and me, as they viewed my Senate campaign as a competitive fundraising threat. Moreover, Fitton, who assumed control and—having begun as my assistant—had always been in my shadow at Judicial Watch was, in my reasoned opinion, jealous of my stature and set out to try to take me down, so he could someday be the "big man on the conservative campus."

To further his ends, Fitton even instructed his counsel to threaten me with public lawsuits to harm my Senate campaign if I ever referred to myself as the founder of Judicial Watch, an absurd proposition. Without belaboring all of the gory details, let it be said that when I could not convince Fitton and his pliant fellow directors Orfanedes and Farrell to lay off, I was forced to file suit. After I left Judicial Watch to run for the U.S. Senate, I have often asked rhetorically and in joking fashion, "What is the only thing that can separate the boys at Judicial Watch, particularly Fitton and Orfanedes, the latter of whom began his early legal career with my early law firm Klayman & Associates and worked with me for over fifteen years?" My answer, "a crowbar!"

The case landed with, you guessed it, Judge Kotelly and it dragged on for now going on seventeen years and counting, thanks

---

70.   See Judicial Watch 990 tax returns at www.judicialwatch.org.

in large part to her own misdeeds. Along the way, this very biased and prejudiced federal judge ruled that I could not present any witnesses or evidentiary exhibits at the eventual trial. The improper and phony reason: I had refused to produce the personal confidential information necessary for me to prove damages without a court-ordered protective order that the information, including personal tax returns, would be kept confidential. I did not trust Fitton and company and believed they would publicly use this confidential information to harm my family and me further.

Kotelly did, of course, gleefully allow the testimony of Fitton and Orfanedes at the eventual trial, finally held in 2018, where they were allowed to publish to the jury, with Kotelly's approval, false and incendiary charges that had no relevancy to the case, made by my former estranged wife that I had physically assaulted her. In other words, and to use the old adage, I beat my wife, an outrageous and fraudulent charge. They also leveled their own manufactured false and incendiary claims that I was forced to leave Judicial Watch because I had an affair with and sexually harassed Judicial Watch's office manager, who, to this day, does not know about this slander of her, a married woman with children. These false charges were later typically repeated and published by the self-styled and defiantly proud dirty trickster Roger Stone, now a seven-time convicted felon who has been sued over his defamation of Dr. Jerome Corsi and me as his lawyer.

Stone feared that Dr. Corsi would testify against him at his criminal prosecution, where he had been charged with perjury, witness tampering, and obstruction of justice, and apparently decided, for tactical reasons, to try to damage my client and me as a result. But divine justice stepped in: Stone was indicted and later convicted in rapid time at trial but Dr. Corsi was not, largely due to my legal representation, where we went on offense and sued and filed ethics complaints before DOJ's Office of Professional

Responsibility and Inspector General against Special Counsel Robert Mueller, discussed in greater detail later in this chapter. Jerry also was no perjurer.

As a result, the jury hearing the Judicial Watch case before Judge Kotelly reacted and ruled against me with a $2.8 Million Dollar verdict, so inflammatory and prejudicial was this slander. As egregious, when I appealed the verdict and judgment, Kotelly's "judicial friends" on the three appellate panel which reviewed her conduct, called her conduct on the then sixteen-year-old case "commendable" and affirmed her rulings, without any real, much less honest, legitimate analysis. This has forced me to sue these fellow judges, with claims that they have violated my constitutional Fifth and Fourteenth Amendment due process and First Amendment free speech rights, since their obvious intent is to bankrupt my family and me. This is an obvious way to attempt to end my public interest advocacy, which has been critical of federal judges like them.

In my complaint I cite the severe criticism contained in the first edition of this book, which was published on October 27, 2020, and heavily publicized by Post Hill Press and other publishing houses, months before, as a primary reason for their retaliation in addition to their circling the wagons to protect one of their own. Ironically, I now have to laugh that virtually every federal judge and their law clerks in the courthouse at 333 Constitution Avenue, N.W., which is shared by the lower and appellate courts, with common dining facilities and meeting rooms where they mingle and stir their legal caldrons together, likely will now purchase and read my book. But don't count on them learning something. I hope they choke on the read while eating taxpayer subsidized third rate surplus food, but this sarcasm is just that, as federal judges are not used to being taken to the woodshed in print, as they are more accustomed to vindictively harming and smearing others they do not like with their biased and frequently corruptly written published opinions and findings. But what is good for the goose, is now good for the gander. As President Harry Truman would often say, quoting General Harry H. Vaughan, "If you can't stand the heat, get out of the kitchen."[71] More on this later when I expose the three judges on the panel as well as the rest of the appellate court judges—who rubber-stamped Kotelly's misconduct—as the dishonest, unethical, and inherently dangerous federal judicial hacks they have proven to be, in goose step with Thomas Jefferson's dictatorial predictions!

In short, Judge Kotelly's vindictive, dishonest, and patently prejudicial misconduct in this case with Fitton and Judicial Watch was the final qualification necessary to secure her place in the annals of gross judicial malfeasance, allowing me to nominate her for and cinch her induction into the Federal Judicial Hall of Shame as the worst and most corrupt federal judge of my lifetime—and that is saying a lot given my long career! I turned seventy on July 20, 2021.

Now on to the other contenders for this prize—federal judicial hacks of the highest or should it more aptly be said lowest order. The first runner-up is the Honorable Amy Berman Jackson, an Obama appointee and one of Judge Kotelly's leftist and/or Republican establishment "soul sisters" on this same court in the murky and uber sleazy swamp known as the District of Columbia.

Number Two and First Runner-Up—Honorable Amy Berman Jackson (Obama Appointee)

The Honorable Amy Berman Jackson, who also sits on the U.S. District Court for the District of Columbia, along with Judges Lamberth and Kotelly and the cavalcade of many other compromised

---

71	. Favorite saying of Harry S Truman, https://www.dictionary.com/browse/if-you-cant-stand-the-heat--get-out-of-the-kitchen.

and intellectually corrupt "geniuses" that we will dissect in this chapter, is an appointee of President Obama. Ironically, before ascending to the federal bench, she was aptly the criminal defense counsel of William J. Jefferson, the African American congressman who was caught red-handed by the FBI stashing bribe money in his freezer and obviously later convicted. Jackson was also the federal judge who presided over the prosecution of now-convicted felon Roger Stone. Prior to trial, Stone posted an Instagram photo of a gun crosshairs next to Jackson's head, a "nicety" that, along with his other threatening coercive bag of tricks, earned him not just a rebuke but also a gag order.[72]

I first came upon Judge Jackson, who contributed a thousand dollars to the Clinton for President Committee in 1992, in a case that I filed for the Gold Star parents of two American heroes, Ty Woods and Sean Smith, who were murdered by Al-Qaeda terrorists along with Ambassador Christopher Stephens in the U.S. consulate at Benghazi, Libya.[73] At the time, Hillary Clinton was secretary of state. Hillary, who initially lied about who perpetrated the fatal attack, was sued by the parents of these patriots, Charles Woods and Pat Smith. The case hinged on Hillary's illegal use of a private, unsecure email server to do government business. This server, it was later revealed by former FBI director James Comey, was predictably hacked by adverse powers, such as Iran, Russia, and China, the primary suspect being Iran, who then transmitted the location of Ambassador Stevens to the terrorists in Benghazi. These terrorists then murdered not just Stephens but our clients' sons, who were part of the ambassador's detail.

The theory of the case against Hillary was that she, through her reckless and, at a minimum, negligent use of a private email

---

72. Julia Jacobs, "Roger Stone Posted A Photo of a Judge Beside Cross Hairs. She Ordered Him to Court," *New York Times* (February 19, 2019), https://www.nytimes.com/2019/02/19/us/roger-stone-instagram-judge.html.

73. Smith et. al v. Hillary Clinton, 1:16-cv-1606 (D.D.C.), https://law.justia.com/cases/federal/appellate-courts/cadc/17-5133/17-5133-2018-03-27.html.

server that was not secure, caused the wrongful death of Ty Woods and Sean Smith. Clinton had also publicly defamed their parents at the height of her presidential campaign in 2016: she called them liars when they revealed that she told them that the deaths were the result of Muslims becoming angry about a video broadcast by someone in California denigrating the Islamic prophet Mohammad—an absurd claim—especially since it later was disclosed that Hillary knew that Al-Qaeda terrorists had done the dirty deed. Hillary even told Charles Woods that she was going to see to it that the videographer would be criminally prosecuted. Charles, a former administrative law judge with legal training, recorded all of this in his diary to preserve it as evidence.

To the contrary, what the public later learned was that Clinton knew all along that the tragedy was carried out by Al-Qaeda and not some random Muslims who had gotten "indigestion" after watching the Muhammad video while eating rancid hummus. Thus, Hillary's famous line, broadcast during a congressional hearing, "What difference does it make!?"[74]

In the complaint, we pled that Hillary did not have immunity from suit because, first, she had acted outside the scope of her government authority by using an unauthorized, and thus illegal, private and unsecure email server. Second, we claimed that she had defamed my clients when she no longer was secretary of state, but rather a private citizen, albeit running for the presidency. It was a strong case with a strong pretext and perhaps the one chance to ever have Clinton pay legally for her actions.

When I filed the case for my clients, it was assigned to who I thought at the time was an unbiased and honorable federal judge, Richard J. Leon—a jurist who had twice ruled in my favor over

---

74. Feliks Garcia, "Why Did Hillary Clinton Ask 'What Difference Does It Make'?" *Independent* (July 21, 2016), https://www.independent.co.uk/news/world/americas/us-politics/hillary-clinton-what-difference-does-it-make-rnc-2016-benghazi-a7148706.html.

illegal surveillance and spying by Obama's Deep State intelligence agencies and who was then presiding over a Freedom of Information Act complaint that dealt with the similar issue of who had perpetrated the attack and what Clinton knew when she lied about the cause of the deaths. (My opinion of Leon later changed, as previously discussed.) But Leon, who was then approaching senior status on the bench and apparently wanted to lighten his caseload as a prelude to retirement, for improper and personal reasons, threw our case back into the clerk's random selection system. It was then sent by this judicial "wheel of fortune," so we were told, to Judge Jackson. In truth, I do not think that the case was assigned randomly to Berman Jackson, but was sent to her by the very politicized Chief Judge Beryl Howell, a leftist Democrat and undoubtedly a supporter of Hillary Clinton.

At the outset of the case, Hillary's legal counsel, David Kendall of the infamous law firm of Williams & Connolly—they helped her destroy the 33,000 plus emails generated by her unsecure private email server—routinely filed a motion to dismiss. And as has always been true when I sued the Clintons, he attacked me savagely and personally. I pushed back before Judge Jackson and pointed out how Kendall's client had committed many other crimes in the past and had lied repeatedly to courts, and that Kendall himself admittedly helped Hillary destroy much of her missing emails. But Judge Jackson chose not to even criticize Kendall for his unprofessional ad hominem attacks on me; instead, she pointedly warned me not to sharply criticize Hillary and Kendall again, else I would pay a price!

It was thus apparent that Jackson, appointed by Obama and a donor to the Clintons, was a typical, biased, leftist federal judge. Indeed, this proved to be true when, on the eve of Memorial Day in 2016, she predictably dismissed the case, taking the decision to rule on the wrongful death and defamation claims away from the jury Woods and Smith had requested, as was their constitutional right. With regard to the powerful wrongful death claim, she unethically strained to find that Clinton had government immunity for her nefarious actions—that is, she was acting within the scope of her employment when she illegally used a private, unsecure email account and server that gave up the location of the consulate to the terrorists. To the contrary, established case law clearly provides that even a secretary of state cannot claim immunity if she is acting illegally at the time.

And as for the dismissal of the defamation claim, this also was a flagrant violation of law, as the issue of who told the truth about the cause of the murders of my clients' sons—Hillary or Charles Woods and Pat Smith—was one for a jury to decide, not a politicized, leftist, pro-Hillary, Obama-appointed judge.

In short, I believe that this important case was dismissed to curry favor with Hillary Clinton during the 2016 presidential campaign with the obvious hope that Judge Jackson would be rewarded with a higher appointment, perhaps a seat on the U.S. Court of Appeals for the District of Columbia Circuit—widely considered however disingenuously the most "prestigious" tribunal short of the U.S. Supreme Court—should Hillary have been elected president. But what was far worse is that this hack leftist federal judge dismissed the suit on the eve of Memorial Day, despicably and disrespectfully sticking it to these Gold Star parents as they grieved for their heroic fallen sons.

With Judge Jackson's dishonest and politically motivated dismissal, I took her contrived and frivolous ruling up on appeal. The panel of three judges assigned to the appeal were "mysteriously" comprised of two Obama appointees and one establishment Republican jurist. Incredibly, I learned by accessing Federal Election Commission records that one of the Obama appointees had donated money, one thousand dollars to be exact, to

Hillary to further her 2008 presidential bid! Her name is Patricia Millet. In fact, Millet has donated boatloads of contributions to other leftist Democrat politicians' interests as well, such as Obama for America, Obama Victory Fund, Gilibrand for Senate, Kaine for Virginia, Moran for Congress, and, conveniently, even the now-deceased chairman of the Senate Judiciary Committee, Republican-turned-Democrat Senator Arlen Specter, who if she was ever nominated for a federal judgeship would hold confirmation hearings.

Politely, I first asked Judge Millet to recuse herself for her obvious conflict of interest in donating to Hillary Clinton, a violation of the Code of Judicial Conduct. She predictably refused, as federal judges in particular feel that they can do as they please given their unelected life tenure and immunity from suit. But when I filed a formal motion to disqualify her, incredibly and arrogantly ruling on the motion herself, Millet again refused to get off the appeal. And when I then went to the full court with a petition for en banc review—meaning, every judge on the appellate court, all eleven, including those appointed by Republican presidents, would review the case, they predictably circled the wagons and took no action to unseat this corrupt hack leftist colleague.

It thus came as no surprise that the appellate court, compromised politically to the core and entrenched in the smoldering stench of the swamp in our nation's capital—the "Capital of Corruption"—affirmed Judge Jackson's dismissal of the suit. The ruling reeked of dishonesty and disdain for anyone who would dare challenge and hold legally accountable, even in civil court, a fellow elite, that is, a "protected political insider species," like Hillary Clinton.

Needless to say, when I then took the matter to the U.S. Supreme Court, the nine politically appointed justices there also ran for cover. How dare my Gold Star parents, with needlessly murdered sons, sue the high priestess of deceit, trickery, and crime, a fellow swamp creature named Hillary Clinton. But for the grace of God, so goes the rest of the Washington, D.C. federal, judicial, and law enforcement establishment, the ethical and moral equivalent of Hollywood, only for ugly people!

Predictably, this Obama judge, in the accurate words of The Donald, protected the high priestess of crime, Hillary Clinton!

Now, in the aftermath of the January 6, 2021, uprising, Berman Jackson is hard at work doing the bidding of the Biden-Harris regime and the left. In this regard, she is gleefully and hatefully throwing even peaceful protesters in prison after they have been charged and arrested by a corrupt Department of Justice, more akin to a "Gestapo," that our justice ministry, now run by a "yes man" of an Attorney General Merrick Garland—not coincidentally previously a judge on the U.S. Court of Appeals for the District of Columbia Circuit. Garland's lackey is the disgraceful director of the FBI, Christopher Wray, a zero—nebbish in Yiddish—and a virtual legal chameleon who goes with the flow of whomever is in power.

Here is what Berman Jackson proclaimed from the bench in denying bail to one of the many peaceful protesters who were primarily charged with trespassing on the grounds of a Capitol Building, which incidentally belongs to the American people. CNN, which I have come to rename the Communist News Network, reported:

> In presiding over the cases of hundreds of people accused of breaching the U.S. Capitol on January 6 in support of then-President Donald Trump, federal judges have not held back when describing the unprecedented nature of the events that day.

> "You called yourselves patriots, but that is not patriotism," Judge Amy Berman Jackson told defendant Karl Dresch

earlier this month. "Patriotism is loyalty to country, loyalty to the Constitution—not loyalty to a head of state (meaning then-President Trump). That is the tyranny we rejected on July Fourth."

Earlier in Dresch's case, Jackson had denied his bond, in part because Trump "continues" to spew the (big) lie that inspired the attack on a near daily basis, according to her May 5 opinion.

That Trump continues to argue that he likely won the presidential election, and I share this view that absent cooked mail-in ballots, other election games and irregularities and perhaps massive fraud, he indeed probably did win, Berman Jackson's hatred of The Donald was not a valid reason to deny Dresch bail and keep him in prison while he awaited trial. And, her gratuitous proclamation that patriotism and loyalty to country means slavishly obeying the established government would have fallen on the deaf ears of our Founding Fathers, who themselves waged a literal coup against King George III and his corrupt government. Of course, for this dishonest leftist judge, unbridled obedience to a corrupt sovereign translates into her brand of patriotism and loyalty, "Sieg Heil" style.[75]

But Berman Jackson is not alone in this view. In addition to her other leftist hack colleagues on this court, Judges Beryl Howell, Emmet Sullivan, and Randolph Moss, Tanya Chutkan, Amit Mehta, James Boasberg, and Reggie Walton, to name just a few among many, both Democrat and Republican appointed, and coming from the presumed opposite side of this federal lower court in the capitol of corruption, Judge Royce Lamberth, a Republican appointee who, as previously discussed, pushed me over the edge

75. Tierney Sneed, "US Capitol Riot Judges Step Up as the Conscience of Democracy While Lawmakers Squabble," *CNN* (August 13, 2021), https://www.cnn.com/2021/08/13/politics/judges-riot-court-describe-january-6-chilling-disgrace-tyranny/index.html.

in tolerance for the comprised and politicized minions on the federal bench, pronounced this to another peaceful protester charged primarily with mere trespassing by the Biden-Harris Gestapo, as reported by *The Hill*, a centrist publication:

> "Quoting Washington, Lamberth wrote in his decision released Thursday (also denying bail to a January 6, 2021, protester) that 'The very idea of the power and the right of the people to establish government presupposes the duty of every individual to obey the established government.'"[76]

Lamberth's quotation, taken wholly out of context of what George Washington was trying to convey at the outset of the republic when many like Alexander Hamilton wanted to return to a limited monarchy after things were not going too well, belies the hard fact that the general and his colonial militias declared war on an established government and with the help of France won this war, after having defied the tyrannical edits of the King, rubber-stamped by his yes men on the Court of Saint James.

Lamberth, this once-clear-minded "patriotic" judge must have been smoking pot prior to the sentencing of this protester Eric Munchel, among the several other sentencing proceedings where he effectively equated peaceful protesters with white and other so-called domestic terrorists. If Lamberth persists, even at the more-than-ripe old age of seventy-eight, and even as a Reagan appointee to the federal bench, tongue in cheek he even could be considered as a candidate for the Supreme Court when the Biden-Harris regime if and when the Democrats inevitably try to pack it.

Indeed, Lamberth was recently praised by Biden Attorney General Merrick Garland during a House Judiciary Committee

76. Joseph Choi, "Federal Judge Blocks Release of Man Accused of Carrying Plastic Restraints Into Capitol During Riot," *The Hill* (February 18, 2021), https://thehill.com/homenews/state-watch/539493-federal-judge-blocks-release-of-man-accused-of-carrying-plastic.

Hearing under questioning by Republican congressmen about the mistreatment of January 6, 2021, peaceful protesters. The context: Garland used Lamberth to try to deflect from prison officials denying medical care to a wrongfully incarcerated protester pending trial who was seriously ill, by suggesting that Lamberth's meaningless referral of this criminal conduct to the DOJ's Civil Rights Division would solve the problem. However, sending the matter to the Biden-Harris Gestapo to investigate is like asking the fox to look into his own hen-house massacre. Garland and Lamberth are indeed birds of a feather, even if coming from a professed different ideological persuasion. You cover my derriere and I will cover yours, which is the primary modus operandi of sitting federal judges, Garland having been the chief judge on the federal appellate court in the swamp before Biden put him in charge of his Gestapo.[77]

Such is the arrogant, perverse, and patrician-like mindset of the establishment of judges on the federal bench—both Democrat- and Republican-appointed—fearing that they finally will be held accountable and "taken to the guillotines" when it comes to what inevitably will be further rebellion by We the People as the nation sinks further into a sea of deceit, corruption, and virtual dictatorship by the so-called ruling class, which tyranny is not to be questioned even through peaceful protest!

Number Three and Second Runner-Up—Honorable Ellen Segal Huvelle (Clinton Appointee)

The Honorable Ellen Segal Huvelle was appointed by President Bill Clinton and is a dyed-in-the-wool leftist Democrat. She is now

---

77. Kate Benner, "Garland Parries Pressure From Both Sides in Congressional Testimony: Appearing Before the House Judiciary Committee, the Attorney General Sidestepped Questions From Democrats About the Jan. 6 Investigation and Battled Away Criticism from Republicans," *New York Times* (October 21, 2021), https://www.nytimes.com/2021/10/21/us/politics/garland-testimony-jan-6.html.

on senior status on the same district court, the most politicized in the land, as are her rabidly leftist soul sisters Kotelly and Jackson.

I first encountered her when I ran Judicial Watch, when we received a notice of audit from the IRS, after our impeachment report over the myriad of Clinton scandals was accepted into the congressional record during the lead-up to Slick Willy's impeachment. The IRS notice of audit asked for my and the other directors' political party affiliations, which clearly evidenced a political motivation for the audit.

After attempting to negotiate a suitable solution with the most-feared Deep State agency in the executive branch, on par with the intel community, and an audit having been instituted, Judicial Watch was forced to file suit. The complaint regrettably landed before Judge Huvelle.

Predictably, given Judge Huvelle's apparent political bias and appointment to the federal bench by President Clinton, she ultimately dismissed our complaint, despite overwhelming evidence of the IRS's political and improper motivations. Indeed, Judicial Watch was not the only conservative group or publication to receive notices of audits and, of course, audits during the Clinton administration. I had represented my friend Joseph Farah in this regard concerning one of his entities, the Western Journalism Center (WJC), a conservative news service.

In representing Farah's WJC, I uncovered that the Clinton White House had triggered WJC's audit by sending a letter it had received from one of Slick Willy's supporters questioning the legitimacy of the publication's tax-exempt status to the president himself, which he then had forwarded to the commissioner of the IRS—a not-too-subtle suggestion to begin an audit and remove WJC's tax exemption in retaliation for its negative coverage, particularly over the death of Deputy White House Counsel Vince Foster. By the way, the president's actions were yet another one of his myriad crimes while in office, and the misuse of the IRS was an integral part, not coincidentally, of Judicial Watch's impeachment report.

Judge Huvelle was given considerable evidence concerning the political motivations for Judicial Watch's audit. There was also evidence of the Clintons' pattern and practice of having their adversaries audited. Included in their list of IRS victims, in addition to WJC, were many of President Clinton's female victims, women such as Gennifer Flowers, Juanita Broaddrick, Kathleen Willey, and Paula Jones, some of my clients at the time.

Thus, when Judge Huvelle summarily dismissed Judicial Watch's complaint before we could even take discovery and obtain documents in the agency's files, as well as take sworn deposition testimony from its officialdom, it was clear that Huvelle's dismissal was without legal merit and simple partisan payback for Bill having put her on the federal bench.

Judicial Watch was ultimately cleared of improper charitable conduct by the IRS after George W. Bush won the presidency in 2000. At least the litigation against Clinton's Deep State IRS had delayed things for enough time, five years to be exact, to get Bonnie and Clyde out of office.

Many years later, at the height of Special Counsel Robert Mueller's Russian collusion investigation, I again had the displeasure of having Judge Huvelle on a high-profile politically charged case, when I filed a lawsuit that was assigned to her concerning my client, Dr. Jerome Corsi.[78] The complaint, even though not ultimately successful before Huvelle, as discussed, effectively helped to keep Jerry from being falsely indicted by Mueller for perjury if he did not agree to lie and implicate President Donald J. Trump.

---

78. Corsi v. Mueller et. al, 1:18-cv-2885 (D.D.C.), https://www.courtlistener.com/docket/8378291/corsi-v-mueller/.

Specifically, the case before Judge Huvelle concerned the issue of whether Mueller could be held personally liable for the acts of his top prosecutors with regard to the threats leveled against Dr. Corsi. I had primarily alleged on Corsi's behalf that Mueller, both in his personal and governmental capacities, had violated the First and Fourth Amendment constitutional rights to free speech and to be free of illegal surveillance. The complaint also challenged the violation of criminal grand jury secrecy rules.

Specifically, for the First Amendment claim, Mueller's top prosecutors had abridged Jerry's free speech by threatening him with indictment if he did not falsely testify that he had been in touch with WikiLeaks on behalf of Trump. With regard to the Fourth Amendment claim, the complaint alleged that Mueller had illegally surveilled Jerry without probable cause. And as for the violation of grand jury secrecy, I alleged that Mueller had leaked grand jury information to try to coerce the good doctor into rolling over and lying. There were other counts to the complaint as well, namely abuse of process, tortious interference with Jerry's business relationships, and intentional infliction of emotional distress.

During the pendency of Mueller's witch hunt, Jerry, who is well into his seventies, experienced severe health issues, had to see physicians over chest pains, and virtually lost his means to make a living. The damage callously inflicted by Mueller and his prosecutors was significant and remains ongoing, including unjust harm to Jerry's reputation and good will. Indeed, during the interrogation process, Jerry was browbeaten by Mueller's prosecutors, who mocked his Christian faith and disparaged him as a so-called birther, among other insults and taunts, all the while repeatedly chastising him as a liar. I had locked horns with one of the prosecutors, Jeannie Rhee, who had been Mueller's partner at the D.C. mega-firm of Wilmer Hale, years earlier when I sued the Clinton Foundation on racketeering charges. She was the foundation's lawyer, not coincidentally. She and her colleagues in the special counsel's office were out for blood at all costs to take the president down by using Jerry as their tool.

As for Rhee, of some humor is that during one grand jury interrogation session with my client Corsi, she showed up wearing a see-through blouse, perhaps trying to distract Jerry. But my client told me that he was unimpressed and paid little attention to her nonlegal assets.

Importantly, Judge Huvelle, who was assigned to administer to the complaint after another judge declined to hear it as related, had issued a precedential ruling in the past that supported Jerry's claims of being able to sue Mueller personally for violation of his constitutional rights. There was a multitude of other legal precedent as well that stood for this proposition, including a case I brought for Notra Trulock, the Department of Energy's top investigator during the Clinton administration, who had uncovered Wen Ho Lee's theft of nuclear codes at Los Alamos Nuclear Laboratory. There, I had sued then-FBI Director Louis Freeh, alleging that he ordered his agents to illegally seize Trulock's computer and assault his dog to "convince" my client against writing a book about the FBI's incompetence in giving Wen Ho Lee a free pass. The Trulock complaint thus pled violations of the First and Fourth Amendments, just as I did for Jerry. Importantly, the courts held that my Trulock complaint was viable and let it go forward.

Thus, the only way Judge Huvelle could seek to sidestep allowing the Corsi complaint to move forward into a discovery phase and later trial was for her to dishonestly claim that I did not have direct evidence at this stage of Mueller having ordered his prosecutors to violate Jerry's constitutional rights. I told Jerry that Judge Huvelle may attempt this gambit before the hearing on Mueller's predictable motion to dismiss.

Breaking with accepted protocol, Judge Huvelle asked me to answer questions first even though ordinarily Mueller's lawyers would go first, since it was their motion to dismiss that was primarily at issue. It seemed that she had already made up her mind to dismiss Corsi's complaint and just wanted to put on a show for the gallery of leftist reporters watching in the courtroom. Sure enough, Judge Huvelle's first question to me was to ask sarcastically whether I had any proof Mueller ordered his prosecutors to violate Jerry's constitutional rights.

In response, I argued strongly that at this stage of the case I need only have pleaded that this was so, and indeed for anyone to believe that Mueller was not in charge of the case, one had to live on Pluto. The judge shot back that she lived on Mars! I then reacted politely and dared Judge Huvelle to bring Mueller into court and put him under oath to testify.

As I vigorously argued to Judge Huvelle, we now live in a compromised world where the elite privileged circle the wagons and protect each other. I implied, not too indirectly, that she was predisposed to do just that. Mueller, I argued, should be treated no differently than anyone else.

Of course, given all of Jerry's other claims, much more was said and done at the hearing.

But the moral of my client's story is this: In today's day and age, one cannot sit back and take it anymore from not just a corrupt government but from its equally corrupt law enforcement and legal establishment—run by so-called elites of both political parties.

Jerry challenged "the law"—which, of course, is not the law at all—and won! By fighting back, he stood Mueller and his prosecutors down and avoided indictment. Now he deserves to be made whole again!

Judge Huvelle thwarted Dr. Corsi's ability to obtain damages and did so in a very partisan and dishonest fashion. And, when we took an appeal, the establishment jurists on the higher court, Judges Sri Srnivasan, David Tatel, and Laurence Silberman, two ultraleftists appointed by Bill Clinton and Barack Obama, and a Republican establishment hack appointed by Ronald Reagan, affirmed her outrageous and illegal ruling. Both Democrat and Republican federal judges, installed by the establishments of both parties, are more than inclined to scratch each other's backs, circle the wagons, and rubber-stamp each other's' rulings when someone like their swamp colleague Robert Mueller is involved.

Number Four and Third Runner-Up—Honorable Beryl Howell (Obama Appointee)

The Honorable Beryl Howell, now the chief judge of the U.S. District Court for the District of Columbia, the same court that houses Judges Lamberth, Kotelly, Berman Jackson, and Huvelle—clearly a clubbish swamp-infested epicenter of rank judicial deceit—is a graduate of uber leftist Bryn Mawr College and Columbia Law School. As chief judge, she presided over the grand jury of Special Counsel Robert Mueller during his out-of-control Russian collusion witch hunt, where she let Mueller's prosecutors run wild, allowing them to do virtually anything that suited their partisan ends. It is no wonder that Judge Howell, an Obama appointee, did not even bother to respond when I wrote to and then filed a motion with her to rein in the grand jury leaks that were severely damaging my client, Dr. Jerome Corsi, who was a target of Mueller's grand jury investigation. She could not have cared less!

While this federal judge, also a financial contributor to Democrats, has a nice and friendly demeanor, she is a leftist political hack through and through. For this, she wins at least third runner-up in my Federal Judicial Hall of Shame. One case in particular, in addition to her slavish acquiescence to the crimes committed by Mueller and his prosecutors—it is illegal to release secret grand jury testimony under Rule 6 (e)(2) of the Federal Rules of Criminal Procedure—involved "her" president.

The "emperor in chief," President Barack Hussein Obama, had reared his head again. His appointed federal judge, Beryl Howell, issued a ruling on the eve of Christmas 2014, a Christmas gift to her "führer," dismissing the lawsuit Freedom Watch and I, on behalf of Sheriff Joe Arpaio of Maricopa County, Arizona, filed against Obama, Attorney General Eric Holder, and the immigration enforcement arm of the U.S. Department of Homeland Security.[79] This case challenged what even the emperor had confessed, over twenty-two times in the past, would be an unconstitutional grab of power if he unilaterally took executive actions, bypassing Congress's legislative prerogative, to modify the current immigration laws, which require that illegal aliens generally be deported, rather than be granted what is referred to as "deferred action."

The professed grounds for Judge Howell's Christmas present for the emperor: the courts have no say in stepping in to break up what she ruled was simply a political dispute between the executive branch and the legislative branch of government, even if constitutional issues are involved. For good measure, with lots of yuletide pro-Obama sugar and spice, she added that Sheriff Arpaio could not demonstrate any injury from Obama's amnesty for over five million illegal aliens, many of whom are criminals who wind up back in the sheriff's jails, since they are not deported, at great expense to the Maricopa County taxpayer. Indeed, this increased strain on his office's resources is clearly a harm that conferred standing on the sheriff to bring suit.

---

79. Arpaio v. Obama et. al, 14-cv-1966 (D.D.C.), https://www.clearinghouse.net/ch-Docs/public/IM-DC-0023-9000.pdf.

The legal absurdity and rank politically based hackery of Judge Howell's ruling were self-apparent. But regrettably, it can also be explained by her past political background. For many years, she was a top legal aide to Sen. Patrick Leahy (to whom she also contributed monies for his Senate reelection), the Democrat chairman of the Senate Judiciary Committee—that is, until a Republican-controlled Senate was sworn in on Jan. 6, 2017. Sen. Leahy, who is just slightly right of Fidel and Raul Castro, two other "gentlemen" favorites of our emperor, as demonstrated by his having opened relations with Communist Cuba (which Trump ended with this presidency subject to Biden now likely reversing course Obama-style), is a big backer of open borders and increased immigration. While I like Judge Howell as a person—indeed in a friendly way, we traded niceties at the hearing on our motion to preliminarily block Obama's unconstitutional power grab—she clearly is the product of Leahy's lobbying the president to make her a federal judge. And, indeed, this paid off for Obama, Leahy, and their leftist friends.

After her ruling, the Obama White House boasted that the emperor's new clothes—ones that allowed him to flout the Constitution on immigration law despite his Justice Department's prior advisory rulings and his own past admissions that this would be illegal—were the appropriate fit for the nation. But as the old expression goes, he who laughs last laughs best.

In this regard, within twenty minutes of Judge Howell's legally bizarre, politically based ruling, I filed an appeal before the U.S. Court of Appeals for the District of Columbia Circuit. I then sought to accelerate this appeal by filing a motion for expedited review and also filed a petition for writ of certiorari prior to judgment to ask the U.S. Supreme Court to permit Sheriff Arpaio and me to "leapfrog" the D.C. Circuit and have the High Court decide the constitutional and other related issues. Time is of the essence, I argued, since by the Obama DOJ's own admissions at the ensuing hearing held before Judge Howell, the full force of the emperor's executive actions effectively granting amnesty for over five million illegals would have gone into effect rapidly. This needed to be stopped in its tracks before further damage was done to Sheriff Arpaio's office, the people of Maricopa County, Arizona, and the nation as a whole.

Coming as no surprise, the leftist D.C. Circuit took no action and refused to reverse Judge Howell's politically based ruling. But there remained another avenue for possible victory, a copycat case fashioned after the one I had filed in Howell's court that was pending, having been instituted by the Republican governors of twenty-five states in the U.S. District Court for the Southern District of Texas.

This case had been assigned to the Honorable Andrew Hanen, an appointee of President George W. Bush and a graduate of Denison University and Baylor Law School. Hanen is seen as conservative, and I thought that my client Arpaio might get a "fair shake" in his courtroom.

So, on behalf of America's Toughest Sheriff, I intervened in this case and, along with the twenty-five states, ultimately prevailed in having Judge Hanen impose a preliminary injunction restraining the implementation of President Obama's illegal and unconstitutional executive order.

The grounds upon which Hanen's ruling rested was that Obama, in fashioning and implementing his executive order, which effectively granted amnesty to over five million illegal aliens, had violated the Administrative Procedures Act; that is, he simply went about his executive order the wrong way by not allowing for a period of notice and comment before it was implemented.[80]

---

80. Bill Chappell, "Federal Judge Blocks Obama's Executive Actions On Immigration," *NPR.com* (February 17, 2015), https://www.npr.org/sections/thetwo-way/2015/02/17/386905806/federal-judge-blocks-obama-s-executive-actions-on-immigration.

While Hanen's ruling was a constitutional "cop-out," as it ignored the hard fact that the "Emperor in Chief" had overstepped his constitutional lack of authority to even issue any such order, as this was the prerogative only of Congress, the legislative branch of government, at least we had stopped the president in his politically based tracks, so we thought.

But wait! Obama and his leftist minions in the administration defied Hanen's order in any event, with even the Obama Justice Department caught lying to this federal judge, denying that its "fearless leader" had secretly continued to carry out the amnesty plan. While Hanen then sanctioned the DOJ's lawyers, he did so only mildly, by ordering them to take courses on legal ethics—that is, teaching them not to lie. *What a joke*, I thought at the time. Even a Republican-appointed judge did not have the courage to put his foot down on the Deep State dishonest tactics of the Obama DOJ. And, to make matters substantively worse, he had avoided ruling that President Obama had acted unconstitutionally. But after all, Hanen was an appointee of President George W. Bush, a "blue blood" establishment Republican. In the prescient words of then-incumbent Texas Governor Ann Richards during the 1994 Texas gubernatorial election that W miraculously won, W was born with a "silver spoon in his mouth." It would seem that Hanen, a "country club" Republican establishment W appointee, lacked the courage to go the country mile in his decision, however welcome it was.

Judge Hanen's ruling was then appealed by the Obama DOJ to the U.S. Court of Appeals for the Fifth Circuit, a generally pro-Republican and conservative appellate court, and was sustained. Later, Obama's lackeys at his DOJ took Hanen's ruling to the U.S. Supreme Court, and with only an eight-justice panel—deceased Justice Antonin's seat had yet to be filled—the High Court deadlocked, four justices to four, with the so-called conservative wing voting to uphold Judge Hanen's ruling predictably along ideological lines. A tie vote at the Supreme Court goes to affirming a lower court's ruling. Thus, the good sheriff, the twenty-five states attorneys general, and I ultimately prevailed. But you patriots can see how politics, left and right, played a major role in our victory in the end.

Such is the inherent nature of the highly politicized federal judiciary. Win some and lose some, generally not on the merits of the case but the politics involved. Just what Jefferson predicted on the federal bench! A bunch of political hacks not accountable to We the People but instead doing as they please, slivering around as the judicial snakes they are.

Judge Howell's initial ruling and its affirmance by her D.C. Circuit appellate court, packed with leftist Democrat appointees of Presidents Clinton and Obama, tells the sad tale. And the "lukewarm" rulings of Judge Hanen, while welcome, were hardly a *Profile in Courage*, the title of the famous book of President John F. Kennedy.

But wait, Judge Howell has again predictably reared her ugly leftist head in the aftermath of January 6, 2021, following the lead of other previously fingered court jesters including, you guessed it, Judge Kotelly, on the federal bench in the swamp. Lecturing even the Biden-Harris "Gestapo" at the Justice Department that the primarily trespass charges leveled against the peaceful protestors were too lenient, arguing for more felony indictments as opposed to misdemeanor charges, Judge Howell ranted:

> "This is a puzzle for this petty offense charge...It's to parading, demonstrating or picketing … Demonstrating is typically about something. It's parading about something."[81]

---

81.   Josh Gerstein, "Judge Suggests Feds Are Too Lenient Toward Jan. 6 Defendants," *Politico* (August 9, 2021), https://www.politico.com/news/2021/08/09/judge-feds-lenient-jan-6-503052.

So, there you have it, now even simple protesting is a felony, especially when the corrupt swamp establishment's ox is being held to peacefully account. Mussolini would be proud!

Number Five and Six—Tie for Fourth Runner-Up— *Honorable Karen Gren Scholer (Trump Appointee)* *and Honorable Sam Lindsay (Clinton Appointee)*

The Honorable Karen Gren Scholer was nominated to the federal bench in Dallas, the U.S. District Court for the Northern District of Texas, by President Donald J. Trump on September 7, 2017, and was confirmed in the U.S. Senate by a vote of 97–0, as these days female appointees generally sail through confirmation easier than white males, increasingly a "suspect species." She is a graduate of Rice University and Cornell School of Law, but that is where the distinguished credentials end. Typically, like her Democrat colleague on the federal bench, she conveniently has a history of donating to politicians—in this case, Republicans who helped persuade President Trump to nominate her for a judgeship, most notably Senator Ted Cruz and the Dallas County Republican Party.

What I am about to tell you undercuts The Donald's constant boasts about the "great" judges, in terms of integrity, competence, ideology, and numbers, that he has put on the federal bench. This simply is not reality but, sadly, merely misinformed political hype. His judges are as politicized and as intellectually dishonest as the rest. As I will also discuss later, the ones I have encountered thus far are pantywaists, lacking not just courage but principles—in effect, judicial groundhogs like Punxsutawney Phil, who usually are scared of their shadows and crawl back into their holes, and not just every February 2. For these federal judges, their holes are their chambers. They are, by and large, Republican RINO (Republican in Name Only), pseudo-conservative, dangerous clowns. And the problem stems from the president not knowing who he put on the federal bench; the nominations have been put in front of him by RINO-establishment Republican advisors and lobbyists who greased their nominations, and Trump has been urged if not pushed to "sign here."

For instance, at the highest level of the federal judiciary is Justice Brett Kavanaugh, who is a prime example of a politician in robes and ideologically is a limp fish and not a real conservative. Since his rocky confirmation hearing, which involved incendiary and likely false leftist charges of sexual abuse of women, he has reflexively moved to the left to appease those who tried and almost succeeded in taking the justice out and, to this day, have not given up on finding an excuse to impeach him. Kavanaugh has joined another phony "closet liberal" on the High Court, Chief Justice John Roberts, who rubber-stamped Obamacare—just one example of the federal judiciary's collective two-faced decision-making.

On the other side of the political nomination spectrum on the U.S. District Court for the Northern District of Texas, the same tribunal as Trump Judge Scholer, is Clinton appointee, the Honorable Sam Lindsay, an African American and a graduate of St. Mary's University and the University of Texas School of Law.

Of more than note is Judge Lindsay's daughter, Rachel Lindsay, who followed in her father's footsteps and has a law degree. She also was a contestant on the television show *The Bachelor* and won third place. This then got her a leg up and a role on ABC's *The Bachelorette*, where she was the first African American star on the show in its history. This may have factored into what I am now going to reveal, joining together like Siamese twins the rank dishonesty and cowardly decisions of both Trump-appointee Scholer and Clinton-appointee Lindsay. For this, they both are tied for the spots of fourth runner-up in my Federal Judicial Hall of Shame.

What do these two federal judicial hacks have in common to win such a "coveted" award? They both gave radical black racists, race baiters, extortionists, conmen, vigilantes, anticop, antiwhite, anti-Semitic, and anti-Christian persons and groups a free pass to murder and wound seven Dallas policemen in the widely publicized heinous massacre in Dallas, Texas, on July 7–8, 2016. This massacre was perpetrated by a disciple, Micah Johnson, of the hate-filled and vile Black Muslim, Neo-Nazi, and "primo" racist, the so-called Minister Louis Farrakhan of the Nation of Islam. Farrakhan is a dangerous creep akin to, but far worse than, the Joker in *Batman*, only Farrakhan is for real! Many believe Farrakhan played a principal role in murdering his fellow black Muslims, Malcolm X and Elijah Mohammad, to become the "top dog" of the Nation of Islam and the newly minted religion in general. In effect, both federal judges took it upon themselves to issue "licenses to kill" to Farrakhan and his radical black comrades, but the persons and groups who received this "privilege" were not the equivalent of the Hollywood's noble and brave British Secret MI6 Agent 007, James Bond, but instead lowlifes and societal degenerates of the highest order. So much for their federal judicial precedent, which I am about to disclose, that will dangerously carry far into the future. Let's turn to Judge Scholer first.

The case before Judge Scholer was brought by me for the father of one of the police officers slain at the hands of Micah Johnson, the disciple and follower of Farrakhan. Included as defendants in the wrongful death suit, which also included a count for the intentional infliction of emotional distress, were none other than Farrakhan himself and his Nation of Islam, the "Pigs in Blankets Fry 'Em Like Bacon" group that emerged after Trayvon Martin's death, Black Lives Matter, the New Black Panthers Party, their founders and leaders, and the race baiter, extortionist, and conman, the so-called Reverend Al Sharpton and his antiwhite racist group, the

National Action Network. Last but hardly least was George Soros, the ultraleftist philanthropist who funds many of these vigilantes and radical groups. Not coincidentally, Soros is a self-hating Jew and was a Nazi collaborator during World War II, where he and his father confiscated the property of Jews on their way to Hitler's gas chambers and ovens to save their own disgusting skins.

Soros and his father were fortunate not to have been prosecuted in Israel for their alleged war crimes, but then again, money talks, and with the Soros' prominent perch in the financial world, they somehow walked. Israeli justice for alleged Jewish Nazi collaborators is discussed in a prominent article recently written by Dan Porat of *Time Magazine* and published on October 25, 2019, titled "How Israel's Justice System Dealt with Alleged Jewish Collaborators in Concentration Camps—And Why That Still Matters Today." In a CBS *Sixty Minutes* interview, George Soros unabashedly admitted to his Nazi collaboration and infamously expressed no remorse for it.[82]

For Soros and the other defendants in my lawsuit, brought by Enrique Zamarripa, on behalf of his fallen Hispanic son, Patrick, they were clearly birds of a feather who flocked together, fomenting hatred, effectively calling for the death and destruction of not just white cops but cops in general.

Here are some passages from Enrique's complaint, which tell only part of the story. I urge you to read all of it by going to www. larryklayman.com. Of primary importance, since the murderer was Farrakhan's disciple of the Nation of Islam, as boasted by the killer Micah Johnson himself on his Facebook page, are the paragraphs of the complaint that tie Farrakhan to the tragic deaths of not just the Dallas cops but many others.[83]

---

82. "George Soros Interview," CBS, 60 Minutes (1998), https://www.youtube.com/watch?v=QSyczwuTQfo.

83. "Dallas Cop Murderer Was Follower of Nation of Islam," *Geller Report* (July 8, 2016), https://gellerreport.com/2016/07/dallas-mass-cop-murderer-was-follower-of-nation-of-islam.html/.

In nearly every other highly charged incident, from Trayvon Martin to Ferguson, Missouri, to Charleston, South Carolina, to Baltimore, Maryland, this antiwhite, anti-Semitic racist called for the deaths of cops, whites, gays, and Jews. Focusing here just on Dallas, just days before the massacre, Farrakhan stoked violence among his tribe, as reported by *The Blaze* on July 8, 2016:

> Hours before gunmen opened fire on police officers in downtown Dallas, killing five cops and injuring seven others, Louis Farrakhan posted a message of hatred and violence against white people on social media.
>
> Dallas Police Chief David Brown said on Friday...Xavier Johnson, told officers he was angry about recent police shootings and wanted to kill white people.
>
> "When you are willing and not afraid anymore to pay the price for freedom—don't let this white man tell you that violence is wrong," Farrakhan said. "Every damn thing that he got, he got it by being violent—killing people, raping and robbing and murdering. He's doing it as we speak, and then he has the nerve to come and tell us that violence and hatred won't get it. Don't buy that!"
>
> Speaking about white people as one entity, Farrakhan proclaimed, "He is worthy to be hated." He also claimed that "God hates," and man is no better than God.
>
> The shocking video was posted on Twitter at around 5 p.m. on Thursday.[84]

This was more than hate speech but was in fact a call to murder among his disciples and other like-minded radical blacks. It was not the first by Farrakhan. Here are several other examples, as set

---

84. Jason Howerton, "Hours Before Officers Were Gunned Down in Dallas, Louis Farrakhan Posted This Shocking Message of Racism and Violence," *The Blaze* (July 8, 2016), https://www.theblaze.com/news/2016/07/08/hours-before-officers-were-gunned-down-in-dallas-louis-farrakhan-posted-this-shocking-message-of-racism-and-violence.

forth in numbered paragraphs of the Zamarripa wrongful death complaint, which was filed against him and his racist and pathologically venomous allies:

Paragraph 51. On November 22, 2014, Farrakhan spoke to a packed auditorium at the Murphy Fine Arts Center at Morgan State University in Baltimore, Maryland. More than 2000 people including student community leaders and distinguished guests came to hear the lecture by the 81 one-year old [*sic*] Nation of Islam leader.

Paragraph 52. During the speech, Louis Farrakhan urged retaliation by violent conflict for the death of Michael Brown, a thief who was shot and killed by a Caucasian police officer in Ferguson, Missouri.

Defendant Farrakhan explicitly and specifically sought to stop black community leaders from discouraging the violent revolution, riots, and crime waves that he was calling for.

Paragraph 54. Defendant Farrakhan directed his attacks at other black leaders, but attacked them for discouraging riots and violence:

"But time has moved on. Your day of leading our people is over," he said. Then he turned to his fellow preachers—your day of being the pacifier for the white man's tyranny on black people is over. You've got to know they're not going to hear you anymore."

Paragraph 55. Defendant Farrakhan called for further violence in Ferguson, Missouri, and clarified his condemnation of other leaders who are trying to avoid the violence:

"They know an explosion is going to come," the Nation of Islam leader said to cheers from more than 2000 people crowding the university's Murphy Fine Arts Center. "You leaders are the worst."

Paragraph 56. At one point, Defendant Farrakhan held up what resembled a Quran inside the public school, saying that both the central religious text of Islam and the Bible require a "law of retaliation" and the punishment of "a life for a life."

Paragraph 57. In response to Defendant Farrakhan's calls for "a life for a life", Ismaaiyl Abdullah Brinsley ("Brinsley") brutally executed two New York City police officers only 28 days after Farrakhan's November 22, 2014, incitement to violence. Those two uniformed NYPD officers were shot dead as they sat in their marked police car on a Brooklyn street corner by Brinsley's assassination-style mission to avenge Eric Garner and Michael Brown. There was no warning, no provocation no other interaction—the two police officers were simply assassinated, targeted for wearing a police uniform.

Paragraph 58. Just three hours before shooting of the two police officers the vile anti-police threats were posted to Brinsley's Instagram page. The threats referenced the recent police-involved killings of Eric Garner and Michael Brown. Brinsley wrote, "I'm Putting Wings on Pigs Today' and 'They Take 1 Of Ours … Let's Take 2 of Theirs."

Paragraph 68. Defendant Farrakhan continued by saying, "Death is sweeter than watching us slaughter each other to the joy of a 400-year-old enemy. Death is sweet. The Quran teaches persecution is worse than slaughter."[85]

Of course, death in an Islamic jihad is dandy unless it is the death of Farrakhan himself. So much better to get your followers to kill and maim the white man, cops, Jews, Christians, gays, lesbians, and transgenders, which apparently squares with this bigot's interpretation of the Holy Quran. It is telling that President Obama has been proudly photographed with the leader of the Nation of Islam, a photo that was suppressed and did not surface until just recently.

---

85. Zamarripa v. Farrakhan et. al, 3:16-cv-3109 (N.D. Tx.), https://cas etext.com/case/ zamarripa-v-farrakhan; Complaint can be found at www.larryklayman.com.

I can go on and on, but you see how strong the Zamarripa case was against Farrakhan and the Nation of Islam. The two had directly called for the murder of Dallas cops, most of whom were white.

As pled in the Zamarripa complaint, the other defendants were equally guilty, but the master black racist and Al-Qaeda-like Islamic fomenter of hate, Farrakhan, won the prize, particularly since his disciple, Micah Johnson, slavishly did the homicidal dirty deeds. Johnson was not sued, as he was shot dead by the Dallas police during the massacre.

Despite the overwhelming evidence that Farrakhan and his co-defendants had either directly called for or fomented enough hate to cause this Nation of Islam disciple to kill, as pleaded in the Zamarripa complaint, Judge Scholer sat on the case for many months before taking up motions to dismiss, filed by Farrakhan and the others. When this Trump appointee finally got around to meting out justice and considering whether to allow the case to go forward, at least into the discovery phase where evidence could be gathered to go to trial before a jury, she ran for the door, probably because the case was too hot to handle, and she feared for her own safety—and that is the best possible explanation. And to be honest, in today's world, if you are a minority, such as African American or Muslim, and Farrakhan is notably both, courts and other venues in society will usually give you a free pass for fear of being smeared as racists if, God forbid, race baiters, conmen, and vigilantes are held to account. That is the brutal unvarnished truth, and everyone knows this, particularly persons like Farrakhan, Sharpton, Black Lives Matter, the New Black Panthers Party, their leaders, and the rest—and they use this repeatedly to their advantage.

Here, incredibly, is what this federal judge wrote in dismissing the wrongful death complaint of Enrique Zamarripa, who had lost his beloved and only son, a valiant Dallas cop, to these societal misfits and lowlifes. In her order of July 6, 2018, almost two years exactly since the Dallas police massacre, Scholer spewed completely dishonest crap on the record:

> Enrique Zamarripa ("Zamarripa") filed this lawsuit after the July 7, 2016, fatal shooting of five police officers in Dallas, Texas, by gunman Micah Johnson ("Johnson"). Comp. para. 7. Zamarripa's son, Patrick Zamarripa, was one of the police officers killed in the shooting. Id. Zamarripa accused Farrakhan, the NOI ("Nation of Islam"), and 12 other defendants of conspiring to start a race war in the United States. Id. Paras. 8–12. Zamarripa further alleges that Johnson was acting as an "agent of" and "under the direction of Farrakhan and the NOI, among others. Id. Par. 1. Based on these allegations, Zamarripa brings claims for wrongful death and intentional infliction of emotional distress.
>
> ...
>
> Dismissal for lack of subject matter jurisdiction is warranted when "it appears certain that the plaintiff cannot prove any set of facts in support of this claim that would entitle plaintiff to relief." *Gilbert v. Donahue*, 751, F. 3rd 303, 307 (5th Cir. 2014) (quoting *Ramming v. United States*, 281 F. 3rd 158, 161 (5th Cir. 2001)).
>
> ...
>
> To support his standing argument, Zamarripa alleges that "Defendant Farrakhan and NOI directed his disciples, such as Micah Johnson, to kill cops just hours before the Dallas Massacre." Pl.'s Br. 9. In support of this proposition Zamarripa points to a video in which Farrakhan allegedly published racist endorsements of violence.
>
> ...

However, Zamarripa attempts to hold Defendants liable because Johnson allegedly was one of their "disciples." Pl's Br. 9. Zamarripa's allegations against Farrakhan and the NOI, like his allegations against the Defendants dismissed pursuant to the Godbey Order, "are wholly conclusory and fail to reasonably trace the words and actions of (Farrakhan and the NOI) to the death of Zamarripa's son." Godbey Order 8. Zamarripa fails to explain how the injury at hand resulted from anything other than "the independent action of Johnson, who is not before the Court. *Simon*, U.S. at 42.

...

Here, other than conclusory statements, Zamarripa has not pleaded any facts to suggest that Johnson's conduct was dependent on or incentivized by Farrakhan or the NOI.

...

For the foregoing reasons, the Court grants Farrakhan and the NOI's motion to dismiss.

SO ORDERED.

SIGNED JULY 6, 2018

KAREN GREN SCHOLER

UNITED STATES DISTRICT JUDGE[86]

So, there you have it. Despite excruciating detail in the Zamarripa complaint setting forth Farrakhan's and his Nation of Islam's call, if not order, to kill cops and others just hours before the Dallas massacre, this Trump federal judge went through the monkey business and act of "seeing no evil, hearing no evil, and doing no evil" and trashed the case of my client, the father of slain officer Patrick Zamarripa. And if Scholer had any doubt about our

---

86. Ibid.

so-called allegations, which were not allegations at all but verifiable calls for violence by Farrakhan himself, she clearly could have allowed the case to at least go forward to discovery, where we could have confronted Farrakhan and his racist group by taking oral testimony and showing him the video of his statements to confirm they were his, not that any confirmation was needed.

But Judge Scholer did not want the case of Patrick Zamarripa's wrongful death to proceed; rather, she wanted it to be killed for her own improper, unethical, and obviously unlawful reasons. Such is the unaccountable despotic power bestowed upon a federal judge, which Jefferson feared! Do as I please without apparent consequences, even if the father of a slain hero gets the shaft! Whether it's a Trump federal judge like Scholer or an Obama federal judge like Amy Berman Jackson in the wrongful death Extortion 17 suit against Hillary Clinton, let the grieving parents of fallen heroes be damned! Protect yourself at all costs of decency and humanity, not to mention the rule of law!

Then, there was the earlier case that I brought in Dallas federal court for a courageous African American police officer, Sergeant Demetrick Pennie, one of Patrick Zamarripa's brothers on the force. Pennie had been assaulted during the massacre by the likes of Black Lives Matter and the New Black Panthers Party, and his case was structured in a similar fashion to the Zamarripa case. Demetrick holds a doctorate degree in higher education from Texas Tech, having written a doctoral thesis that in part dealt with black separatist ideology of the sort practiced by the defendants in both cases. And it was Demetrick, whom I consider my "brother" after all these years, who introduced me to Enrique Zamarripa, Patrick's surviving dad.

As I alluded to earlier, the case was supposedly randomly assigned to federal judge Sam Lindsay, an African American appointee of President Bill Clinton.

After considerable delay in the early stages of the suit, Lindsay, who had virtually the same facts before him as Judge Scholer, dismissed Demetrick's case as well. In so doing, he called the facts we set forth in the complaint, which concerned Farrakhan's and the other defendants' call for violence and for the killing of cops, whites, and assorted other shades of humanity or religious beliefs (mostly Jews) they do not like, simply our "personal beliefs."

Hearing this obvious bias and prejudice—if not more simply put, complete garbage—from Judge Lindsay, I moved to have him disqualified. But predictably, he denied my motion, even though under the law he should have allowed another federal judge in the courthouse to make that decision and take over the case. The statute that requires disqualification is 28 U.S.C. 144 of the United States Code and is crystal clear in this regard:

> Whenever a party to any proceeding in a district court makes and files a timely and sufficient affidavit that the judge before whom the matter is pending has a personal bias or prejudice either against him or in favor of any adverse party, such judge shall proceed no further therein, but another judge shall be assigned to hear such proceeding.

In compliance with this federal statute, on behalf of Demetrick, I filed the requisite "sufficient affidavit," but Judge Lindsay ignored it. Regrettably, this federal judge is no different than his colleagues on the bench. Having attempted to disqualify a number of federal judges under 28 U.S.C. 144 during my long legal career—God only knows how many biased and prejudiced federal judges my clients and I have been forced to endure—they all refuse to follow the law and instead rule on the disqualification motions themselves and continue on thumbing their arrogant noses at the law.

And when I have attempted to take this matter before higher appellate courts, including the U.S. Supreme Court, they all refuse to address the obvious inherent conflict of interest with a federal judge ruling on the merits of his or her own alleged biases and prejudices. This is yet another Jeffersonian example of the unchecked authority and unaccountability of federal judges put on the bench as a result of greasy political patronage, forcing We the People to serve lifetime sentences for their unethical and frequently illegal actions and rulings.

As icing on Lindsay's dishonest cake, he even threatened me not to file another disqualification motion should the need arise:

> Plaintiffs have thus, failed to establish that the undersigned has succumbed, or is likely to succumb, to any extrajudicial influences or pressure from any Defendant in this case. Instead, Plaintiffs have done nothing but rely on rank speculation, conjecture and hyperbole to make irrational and impermissible inferences that the undersigned had a personal bias against them or in favor of an adverse party.[87]

And here was the "kicker" from this very defensive and hostile federal judge:

> Plaintiffs shall not file another motion to recuse or disqualification of the undersigned. If Plaintiffs or their counsel files another motion for recusal or disqualification of the undersigned, the court will issue an order for them to appear in court and show cause why they should not be held in contempt of court and sanctioned (Order of October 20, 2016).[88]

What got under Judge Lindsay's skin was a suggestion, in particular, that he was afraid to rule in favor of my client, given the violence espoused by Farrakhan and the Nation of Islam, who

---

87.   Klayman and Pennie v. Obama et. al, 3:16-cv-2010 (N.D. Tx.), https://casetext.com/case/klayman-v-obama-8.

88.   Ibid.

had chastised even black leaders for their cowardice to violently seek retribution against the white man, cops, and others on his list of "undesirables," to use a phrase coined by Hillary Clinton during the 2016 presidential campaign. Indeed, last May, we saw, in real-time, living color, the "persuasive coercion" of the likes of Farrakhan, Sharpton, Black Lives Matter, the New Black Panthers Party, and Antifa, whom Trump has declared a domestic terrorist group, with the looting, burning, mayhem, and physical violence that began in Minneapolis, Minnesota, over the death of a black man, George Floyd, at the hands of the police—violence that quickly spread nationally. Judge Lindsay, it appeared to me, was one scared jurist.

And it seemed to me that Lindsay, in throwing out Demetrick's case, was also seeking to protect his daughter, a budding television star. Leftist Hollywood certainly would not look kindly on a black man and federal judge taking on and holding legally accountable the likes of Farrakhan, Sharpton, Black Lives Matter, and the rest—second only to Marx, Mao, and Castro in the leftist entertainment industry's list of heroes. This could result in fallout and perhaps shunning for his offspring among the beautiful leftist elites in Tinseltown.

Indeed, after Demetrick bravely authorized me to file suit, he was called every antiblack, racist name in the book by radical blacks and stupid leftist whites, ranging from "Uncle Tom" to "House Nigger." And his life and the lives of his family as well as me and mine were threatened by the likes of the New Black Panthers Party and their defendant allies. But, of course, Judge Lindsay refused to hear that and, again, called our well-documented allegations against Farrakhan and his racist comrades merely our "personal beliefs"!

Numbers Seven and Eight—Tie for Fifth Runner-Up—
Honorable Gloria Navarro (Obama Appointee) and
Honorable Jay Bybee (George W. Bush Appointee)

The two Sin City "love bird" federal jurists, hailing from Las Vegas, Nevada, in a one-two punch, caused considerable legal harm to my client Cliven Bundy and thus to the other defendants in the criminal prosecution against him, his sons, and the peaceful protesters who were indicted by the Obama DOJ.

Chief Judge Gloria Navarro's role in this travesty was as the presiding trial jurist over this prosecution before the U.S. District Court for the District of Nevada.[89] Judge Jay Bybee, on the other hand, sits on the U.S. Court of Appeals for the Ninth Circuit, and he happily obliged his friend Navarro in rubber-stamping some of her outrageously unconstitutional orders, whereby in violation of Cliven Bundy's Sixth Amendment right to the counsel of his choice, she kept me from formally appearing for Cliven as his primary criminal defense attorney.[90] Given the seventeen counts leveled against Cliven and the other defendants, ostensibly for allegedly threatening federal officers and thus various permutations of obstruction of justice, they all faced, if convicted, the prospect of life imprisonment.

Judge Navarro is a graduate of the University of Nevada at Las Vegas and holds a law degree from Arizona State University, which is located in Maricopa County, where my client Joseph Arpaio was the sheriff for decades. As she was a Latina and given the false smears in the leftist media that Arpaio is racist toward Hispanics, I was wary whether my representation of Arpaio could affect her conduct toward me as Cliven Bundy's criminal defense counsel, particularly since she had been nominated to the federal bench by

---

89.   United States of America v. Bundy et. al, 2:16-cr-46 (D. Nev.), https://casetext.com/case/united-states-v-bundy-45.

90.   Bundy, 16-72275 (9th. Cir.), https://www.govinfo.gov/app/details/US-COURTS-ca9-16-72275/USCOURTS-ca9-16-72275-0.

President Obama, whom I had sued on multiple occasions while at Freedom Watch. Indeed, as I explain below, that happened, with even the *Las Vegas Review-Journal*, the hometown newspaper, opining that she had little respect for the constitutional rights of my client and his co-defendants, the peaceful protesters at Bunkerville. It observed:

> Government prosecutors have a friend in U.S. District Judge Gloria Navarro.
>
> The judge is presiding over the retrial of four [peaceful protester] defendants charged with various crimes stemming from their participation in the 2014 Bunkerville standoff near Cliven Bundy's ranch. The first trial ended in April with the jury deadlocked on all counts involving the four men.
>
> On Monday, the judge eviscerated the defense's legal strategy, putting off limits a host of issues that might make it more difficult for the government to win convictions. The defendants will be forbidden from arguing that they were exercising their constitutional rights to peacefully assemble and bear arms. They may not highlight the actions of BLM agents in the days leading up to the incident or mention federal gaffes such as the ill-advised "First Amendment" zone created for protesters.
>
> And if imposing these restrictions on the defense wasn't enough, Judge Navarro ruled that prosecutors may introduce testimony about the four accused men and their associations with so-called militia groups.
>
> Judge Navarro made a similar ruling before the first trial. She is going to extraordinary lengths to address prosecution fears of "jury nullification," in which jurors refuse to convict based on a belief that the law or potential punishment is unjust. The practice dates to 1734, when a jury ignored statutes and acquitted publisher Peter Zenger on charges of criticizing

New York's new colonial governor, accepting arguments from Mr. Zenger's attorney, Alexander Hamilton, that the newspaper has simply published the truth.

Federal prosecutors have encountered unexpected difficulty—both here and in Oregon [where Ammon and Ryan Bundy, Cliven's sons were also indicted and tried]—in securing convictions against those protesting federal control of Western public lands. But the issue here isn't whether one believes the Bundy defendants are courageous freedom fighters or zealous lunatics. Rather it's whether a judge should usurp the rights of the defendants to have a jury of their peers consider their arguments alongside the law, evidence and other testimony.

Judge Navarro's sweeping order reflects a deep mistrust of the American jury system.[91]

Judge Bybee graduated with an undergraduate degree from Brigham Young University and holds his law degree from the J. Reuben Clark Law School. He was nominated to the federal bench by President George W. Bush. Prior to becoming a federal judge, Bybee was an assistant attorney general for the Office of Legal Counsel in W's DOJ, and undoubtedly, that is where he made the political connections to be nominated by the president.

During his tenure at the DOJ, Bybee was strongly criticized for running interference for Bush and Cheney, for which he was likely rewarded with his federal judgeship, by writing the so-called "Torture Memos" justifying the legality of the use of torture with regard to the interrogation of terrorists at Guantanamo Bay, Cuba, and the Abu Ghraib prison in Iraq after Saddam Hussein was deposed, post September 11. Later, once on the federal bench, Bybee also has been severely criticized for writing a dissenting opinion that held that it was not a violation of the Sixth Amendment or the attorney-client privilege for federal prisons to open and read mail

91. "Judge Bans Defense Arguments in Bundy Retrial," *Las Vegas Review-Journal* (July 13, 2017), https://redoubtnews.com/tag/las-vegas-review-journal/.

to prisoners from their legal counsel, a particularly outrageous if not illegal ruling. He also, in a majority opinion, ruled against Sheriff Arpaio's claim of government immunity in a case where America's sheriff had allegedly falsely arrested two newspaper publishers who had defamed him.

Navarro and Bybee thus have a history of having a very limited view of the constitutional and other rights of defendants, while ironically politically being polar opposites. Their actions with regard to Cliven Bundy are consistent with their being the textbook judicial despots Jefferson feared would come to pass.

In the Bundy prosecution, which followed the trials of the four peaceful protesters that were the subject of the *Las Vegas Review-Journal's* opinion piece, Navarro racked up an indoor record of even more constitutional law violations, that today stands unchallenged in Nevada federal court history. First, she denied the defendants' bail without any credible showing that they were a flight risk or a danger to society. In fact, government threat-assessment reports, which had been hidden by the prosecutors but later turned up during the trial, showed otherwise. Then she had the Bureau of Prisons, a part of DOJ, throw Cliven, and later his son Ammon, into solitary confinement, the latter being put on ice for expressing his religious rights with regard to an undergarment that can only be removed in the Mormon faith by one's wife, but that prison guards took it upon themselves to remove. Finally, for "good measure," she denied them a right of counsel and speedy trial in violation of the Sixth Amendment, resulting in them being incarcerated for nearly two years, mostly in a maximum-security prison in Pahrump, Nevada, in the midst of the infamous Area 51.

Interestingly, leaving the penitentiary one evening after having visited with Cliven for several hours, I walked out the gate with a security guard at my side. I joked with him that this maximum-security prison was like the modern-day Alcatraz, difficult to try to escape since it was located in remote rattlesnake-infested desert. He responded, "Mr. Klayman, I am not afraid of the rattlers, but I see UFOs every night here!"

Ironically, the Bundy prosecution had turned into more of an extraterrestrial "out-of-body" experience. This was evidenced by what later occurred for all to see and hear in the courtroom, when the U.S. Attorney's Office suborned perjury by government witnesses, with themselves telling their own lies to Navarro and their clients being caught hiding exculpatory evidence. To top it all off, a whistleblower came forward to blow the lid off the case by revealing that there was a BLM kill list that included the heads of the Bundys resulting from their vile prejudice toward the Bundys' Mormon faith. All of this was like several episodes of the *Twilight Zone*. And even this Obama-appointed leftist hack of a federal judge was then—to save herself from going down with a sinking Obama DOJ ship—forced to throw out the indictment. To cap it all off, the Trump DOJ later approved an appeal of the dismissal by the same prosecutors who had committed crimes which, if successful, could have resulted in life imprisonment for Cliven, his sons, and the peaceful protesters indicted along with them.

But perhaps the worst of Navarro's constitutional indiscretions was her order preventing me from being Cliven's trial counsel, based on contrived reasoning that my application to appear "pro hac vice" contained false statements. Tom Fitton, who I regrettably left behind at Judicial Watch when I left to run for the U.S. Senate in Florida in the fall of 2003, and who did everything he could to harm my family and me—since I believe that he feared, after my unsuccessful U.S. Senate campaign, that I might want to return to Judicial Watch as its head—had filed a decade-old bar complaint against me that at the time still had not been ruled upon by the Board of Responsibility of the District of Columbia Bar.

At issue was an alleged conflict of interest in my representing a donor of Judicial Watch, Louise Benson, who is like my adopted mother. She had made a large donation that was intended to, along with donations from other donors, buy the building in which Judicial Watch rented office space. Judicial Watch to this day, nineteen years and almost two decades later, has not bought the building it promised to buy. In addition, I also represented a client who, after I left, had been abandoned by Fitton in a criminal case, that contributed to him ultimately being convicted of stock and bank fraud and then doing ten years in federal prison. The client was Peter Paul, the man I wrote about in *Whores* who put on the Hollywood Tribute to Bill Clinton and had the goods on Bonnie and Clyde for their illegal campaign contributions to Hillary's 2000 U.S. Senate campaign in New York. In addition, I represented the director of Judicial Watch's Miami office, Sandy Cobas, who had been harassed and forced out of Judicial Watch by Fitton after I left, as he then fired many of the people I had hired to run the organization's field offices in Texas and Los Angeles. I agreed to represent these victims of Fitton's conduct because they could not afford to hire a lawyer on their own, as well as to protect my own reputation.

Since I am not licensed in Nevada, I had to apply for what is called pro hac vice entry into Cliven's case. Navarro, in reviewing my application, falsely claimed that I had misrepresented the state of Fitton's vindictive ethics complaint to her because a low-level bar hearing committee had found a conflict of interest. I disclosed this simple recommendation and predicted that I would ultimately prevail on appeal. Despite there being no final disciplinary action, as my appeal was pending, she ruled that I could not be Cliven's criminal defense counsel, despite there being a sacrosanct constitutional right, particularly in a criminal case where the stakes are so high, to have the lawyer of one's choice. Importantly, established law provided that a criminal defendant can only be denied right of an out-of-state lawyer like me, if he or she is subject to disbarment. This clearly did not apply.

I then took the matter up to the Ninth Circuit. But Judge Bybee and one of his colleagues sustained Navarro's ruling, citing false facts that Navarro had provided to them. However, one federal judge on the three-judge panel deciding the case, Ronald Gould, an honest liberal and a rare credit to the federal bench, found in a dissenting opinion that I had done nothing wrong. He wrote:

> I agree with Klayman that he was not obligated to re-litigate the D.C. [bar] proceeding before the district court and that he did not have to provide the district court with the entire record from D.C. And if his disclosures were selective, still he is an advocate, an advocate representing defendant Cliven Bundy, and after submitting a compliant response to the questions in the pro hac vice application, he had no greater duty to disclose any possible blemish on his career or reputation beyond responding to the district court's further direct requests.[92]

What made matters worse for Cliven and me was not just Bybee himself, a friend of Navarro's ruling which kept my client from having the criminal defense attorney of his choice, but that he had also smeared me in his opinion that I had been dishonest with Navarro. And no sooner than Bybee issued his ab hominem attack on me, Fitton then vindictively sent it to the District of Columbia Bar Disciplinary Counsel to try to start yet another bar proceeding against me—even though he and Judicial Watch were not involved in the Bundy case in any way. To make this long story short, a hearing committee later could not find an ethical violation. But the case, given the political partisanship of the Disciplinary Counsel, all leftist Democrats, drags on in any event.

---

92.   Ibid., Bundy, 16-72275, https://caselaw.findlaw.com/us-9th-circuit/1752929.html.

In short, federal judges Navarro and Bybee, a "soul sister" and a "soul brother" from the legal establishment club in sin city, not only tried to do a number on my client Cliven Bundy, but on me. Their conduct, in my opinion, was dishonest and despicable, qualifying them for induction into my Federal Judicial Hall of Shame.

Number Nine and Sixth Runner-Up—Honorable Claudia Wilken (Clinton Appointee)

The Honorable Claudia Wilken, appointed by President Bill Clinton to the federal bench on the U.S. District Court for the Northern District of California and later assigned to the Oakland Division of this federal court in 1993, is a graduate of Stanford University and the University of California at Berkeley School of Law (Boalt Hall). She also was an adjunct professor of Berkeley Law from 1978 to 1984, a span of six years.

Judge Wilken is the presiding federal judge in a widely publicized lawsuit that I filed for a young politically conservative gay woman, Kiara Robles, who tried to attend a speech by controversial and conservative Breitbart writer and reporter Milo Yiannopoulos, who is also gay.[93] Prior to the planned speech on the campus of the University of California at Berkeley, ultraleftist activists and anarchists, predominantly composed of members of a group that calls itself Antifa, which claims to be antifascist but that itself is fascist, rioted, burned buildings and other property, looted businesses, and attacked many people like my client Kiara, who were peacefully waiting to hear Yiannopoulos speak. My client was pepper sprayed in her eyes and assaulted by these leftist thugs as the Berkeley police and university personnel stood and watched,

---

93. Robles v. ANTIFA, et. al, 4:17-cv-4864 (N.D. CA.), https://floridajustice.com/wp-content/uploads/2020/02/Robles-v.-Antifa-et-al-Order-denying-leave-to-file-motion-to-reconsider-Revoke-PHV-and-Recusal.pdf.

based on stand-down orders from the university, much as later occurred with the race-based riots in Baltimore, Maryland.

In the final days of May 2020, Antifa engaged in and instigated mass riots in over thirty major American cities, which resulted in wholesale looting, theft, and destruction. This group, using as its phony pretext the death of Floyd George in Minneapolis, Minnesota, a black man allegedly murdered by police, upped its violent ground game, resulting in it being declared a domestic terrorist organization by President Donald Trump.

At the outset of the case, after Wilken was assigned as the presiding jurist, I asked her politely to consider sending the case to another judge, given the appearance of her having a conflict of interest, since she had attended and taught at Berkeley, who I had also sued along with Antifa. Predictably and regrettably, she refused—as federal judges rarely have the humility to do what is right in these types of situations, thinking that they are untouchable since they are not elected officials, as, again, Jefferson warned.

During the pretrial stage of the case, Wilken quickly saw fit to dismiss her alma mater, the University of California at Berkeley, from the suit, as well as other related defendants and, based on Judge Bybee's ruling in the Bundy case upholding Navarro's refusal to grant me pro hac vice status, revoked my pro hac vice entry into her case, even though it had previously been granted by court officials.

When I advised Judge Wilken that the matter was still under review by the District of Columbia Bar, she could not have cared less. She was intent, like Navarro and Bybee had been, to deny my client her right of counsel. And what added insult to injury was that my local counsel, who had entered the case only for administrative purposes, and who was not equipped financially to take over representation, could not continue. Wilken was informed of this in a sworn affidavit by my local counsel, as well as one that I submitted to her from Kiara. But she ignored both, thus effectively ending the case, as this young gay woman then had no lawyer to represent her. And, as Kiara and I also pointed out to Judge Wilken, no other lawyer other than yours truly could or would take the case given Antifa's violent acts. They were fearful for the well-being of themselves and their families in the ultraleftist Bay area and were not prepared to represent her on a pro bono basis, as I did, given that Kiara was financially unable to pay legal fees and costs. My removal as Kiara's counsel is now on appeal to the Ninth Circuit. Good luck there, as many of the members of this court are graduates of Berkeley law and its undergraduate school and are predominantly leftist. Kiara and I will soldier on, praying that God, quite foreign to the likes of Antifa, will intervene.

Number Ten and Seventh Runner-Up—Honorable Donald Middlebrooks (Clinton Appointee)

The Honorable Donald Middlebrooks graduated with an undergraduate and law degree from the University of Florida. It comes as no surprise that, like most of the other nominees for my Federal Judicial Hall of Shame, his political connections and generous contributions to beaucoup influential politicians landed him on the federal bench. Before being picked by President Clinton for a seat on the Palm Beach Division of the U.S. District Court for the Southern District of Florida, he was assistant general counsel for Governor Rubin Askew from 1994–1997, beginning in the year I founded Judicial Watch. That job, with the Florida governor advocating for his appointment with Bill Clinton, gave him the juice to get his current job, among other acts of political patronage.

As for Middlebrooks's "generosity" to those who could put him on the federal bench, they include the Clinton/Gore '96 Primary Committee, Clinton for President, Kerry for President, the

Democratic Senatorial Committee, DNC Services, Friends of Bob Graham, Askew for President, Biden for President, and a host of others, totaling many thousands of dollars. Google the Federal Election Commission website and see for yourself this disgraceful financial largesse. Middlebrooks even contributed to the National Republican Senatorial Committee in 1996 shortly before he was nominated by President Clinton to the federal bench, obviously to grease the potential skids that could have been caused by Florida's Republican U.S. Senator Connie Mack—who could have put a hold on or even blocked his nomination. Mack, not coincidentally, sat at the time on the Senate Judiciary Committee, the congressional entity that vets the qualifications of federal judges and sends their nomination to the full floor of the U.S. Senate for a final up or down confirmation vote.

Middlebrooks was supposedly randomly assigned to a complaint I filed on behalf of myself against none other than Hillary and Bill Clinton and the Clinton Foundation under the Racketeer Influenced and Corrupt Organization Act, commonly known as RICO. The complaint thus alleged in its preamble that:

> Plaintiff sues the Defendants as individuals operating a criminal enterprise, for violating Plaintiff's statutory rights to obtain documents under the Freedom of Information Act ("FOIA"), 5 U.S.C. 552, for violating Plaintiff's due process rights, vested property rights, constitutional rights, and for misappropriating property. The Defendants have systematically and continuously, over the last ten (10) years and more, conducted a corrupt enterprise in violation of the Racketeer Influenced and Corrupt Organization ("RICO") Act.[94]

My RICO complaint was novel but well-grounded in verifiable facts and the law. I alleged that the Defendants, in refusing to produce documents about Hillary Clinton's illegal if not criminal

94. Klayman v. Clinton et. al, 9:15-cv-80388 (S.D. Fl.), https://casetext.com/case/klayman-v-chairman-bruce-lindsey-or-vice-chairman-chelsea-clinton-mezvinsky.

use of an unsecure private email server while secretary of state, which she used to secretly shake down persons and entities who sought her waivers to do business with the terrorist nation of Iran and other favors, that she, Bill, and the Clinton Foundation, had violated RICO. The Clintons and their foundation had received monies from these bribing parties, and committed, as required by RICO, more than two acts of mail and wire fraud over a ten-year period, necessary to trigger this statute. Indeed, my complaint detailed numerous acts of these Clintonesque "pay-to-play" bribery schemes over this time span.

For instance, as just a few examples of this "pay-to-play" criminal enterprise, the following paragraphs of my complaint set forth these, among many other indisputable facts:

> Paragraph 100—Since leaving the White House in 2001, the Bill and Hillary household has amassed a personal fortune (outside of the Clinton Foundation) of over $105 Million USD, consisting mainly of speaking fees paid to Bill Clinton from many nations, organizations, leaders, and business interests hostile to the United States and U.S. foreign policy and especially hostile to Israel, but flush with cash from oil revenue or from sources doing business with oil rich, Middle Eastern and Arab countries.

> Paragraph 101—While Hillary Clinton served in the U.S. Senate from 2001 through 2009 and as Secretary of State from 2009 through 2013, foreign governments, foreign business interests, and wealthy businessmen and women around the world whose interests are influenced and affected by U.S. government policies and actions have funneled billions of dollars to the Clinton Foundation.

> Paragraph 102—While Defendant Hillary Clinton served in the U.S. Senate from 2001 through 2009 and as Secretary of State from 2009 through 2013, foreign governments, foreign business interests, and wealthy businessmen and women

around the world whose interests are influenced or affected by U.S. government policies and actions have funneled tens of millions of dollars in speaking fees to her husband Bill Clinton and herself. [95]

And these allegations were just the tip of the iceberg in the Clintons' shake-down racketeering enterprise.

RICO, which has both criminal and civil law remedies, was originally enacted by Congress, the legislative branch of our so-called government, to combat the Mafia and other organized crime. In its civil context, it provides a private right of action, where litigants can go before a jury of their peers and seek treble damages, plus an award of attorney's fees and costs.

My complaint was strong. It alleged that by the Clinton Foundation denying me the documents I had sought under FOIA showing the Clintons' "pay-to-play" bribery scheme, they were not just furthering their criminal enterprise by keeping me from obtaining incriminating evidence but also depriving me of earning a living as the head of my public interest group, Freedom Watch, which raises monies based on our uncovering governmental crime to pay for our law enforcement mission as in effect the People's Justice Department.

Entering the case to defend the Clintons and their corrupt Clinton Foundation, as previously mentioned, was Jeannie Rhee, of the mega-law firm of Wilmer Hale. Rhee was, not coincidentally, Robert Mueller's partner at the time. Mueller was later picked by Trump DOJ Deputy Attorney General Rod Rosenstein to be Special Counsel in the Russian collusion investigation. When Mueller was chosen to be Special Counsel, he then plucked Rhee from his old firm to join him, a choice, along with the other Democrat partisan prosecutors he recruited, such as Andrew Weissmann, that caused outrage in the conservative pro-Trump community.

---

95. Ibid.

But while the Clintons and their foundation took my RICO complaint seriously enough to hire Jeannie Rhee and her law firm WilmerHale as their legal counsel, Judge Middlebrooks, for his own politically based reasons, as a Clinton appointee, supporter, and contributor before taking the federal bench, predictably did not!

Sure enough, Middlebrooks, sitting on the case for many months, eventually got around to dismissing my complaint, a pre-ordained outcome given his Clintonesque roots. Here is his contrived justification and legal standard of review of my excruciatingly detailed complaint, based upon his own personal views of the "plausibility" of my allegations—again a hear no evil, see no evil, and do no evil approach to cooking the final result:

> A motion to dismiss under Rule 12(b)(6) challenges the legal sufficiency of a complaint. See Fed. R. Civ. P. 12(b)(6). In assessing the legal sufficiency of a complaint's allegations, the Court is bound to apply a pleading standard articulated in Bell Atlantic Corp. v. Twombly, 550 U.S. 544 (2007) and Ashcroft v. Iqbal, 556 U.S. 662, 678 (2009). That is, the complaint "must … contain sufficient factual matter, accepted as true, to "state a claim to relief that is plausible on its face. (Order of August 11, 2015)[96]

Middlebrooks, like his comrades of politically picked federal judges these days, acted as if he was the sole arbiter of the facts, not the jury I had designated to decide the case. As Jefferson predicted, Middlebrooks took on the role of a despot, acting as if he could do as he pleased. And this is the dilemma! If the nation does not have federal judges who will put aside partisanship and payback to the benefactors who got them their jobs, then We the People are left defenseless, that is, unless we take up legal and peaceful arms unto

---

96. Ibid.

ourselves, assuming that is even possible in today's world of mass surveillance and Deep State government domination.

Hillary Clinton, as usual, was given a free pass to continue her "pay-for-play" criminal racketeering enterprise as secretary of state, shaking down persons, corporations, special interests, and even foreign governments and selling her office at the U.S. State Department to enrich herself, her husband Bill, daughter Chelsea, and the Clinton Foundation, all the while raking in hundreds of millions of dollars in cold cash.

Middlebrooks was recently mysteriously assigned a new anti-trust case, which I filed against the Organization of Petroleum Exporting Countries (OPEC), over what is clear per se price fixing and market division to drive the price of oil and thus gasoline through the roof, thanks to the Biden-Harris regime's virtually eliminating our nation's fossil fuel energy self-sufficiency with the shutdown of the Keystone oil pipeline and other destructive actions to overly promote alternatives of energy at this time. Don't hold your breath on this hack leftist federal judge allowing this case to proceed against the predominantly Muslim, American-hating states that comprise OPEC.

And what did the Deep State Obama DOJ, and later even the Deep State Trump DOJ, do about this terminal corruption? Nothing, nada, zilch. In the words of French King Louis XVI in the months leading up to the French Revolution, of which Jefferson was also an architect, "apres moi le deluge!" Translated to English, "after me the flood" —meaning, I could not care less. The people can be damned, and I will worry about the consequences later. The consequences were that the king's and his lovely bride, Queen Marie Antoinette's, heads later rolled at Place de la Concorde in the center of Paris for all to witness, thanks to the people's guillotine. Again, in the prophetic words of Jefferson, "when the government fears the people there will be liberty, but when the people fear the government there will be tyranny."

Numbers 11, 12, 13, 14, 15, 16, 17, 18, 19 – Tied for Eight Runner-Ups - Honorable Randolph Moss (Obama Appointee), Honorable Thomas Hogan (Reagan Appointee), Honorable Carl Nichols (Trump Appointee), Honorable Linda Parker (Obama Appointee), and Honorable Reggie Walton (George W. Bush Appointee), Honorable Amit Mehta (Obama Appointee), Honorable James Boasberg (Obama Appointee), Honorable Timothy Kelly (Trump Appointee), and Honorable Trevor McFadden (Trump Appointee)

This grouping of politicized establishment federal judges deserve, and there are many more on the federal court in Washington, D.C., like the others referenced in this chapter over their conduct in the wake of January 6, 2021, to be indicted, tried, convicted, and themselves sentenced to solitary confinement through Freedom Watch's citizens grand juries and citizens trials, as they would like to see occur with the peaceful protesters who supported President Trump with primarily peaceful protest. All but one, Linda Parker, sit on the politicized bipartisan federal court establishment cesspool in Washington, D.C. Parker sits on the U.S. District Court for the Eastern District of Michigan.

Let's start with Judge Randolph Moss, a man who paid handsomely, directly and indirectly through his law firm Wilmer Hale, with campaign contributions to Obama and other Democrats to get his judicial appointment, as will be discussed as well later. As gleefully reported by the leftist legal reporter of the leftist publication Politico, Josh Gerstein:

> A federal judge has handed down the first felony sentence in the Jan. 6 storming of the U.S. Capitol, sending a Tampa

man to prison for eight months for obstructing Congress' effort to tabulate and certify the electoral vote.

The sentence Paul Hodkins, 38, received Monday for marching into the Senate floor with a Trump flag during the chaotic Capitol takeover was less than half of what prosecutors recommended, but U.S. District Judge Randolph Moss also turned down the defense's request that Hodkins get no prison time.

As he imposed the sentence, Moss sent a profound and dangerous message by raising the Trump flag by the Senate dias at the hour members of Congress were supposed to be confirming President Joe Biden's victory.

"The symbolism of that act is unmistakable," the judge said. "In that act, he (Paul Hodkins) captured the threat to democracy that we all witnessed that day...."[97]

No, Judge Moss, you and your colleagues, as Jefferson prophesied, have become the cancerous threat to democracy!

Judge Thomas Hogan, a Reagan appointee, like anti-Semite and drunken Judge William Keller, goes to show again that presidents generally do not even know who they have appointed to the bench, only that his advisers, following the financial and other grease applied by lobbyists and other special interests, have put the name of the jurist in front of the fearless leader be "rewarded" with an appointment.

As reported by the *Washington Post* with regard to yet another peaceful protester on January 6, 2021:

> Hogan said he seriously considered jailing Jessica Bustle because her social media posts calling January 6 participants "patriots" were "so inaccurate and misguided."

---

97. Josh Gerstein, "Judge Hands Down First Felony Sentence Tied to Capitol Riot," *Politico* (July 19, 2021), https://www.politico.com/news/2021/07/19/capitol-riot-first-felony-sentence-500149.

"Patriots are not the ones who attack operations of Congress, or attempt to stop elected lawmakers in both parties from performing their duties," Hogan said. "That is revolution, not patriotism."[98]

That is only half right, Judge Hogan! In this circumstance, where We the People have seen and been forced to endure the rank corruption in all three branches of government, not just in Congress but also in your Court, what happened on January 6, 2021, is largely both patriotism and revolution. And, this patriotic event, like the hostilities that broke out at Lexington and Concord in the months leading up to July 4, 1776, and the signing of the Declaration of Independence, symbolizes the beginning of the second American revolution or shall we now say counter-revolution! Take it or leave it!

Like King George III, Hogan and his fellow tyrannical "witches and warlocks" particularly on the District of Columbia federal bench, these despots cannot tolerate the people's dissent in defiance of their establishment masters, even in the form of First Amendment protected social media posts! With this judicial arrogance and complicity within the elitist establishment ruling class, what now is to come surely will be much more than dissent! Stay tuned, federal judges!

Judge Carl Nichols, a new Trump appointee, was not to be undone by other establishment politicized jurists on the swamp's federal bench. As reported by Associated Press:

A federal judge refused Thursday to set bail for a Texas man who was wearing a T-shirt that said, "I Was There, Washington, D.C., January 6, 2021," when he was arrested on charges he stormed the U.S. Capitol on Jan. 6.

---

98. Spencer S. Hsu, "Not Patriots, Not Political Prisoners—U.S. Judges Slam Capitol Riot Defendants at Sentencing," *The Washington Post* (August 4, 2021), https://www.washingtonpost.com/local/legal-issues/capitol-riot-political-prisoners/2021/08/04/9b6adb84-f54d-11eb-9068-bf463c8c74de_story.html.

U.S. Judge Carl Nichols ordered Garrett Miller to remain jailed pending trial, concluding the Dallas man poses a danger to the community.

Miller didn't give a statement to the law enforcement officers who arrested him at his home two weeks after the riots, prosecutors said. But they noted he was wearing a T-shirt that had a photograph of former President Donald Trump and it said "Take America Back" and "I Was There, Washington, D.C., January 6, 2021."

Prosecutors presented a photograph of Miller wearing the shirt during an earlier hearing for his case and cited it in a court filing seeking his pretrial detention.

Assistant U.S. Attorney Elizabeth Kelley said Miller has shown a troubling "lack of respect for any authority."[99]

Then there is Judge Linda Parker, a radical black federal judge appointed by Barack Obama, who literally—foaming at her mouth in a long vitriolic decision—recently rendered an opinion in a post-election challenge case, recommending the disbarment of then-Trump lawyers Sidney Powell, Rudy Giuliani and loyalist Lynn Wood. Parker is a close friend and protégé of the Governor of Michigan, Gretchen Whitmer, a Trump foe and the queen of the early COVID-19 unconstitutional lockdowns and restrictions. As reported by Reuters:

In a highly anticipated ruling, U.S. District Judge Linda Parker in Detroit said the pro-Trump lawyers, including Powell and prominent litigator Lin Wood, should have investigated the Republican former president's voter fraud claims more carefully before what Parker called a "frivolous" lawsuit.

---

99. Michael Kunzelman, "Capitol Stormer, Who Was Wearing 'I Was There' Shirt When Arrested, to Stay in Jail," *Associated Press* (April 1, 2021), https://wset.com/news/local/capitol-stormer-i-was-there-shirt-when-arrested-to-stay-in-jail.

Parker, who dismissed the Michigan suit last December, formally requested that disciplinary bodies investigate whether the pro-Trump lawyers should have their law licenses revoked.[100]

Comrade Judge Parker, your partisan illegal attacks designed to destroy lawyers who oppose the Marxist takeover of the nation are not isolated. The radical leftist District of Columbia and New York Bars are your fellow Bolsheviks, as detailed later. So much for First Amendment rights of association and free speech. Too bad the Soviet Union no longer exists, as this should be your homeland! But wait, if Putin does not oblige, the Supreme Leader in Islamic Iran will welcome you and he might even offer up the medieval Islamic Evin prison as a place you can order lawyers who oppose your ultraleftist agenda to be imprisoned and then tortured, as are those who oppose the regime.

Rounding out the cavalcade of federal judicial deceit and dishonesty on the federal bench in the District of Columbia is one Honorable Reggie Walton, an affirmative action black appointee of the equally intellectually challenged affirmative action white half-wit President George W. Bush.

Notwithstanding his similar persecution of the January 6, 2021 peaceful protesters—who not coincidentally W. has excoriated as well —years ago Walton sat on a case where Freedom Watch had sued the Organization of the Petroleum Exporting Countries (OPEC), my group being a consumer of oil in the form of gasoline like the rest of us, for price fixing and market division. As OPEC clearly illegally fixes prices between its member states— many of whom, like Iran, are either terrorist states or support terrorism, such as the biggest oil-producing member of OPEC,

---

100. Jan Wolfe, "'Profound Abuse': Judge Disciplines Pro-Trump Lawyers Over Election Lawsuit." *Reuters* (August 25, 2021), https://www.reuters.com/world/us/judge-sanctions-sidney-powell-other-pro-trump-lawyers-who-claimed-voter-fraud-2021-08-25/.

Saudi Arabia—this constitutes a per se antitrust violation under Section 1 of the Sherman Antitrust Act. This is the same law that I, along with my fellow lawyers in the Antitrust Division during the Reagan administration, used to create competition in the telecommunications industry when we succeeded in having the AT&T monopoly broken up.

OPEC headquarters are in Vienna, Austria—the home of some of the most brutal and heinous of Hitler's concentration camps. This former Nazi country from which Hitler himself hailed, even had as its president, Kurt Waldheim, also a former United Nations' secretary general. Walheim for many years after World War II had hidden his Nazi past.

Needless to say, Austria had an affinity to the anti-Israel and primarily Jew-hating Islamic members of OPEC and thus lured the Middle Eastern oil producers to its "shores" by legislating that OPEC could not be served with complaints there.

Despite my having traveled to Vienna in any event to serve OPEC with our antitrust complaint, since Austria's law violated international treaties and the agreement between the European Union and the United States, which does allow for service of process of member states such as Austria, Walton ruled that my service was improper and dismissed the complaint. And, when I appealed his ruling and the D.C. Circuit ruled that I could affect service through alternative means, such as through OPEC's mega-law firm, White & Case, who had filed a mountain of pleadings in the case, Walton again ruled that I could not serve OPEC.[101]

This travesty of justice took several years to play out, with Walton sitting on the case and not moving it along, before he killed it altogether when it was sent back to him by the appellate

---

101. Freedom Watch, Inc. v. Org. of the Petroleum Exporting Countries OPEC, 766 F. 3d 74 (D.C. Cir. Sept. 14, 2014), https://casetext.com/case/freedom-watch-1; Jonathan Kandell, "Kurt Waldheim Dies at 88; ex-UN Chief Hid Nazi Past," *New York Times* (June 14, 2007), https://www.nytimes.com/2007/06/14/world/europe/14iht-waldheim.3.6141106.html.

court. The injustice and outrage is that no one, save for Freedom Watch and yours truly, has ever really taken OPEC on for its grossly inflated price-fixing and market division, which causes a detrimental distortion in the oil industry and significantly raises the price of gasoline for consumers. Notwithstanding Walton's hijacking of my prior case, I have recently sued OPEC again over the highly inflated oil prices now severely driving up the cost of gasoline for American consumers. To get the case away from this compromised federal jurist, as discussed previously, I filed the complaint in the U.S. District Court for the Southern District of Florida, where I reside and where Freedom Watch has a Southern Regional headquarters. See Freedom Watch, Inc. v. OPEC, 9:21-CV-82145 (S. D. Fl. 2021).

One has to wonder if the Judge Walton was not doing the bidding of former oilman President George W. Bush and the Bush family, who have always been very close to, if not in bed with, the Saudi Royal family and Middle Eastern interests in general. One can hardly forget how W and his minions flew members of the Saudi Royal family out of the United States just after September 11, 2001, obviously to avoid them being questioned by the FBI about what is now clear was Saudi involvement in the horrific terrorist attack by Osama bin Laden and his fellow Saudi terrorists on the World Trade Center. Also, perhaps not coincidental was the fact that W's dad, former President George H.W. Bush, was a principal in the Carlyle Group, an investment firm that had received over billion dollars from the Biden Laden family to invest for them.[102]

102. Cindy Rodriguez, "Bush Ties to bin Laden Haunt Anniversary," *Denver Post* (September 11, 2006), https://www.denverpost.com/2006/09/11/bush-ties-to-bin-laden-haunt-grim-anniversary/; Craig Unger, "Saving the Saudis: Just Days After 9/11, Wealthy Saudi Arabians, Including Members of the bin Laden Family, Were Whisked Out of the U.S. on Private Jets. No One Will Admit to Clearing the Flights, and the Passengers Weren't Questioned. Did the Bush Family's Long Relationship with the Saudis Help Make it Happen?," (September 28, 2009), https://doczz.net/doc/497480/saving-the-saudis.

This is at a minimum strong circumstantial evidence of the "ownership" of the federal judiciary by those who put them on the bench, either directly as in the case of President George W. Bush and his family, or those special interests such in the oil industry, who grease nominations, through campaign contributions and other forms of "legalized" bribery.

But wait, Judge Walton was not finished with his federal judicial tyranny. Recently, as widely reported, he imposed severe unwarranted punishment on a January 6, 2021, peaceful protesters Lori and Thomas Vinson, husband and wife. Claiming that federal judges had been threatened over their heavy-handedness following the uprising, but not able to place any blame on the Vinsons themselves, this poor excuse of a federal judge outrageously held them accountable for the alleged actions of others. As approvingly reported by CNN, the "Communist News Network":

> A federal judge said Friday that defiant U.S. Capitol rioters, who are still defending their role in the January 6 insurrection, are fueling threats against judges from people who falsely believe the 2020 election was stolen from former President Donald Trump.

> "It bothers me that she (Lori Vinson) would try to associate herself with that type of violence… and then she goes on television on two occasions and is proud of what she did, and says she would do it again," district judge Reggie Walton said at a hearing for Capitol-riot-defendant Lori Vinson.

> "I know that these types of comments have an impact," Walton added. "As judges, we're getting all kinds of threats and hostile phone calls when we have these (January 6) cases before us, because there are unfortunately other people out there who buy in on this proposition, even though there was no proof, that somehow the election was fraudulent."

These comments came at a sentencing hearing for Vinson and her husband, Thomas Vinson. Walton gave them five years of probation and a $5,000 fine—the maximum allowed, and the largest for a Capitol rioter so far.

. . . .

"I want the sentence to hurt," Walton said. "I want people to understand that if you do something like this, it's going to hurt. I know it's a lot of money but hey that's the consequence that you suffer when you associate yourself with this type of behavior."

. . . .

Speaking through tears, Lori Vinson asked Walton for a lenient sentence. She explained that she now has a new nursing job, has been a frontline worker treating patients with COVID-19, and currently takes care of mentally challenged people in her rural community.

. . . .

Tellingly, as reported by CNN, Walton summed up his rantings by declaring:

"It does threaten the future of our democracy. Democracies die, and we've seen it in the past, when the citizens rise up against their government and engage in the type of conduct that happened on January 6."

Really, Judge Walton, tell that to our Founding Fathers, particularly Jefferson, who, because he owned slaves, you also probably hate and want to erase from our nation's history. And as for the alleged threats against you and the other corrupt federal judges in your courthouse, also remember what Jefferson, who wanted to abolish slavery, proclaimed; "When the people fear the government, there is tyranny, but when the government—in this case dishonest federal judges like you and our colleagues—fear the people, there is liberty![103]

Number 16—Honorable Tanya S. Chutkan (Obama Appointee)

This Obama judge's music is regrettably not as pleasing as another Tanya, Tanya Tucker, as this jurist sings badly and dangerously to a different tune. Chutkan's "off key" rulings hardly remind one of the famous conservative country music star. Instead, Chutkan dances to a radically leftist and vengeful jig —bent, but just for starters, on attempting to harm lawyers like me who somehow wind up appearing in her courtroom.

Chutkan is a radicalized black, having been born in Kingston, Jamaica, with affirmative action undergraduate and law degrees from George Washington University and the University of Pennsylvania respectively. And most likely thanks to minority quotas, Chutkan was hired by and worked at establishment mega law firms such as Hogan & Harston (this is where Chief Justice John Roberts hails from), Donovan, Leisure, Rogovin, Huge & Schiller, and last but hardly least the Democrat leftist haven of Boies, Schiller & Flexner, the latter having through its head partner David Boies, of Gore v. Bush 2000 election fame, succeeded in legalizing gay marriage before the primarily godless U.S. Supreme Court.

As just one example of Chutkan's leftist creed, and a simple Google search will easily reveal more, in a case styled Garza v. Hargan, she ruled that a young girl under the jurisdiction of the Office of Refugee Resettlement (ORR) should be able to decide on her own whether to have an abortion. She later certified a class action to allow for abortions by all young girls in ORR's control.

---

103. Marshall Cohen and Holmes Lyrand, "We're Getting All Kinds of Threats: Judge Says Defiant US Capitol Rioters Are Fueling Threats from Trump Supporters," *CNN* (October 22, 2021), https://www.cnn.com/2021/10/22/politics/judge-capitol-riot-threats/index.html.

But one of the persons whom Chutkan has most in her sights recently is yours truly, primarily in an overt effort to shield her left-ist female colleague, Judge Kotelly—the latter being the outright winner of the worst federal jurist of my Federal Judicial Hall of Shame—from my criticism, wrath, and lawsuits for Kotelly's dis-honest rulings in cases I brought against Tom Fitton and Judicial Watch, as previously discussed.

Chutkan's leftist hit on me manifested itself in a case I was forced to bring against Fitton for allegedly publishing falsely to seven-count convicted felon Roger Stone, who was out to harm my client Dr. Jerome Corsi and me, Corsi's lawyer, that I "was ousted at Judicial Watch because of a sexual harassment complaint." Stone then broadcast this smear on Infowars, where he was a paid host, during a show with Alex Jones and Owen Stroyer, Jones's sidekick.

The apparent reason behind this? Stone feared Corsi and thus me as this award-winning conservative author's lawyer because the paranoid self-proclaimed dirty trickster thought that Corsi would provide testimony during Stone's prosecution, implicating him in yet more crimes, something that my client never intended to do. When I would end up suing not just Stone but also Fitton for defamation, Fitton was forced to admit during a deposition, when he was put under oath, that I never was ousted due to a sexual harassment complaint.

All of this was also part of the case I had filed against Judi-cial Watch, which I previously described, that was in Kotelly's court. And, when Kotelly allowed this highly inflammatory and outrageous falsity to be published to the jury, along with another disgusting and outrageously false statement that I had beat my ex-wife, causing the previously described jury verdict against me, I sued Judicial Watch and Kotelly for what lawyers call equitable relief to set aside the judgment for fraud and other litigation mis-conduct. Both cases landed mysteriously and strangely in front of Chutkan, as I suspect that Judge Beryl Howell, the equally leftist chief judge, assigned it to her secretly, circumventing the court's random selection system. Chutkan, apparently communicating with Kotelly over how to screw me—I asked her to disclose any such communications and she refused; then, without basis, she dismissed both cases, disparaging me in the process, snidely and disrespectfully writing for obvious consumption by the leftist media that I had sued Fitton "umpteen times" and never won a case against Judicial Watch. Both statements were outright false, and in fact I obtained a judgment for defamation, which included both actual and punitive damages, years ago in Miami when, at Fitton's direction, a dutiful employee, Connie Ruffley, defamed me as a "convicted criminal."[104]

As a result, I have since sued this leftist colleague of Kotelly for denying me my constitutional rights to bring suit, and I filed an ethics complaint against her with the court's Judicial Council. But do not hold your breath on the Judicial Counsel disciplining Chutkan. Birds of a feather—meaning compromised and corrupt federal brothers and sisters—flock together.[105]

Chutkan's treatment of me, a conservative legal advocate, corresponds with what other leftist federal judges are doing to other activist lawyers on the right in their courtrooms. Their goal: to eliminate our efforts to use the legal system to take on and legally counter their radical socialist and frequently communist comrades on the left—trying, however usually in vain, to use the current legal system to excise this terminal cancer from our body politic.

But Chutkan, notwithstanding my travails before her, also showed her colors in a criminal case involving a peaceful protestor on January 6, 2021. There, this one angry black jurist, who apparently believes in "black privilege" as opposed to equal justice, even went after one of her compromised colleagues on the federal

---

104. Klayman v. Fitton et al, 1:19-cv-02793 (D.D.C.), https://casetext.com/case/klay-man-v-fitton-1.
105. Klayman v. Rao et al, 1:21-cv-02473 (D.D.C) https://www.pacermonitor.com/pub-lic/case/41937376/KLAYMAN_v_RAO_et_al.

bench, Trevor McFadden, a white Irish-American Trump appointee who, as chronicled below, has his own problems. As happily reported again by leftist reporter Josh Gerstein of Politico:

> Federal judges are wrestling with a dilemma as dozens of cases stemming from the Capitol riot move toward sentencing. Should they throw the book at everyone who streamed into the building on Jan. 6, or just those who committed violence and destruction?

> Many of the judges on D.C.'s federal bench have advocated for stiff sentences in most cases on the grounds that breaching the Capitol was an unconscionable crime against American democracy. And they've overwhelming rejected comparisons lodged by accused rioters that the violence of Jan. 6 is akin to the unrest that plagued Portland, Ore., and other American cities alongside last year's racial justice protests.

> The dispute flared anew on Monday when Judge Tanya Chutkan pointedly rejected her own colleague's comparison between the Jan. 6 mob and the rioters who exploited Black Lives Matter demonstrations last year.

> "Some have compared what took place on Jan. 6 with other protests that took place throughout the country through the past year and have suggested that the Capitol rioters are being treated unfairly," Chutkan said during a sentencing hearing. "I flatly disagree."

> Although she did not mention any names, it seemed unmistakable that Chutkan was responding—nearly point by point—to the analysis of Judge Trevor McFadden, who serves alongside her on the U.S. District Court in Washington, D.C., where more than 600 defendants and counting are facing charges for their roles in the Capitol attack.[106]

---

106. Josh Gerstein, "Black Lives Matter Comparison Roils Court in Jan 6 Cases—Judges in the U.S. District Court in Washington, D.C., Are Clashing Over How Harshly to Sentence the Bulk of the Capitol Rioters," *Politico* (October 4, 2021), https://www.politico.com/news/2021/10/04/black-lives-matter-comparison-roils-court-in-jan-6-cases-515086.

Last but hardly least, just before the 2022 New Year, Chutkan, in sentencing a white male Capitol protester, Robert Palmer, to the longest prison sentence yet, over five years to be exact, had this to add to her mounting credentials as a leading force of federal judicial tyranny, even after she had effectively forced a confession from him that he "was horrified, absolutely devastated" at what he had done. "I am so ashamed that I was part of that."

This anti-white federal judge then responded: "I can't look into your heart or your mind.... The way you conduct your life after this case is going to speak volumes about whether you are truly remorseful." She added, "Every day we are hearing reports of antidemocratic factions."

It is clear what Chutkan was referring to; so-called white domestic terrorists.

Given her similar snide attack on her white colleague, Trump-appointed Trevor McFadden, and these comments, it is unlikely that Palmer would have been sentenced by Chutkan to over five years in prison if he had been a member of Black Lives Matter.[107]

Chutkan's venomous self simply cannot resist. This radical black and feminist Obama-appointed judge apparently relishes even stoking hateful racial discord and division with a white Trump appointee on her own federal bench. There truly is no honor among federal judicial miscreants, whether they are black, beige, white, or yellow.

Then there another Obama appointee, James Boasberg, who years ago would not allow for the release in a Freedom of Information Act case of the alleged photo of Osama Bin Laden's corpse,

---

107. Michael Kunzelman, Colleen Long, Jacques Billeaud, and Lindsay Whitehurst, "Capitol Rioters' Tears, Remorse Don't Spare Them From Jail," *Associated Press* (January 1, 2022), https://apnews.com/article/capitol-siege-rioters-prison-95bdc-863812cab48be3d98ada67bd582; Hannah Rabinowitz, "In the Year Since the US Capitol Attack, Judges Remind Us What it Means to Be American," CNN (December 31, 2021), https://www.cnn.com/2021/12/31/politics/judges-us-capitol-comments/index.html.

even though there is no right of privacy to a dead master terrorist. Instead, seeing the January 6, 2021, peaceful protesters as the real terrorists, and sentencing Derek Jancart and his friend Erik Rau to forty-five days in federal prison, Boasberg weighed in on his leftist if not establishment take on the uprising, as approvingly reported by leftist Jewish journalist Hannah Rabinowitz:

> "You attempted with others to undermine one of our bedrock acts, which is the peaceful transition of power after an election… When you try to eliminate that principle, you strike at the heart of democracy."

Really Judge Boasberg! Electing someone fraudulently to the presidency, or at a minimum with massive election irregularities, is no problem! Disgraceful, but to be expected from the reportedly eighteen federal judges on the bench (four appointed by Trump himself) in the nation's swamp, who are on a mission to snuff out all peaceful dissent to the rank corruption in an establishment government which put them in power.[108]

Another Obama appointee on the D.C. federal court, Judge Amit Mehta, echoing an alarm by his judicial colleague, Randolph Moss, that "we are now fearful about the next attack," told peaceful protester John Lolos in sentencing him to fourteen days in federal prison, "You are a pawn. You were a pawn in the game played by people who know better."[109]

Indeed, if anyone is the pawn, he is you, Judge Mehta—a pawn of the left and the establishment, those who paid to get you on the federal bench as an insurance policy to cover up their government tyranny.

Not to be one upped, intellectually limited Trump federal judge Timothy Kelly, discussed more below, threw his establishment

108. Hannah Rabinowitz, "In the Year Since the US Capitol Attack, Judges Remind Us What It Means to be American," CNN (December 31, 2021), https://www.cnn.com/2021/12/31/politics/judges-us-capitol-comments/index.html.

109. Ibid.

special interest credentials in the mix on the D.C. federal court inquisition of January 6, 2021, protesters, in sentencing peaceful protester Jordan Stotts to two years probation.

Kelly declared, "It was more than just property damage and broken windows. It was a blow against the customs that make up our Constitution… it was a national disgrace."

To the contrary, Judge Kelly, it is a national disgrace that an establishment hack like you found his way onto the federal bench.[110]

Finally, rounding out the top twenty worst federal judges is the Trump-appointed Trevor McFadden, also critiqued later for other outrages, who would not let a peacefully protesting Florida "couple," Dana Winn and Rachael, to appear in court for their sentencing by Zoom at the prior height of COVID-19:

> "Defendants found the means to travel to Washington, D.C.
> to commit the crime to which they have pled guilty. …
> Defendants can therefore find the means to return to Wash-
> ington, D.C. to be held accountable for this crime."

McFadden's comments and actions are yet another unnecessary display of federal judicial arrogance and phony moral superiority over We the People, who are on the brink of doing a lot more than January 6, 2021, thanks to the endemic government corruption and deceit that permeates the current greasy establishment government.[111]

If anyone in this country deserves to be held accountable for the breakdown of the rule of law much more the fiber of the nation as a whole, it should be the federal judges, who consistently sell out the citizenry by protecting—secure in their belief that they are immune from accountability to the masses based on their

---

110. Ibid.
111. Zoe Tillman, "A Judge Refused to Let Two Capitol Rioters Appear by Video for Sentencing," BuzzFeed News (October 29, 2021), https://www.buzzfeednews.com/article/zoetillman/judge-capitol-riot-defendants-virtual-hearing.

unelected lifetime tenure—not just their colleagues on the federal bench but also the self-anointed "new American nobility" like the Clintons, the Bushes, the Obamas, and the Bidens and the similar hordes of the other self-styled establishment elite in the ever-degenerating political and social cancer of government and society in general.

And held accountable should be federal judges far beyond the "Twenty Most Wanted" I have cited simply as only a small example in this chapter.

Then there are the federal magistrate judges, also appointed through politics and special interest grease, who like the federal judges whom they serve, feather the nest of the establishment. In a recent case involving a conservative black actor and activist from Hollywood, Siaka Massaquoi, my client had his home raided at 5:45 a.m. by about twenty FBI agents, and he and his close friend who was visiting with children were handcuffed in front of them. Later, when Siaka asked to call a lawyer, FBI Special Agent Chad Warren told him that this was not necessary and then proceeded to interrogate him in violation of his Miranda and other constitutional rights about his peaceful presence at the Capitol Building on January 6, 2021. For good measure the special agent also confiscated his cell phone and computers, depriving him of a means to earn a livelihood.

When Siaka later retained me to bring a class-action suit against FBI Director Christopher Wray and the special agents who raided his home, for himself and all those peaceful protesters who have been mistreated similarly by the Biden-Harris Gestapo, Magistrate Judge Patricia Donahue, an incestuous career government alumnus of the DOJ's U.S. Attorney's Office in Los Angeles, incredibly wasted no time in dismissing the complaint, without legal basis, before it had even been served on the government and before I could even respond to any later government defenses![112]

---

112. Massaquoi v. Christopher Wray et. al, 2:21-cv-05722-SVW-PD (C.D. Cal. 2021), https://dockets.justia.com/docket/california/cacdce/2:2021cv05722/826003.

Indeed, years earlier when I ran Judicial Watch a similar case that I had filed against the then-FBI Director Louis Freeh, whose special agents broke into the home of my client Notra Trulock, who had exposed the stealing of our nuclear codes by a Chinese scientist Wen Ho Lee at Los Alamos National Laboratory and was writing a book about the FBI's negligence in failing to investigate properly, was found to have merit by the U.S. Court of Appeals for the Fourth Circuit, which allowed the case to continue by over-turning an earlier dismissal before the U.S. District Court for the Eastern District of Virginia.[113]

Siaka's complaint was later refiled and the case is in again in progress, but the bias and prejudice and rank dishonestly exhib-ited by Magistrate Judge Donahue corresponds with that of her superior judges on today's federal courts. So don't be surprised if this attempt to hold the Biden Gestapo to account for its rank vio-lations of Fourth and First Amendment constitutional rights again finds its way into the increasingly sordid trash bin of the history of federal judicial infamy.[114]

Of course, there must be—quite by chance given the corrupt way federal judges are selected for the bench—some good and uncompromised federal judges who put partisanship and slavish loyalty to their political masters aside, and they should be spared the "hooded executioner's blade." But, for now, I am hard-pressed to think of any currently serving…!

---

113. Trulock v. Freeh et. al, 275 F. 3d 391 (4th Cir. 2001), https://casetext.com/case/trulo-ck-v-freeh; Of course, Magistrate Judge Donahue could not have cared less about this strong legal precedent.

114. Massaquoi vs. FBI et. al, Civil Action No. LACV21-5722-SVT-PD (C.D. Cal 2021).

CHAPTER SIX

THE "NEW" TRUMP AND BIDEN FEDERAL JUDGES

"Plus ça change, plus c'est la même chose."

(The more things change, the more they remain the same.)

—French writer Jean-Baptiste Alphonse Karr[115]

A mong Donald J. Trump's campaign promises during the 2016 election, which yours truly considered to be particularly important if not compelling, was his commitment to appoint independent-minded federal judges who would be fearless in obeying the Constitution and the rule of law generally. Under Presidents Clinton, George W. Bush, and his dad George H.W. Bush before him, and, of course, Obama and now Trump, the nation experienced highly compromised jurists on the federal bench. Presently, Biden and his comrades are putting forth other challenged and, in their case, highly leftist mostly affirmative action federal judges. And, depending on what politically

---

115. Roger Vertes, "Plus Ça Change Plus C'Est La Même Chose"—"The More Things Change the More They Remain the Same," m. bezinga.com (July 27, 2011).

or socially charged issues were before them, I could gauge with almost certainty how they would rule.

Indeed, President Trump was completely correct when he shot back at our swamp-infected Chief Justice John Roberts, who disingenuously denied there are partisan judges. This happened after an ultraleftist federal judge on the U.S. District Court for the Northern District of California, Jon Tigar, not coincidentally a University of California, Berkeley Law School (Boalt Hall) graduate, ruled against The Donald's immigration asylum policy. Jon Tigar is a chip off the old block of his father, the self-styled and proud communist leftist public advocate, Michael Tigar, who, as Bob Woodward wrote in his book *The Brethren*, in his early career had been fired, at the urging of J. Edgar Hoover, from his High Court clerkship by Justice William Brennan for his alleged subversive ties. To this day, Michael Tigar, whose latest book, *Mythologies of State and Monopoly Power*, a Marxist rant against capitalist law, relishes his time with Fidel and the Castro brothers. His proud thank-you letters from Fidel and a photo with his revolutionary brother Ramon is even housed in the archives of the University of Texas School of Law. Today, Michael Tiger likes to pass himself off as a "distinguished" professor of law, even teaching at Duke Law School, which has become the "Berkeley Boalt Hall of the South."

It thus came as no surprise that the son of this Castro ally and admirer, Judge Jon Tigar—whose portrait adorns the walls of Boalt Hall along with Justice Ruth Bader Ginsburg and other leftist jurists—preliminarily enjoined Trump's executive order with regard to political asylum for illegal aliens. Trump vehemently complained, stating what could one expect of an Obama judge?

While I was hopeful that The Donald would appoint federal judges to counter the likes of Jon Tigar, and that things would be different under him, sadly there are now also many intellectually dishonest, cowardly, and unethical Trump federal judges running roughshod on the nation's courts. And what, in my experience so far, is a Trump judge? Based on my encounters, he or she is no different than those federal judges chosen by Trump's predecessors. I have thus far had the displeasure to come upon at least six of them, one previously critiqued, the less-than-Honorable Karen Gren Scholer of the U.S. District Court for the Northern District of Texas, a jurist who, in summarily dismissing a wrongful death complaint I brought for the father of a murdered police officer, gave Louis Farrakhan, his racist Nation of Islam, and their radical, black, white-and-cop-hating co-defendants a free pass when one of his disciples, Micah Johnson, slavishly followed his execution orders to murder cops in Dallas on June 7, 2016.

Other Trump federal judges before whom I have thus far appeared fare little better. I am talking about federal judges Trevor McFadden, Timothy Kelly, and Dabney Friedrich of the U.S. District Court for the District of Columbia, as well as Roy Altman and Rodney Smith of the Palm Beach Division of the U.S. District Court for the Southern District of Florida.

And how did these judges wind up being rubber-stamped for confirmation by The Donald? In fact, it is clear that the president did not really know who he was appointing. He was predominantly following the advice of the Republican establishment lobbyist tool known as the Federalist Society, whose primary fearless leader is Leonard Leo, who also is associated with CRC Advisors, a slippery Republican public relations firm that I mistakenly employed early in my days at Judicial Watch but that did virtually nothing to promote us—perhaps because I was too conservative, aggressive, and independent in words and action.

Along with Trump's prior and now-terminated White House counsel, Don McGahn, who later submitted to dozens of hours of interviews with Special Counsel Robert Mueller during the Russian collusion witch hunt behind Trump's back, showing little to no respect for his lawyerly confidential communications with the president, The Donald was duped into appointing these, and undoubtedly other establishment Republican hacks, to the federal bench. This was out of Trump's character, since he is the farthest thing from these establishment Republican swamp creatures.

First, let's talk about Trevor McFadden, who dismissed my client Laura Loomer's and my class action suit against Google/YouTube, Facebook, Apple, Instagram, and other social media companies. I had alleged that the social media companies were restraining trade and attempting monopolization over their restraint of trade, resulting in rank discrimination against conservatives. McFadden incredibly found this "not plausible," perverting U.S. Supreme Court precedent in a case styled *Bell Atlantic Corp. vs. Twombly, 550 U.S. 544 (2007)*—based on his own unsubstantiated views.[116] If, in fact, my charges were so "implausible," then why was it later leaked to the media that my alma mater, the Antitrust Division of the DOJ, as well as some state attorney generals, are filing related antitrust complaints at least against Google. In May 2020, President Trump himself, McFadden's "creator," issued an executive order setting policy guidelines to clip the leftist wings of the bigtech giants like Google, who will not allow and will even remove conservative content on their platforms.

I appealed McFadden's dismissal to the appellate court in Washington, D.C., and on May 27, 2020, not to be outdone, the U.S. Court of Appeals for the D.C. Circuit upped the ante in the annals of federal judicial hijinks. Previously, the three-judge panel had cancelled oral arguments on the briefs that we had filed, using the COVID-19 pandemic as an excuse. This would have been a good opportunity for the federal judges to ask questions of the parties to reach a fully reasoned and informed decision. When I reminded them that even the Ninth Circuit was holding oral

116. Freedom Watch, Inc. and Loomer v. Google, Inc. et. al, 1:18-cv-2030 (D.D.C.).

arguments by teleconference and that they could do the same, the three-judge panel shot down this good idea as well. I guess that one could say in some off-color jest, which is what the D.C. Circuit deserves, that while their judges did not give us oral, we certainly were screwed nevertheless.

In this regard, the opinion was issued in a short four-page order that read more like a hastily prepared memo by a first-year law student. Frankly, it could have been written in one and a half hours, maximum, and the ruling was a total affront not just to any semblance of judicial integrity but also to President Trump. Just one day earlier, The Donald railed against the big-tech social media companies for their discrimination against conservative content on their internet platforms and threatened to have his DOJ break them up. It seemed that, in affirming Judge McFadden's dismissal, the federal judges on the D.C. Circuit, establishment greasy appointees who have marinated in the swamp of the nation's capital for decades, simply took the noncontroversial easy way out. One is a Clinton appointee, Judge Judith Rogers, and Judges Arthur Randolph and Judith Rogers are appointees of Daddy Bush and junior, respectively. By and large, the Bush judges were not fans of President Trump, my client Laura Loomer, nor me.

The decision was so tainted that these establishment federal judicial jurists even refused to give any weight to the legal briefs and arguments of the District of Columbia, which supported our claims that the actions by Google and the other big-tech companies constituted illegal political discrimination under the district's own statutory prohibition to such conduct.

Laura Loomer and Freedom Watch later took our appeal to the full court in what is known as en banc review, and when this was predictably denied, we filed a writ of certiorari with the U.S. Supreme Court. There, only Justice Clarence Thomas, the one jurist with any degree of uncompromised real principles on the

High Court, conceded that our case had real merit but then him-self strangely declined to vote, along with the other justices, not to review the matter.

While I will never give up, the "politicians in robes," both on the lower court and most on the Supreme Court, have no love lost for real conservatives and generally couldn't care less if we are frozen off of social media platforms controlled by the leftist likes of Google.

McFadden has had similarly off-based dismissals of cases brought by Ryan Bundy and peaceful protesters Rick Lovelien and Steven Stewart over their malicious prosecutions at the hands of the Obama DOJ, following the successful Bundy Ranch stand-off with the feds.[117] Put simply, McFadden's rulings were not just contrived but cowardly in not wanting to allow in his court cases that involved powerful social media companies and high DOJ officials. Particularly with regard to the DOJ, this sadly came as no surprise, since McFadden is a former Assistant U.S. Attorney for the District of Columbia and counsel to the W. Bush DOJ's deputy attorney general. His dismissals served to protect former DOJ Attorneys General Loretta Lynch and Jeff Sessions, former FBI Director James Comey, and former Director of the Bureau of Land Management Harry Reid protégé Neil Kornze. They also resulted in stopping the cases from moving forward to discovery and then a jury trial. Only forty-three years old, this Republican establishment product of the swamp is more than wet behind the ears; he is wet everywhere!

Then there is federal judge Timothy Kelly, a lazy Republican establishment, not terribly bright, amateurish jurist who dismissed or transferred out of his courtroom cases brought by my client

---

117. Bundy v. Sessions et. al, 18-cv-2520 (D.D.C.), https://law.justia.com/cases/federal/district-courts/district-of-columbia/dcdce/1:2018cv02520/201298/17/; Lovelien v. United States of America et. al, 19-cv-906 (D.D.C.), https://law.justia.com/cases/federal/district-courts/district-of-columbia/dcdce/1:2019cv00906/205767/20/.

Dr. Jerome Corsi over defamation by Roger Stone, his surrogate Michael Caputo, and InfoWars, when they were fearful that Corsi would testify against Stone, who was a host on InfoWars, during Stone's criminal prosecution.[118] Sitting on Stone's, Caputo's and InfoWars's motions to dismiss for almost a year, Kelly—which pleadings only challenged venue, that is the locale where I had sued, but not the merits of these cases—eventually woke up from a deep sleep and got around to dismissing or transferring them to faraway courts during the COVID-19 pandemic, when travel by air was unsafe and also would significantly run up the cost of litigation for Jerry and me. My brave client had been severely financially hurt by Special Counsel Mueller's unsuccessful criminal investigation against him and Stone's unhinged if not apparently deranged vicious defamation of this distinguished conservative author.

In the Stone/Caputo case, Kelly also dismissed on similar bogus venue grounds, claiming falsely that the venue could not lie in the District of Columbia. To the contrary, venue was proper there, since Stone's, and his surrogate Caputo's, defamation was intended to harm Jerry in the nation's capital, where Stone feared he would testify against him but never did. To make matters worse, Kelly's delay of nearly a year resulted in the expiration of the one-year statute of limitations for defamation. Jerry now cannot even refile his case against Stone and Caputo in New Jersey—the only other logical venue and the place where Jerry lives, since that state has an identical one-year statute of limitations.

It is telling and simply despicable that, in issuing his dismissal order in another case filed by Dr. Corsi against Stone for yet more defamation, in a memorandum opinion dated March 1, 2020, Kelly disparaged and mocked Jerry by smugly writing that "Plaintiff Jerome Corsi, a self-styled 'author and political commentator,' sued Roger Stone, an author and political operative

---

118. Corsi v. Caputo et.al, 1:19-cv-1573 (D.D.C.), https://law.justia.com/cases/federal/district-courts/district-of-columbia/dcdce/1:2018cv02520/201298/17/.

recently convicted of various obstruction crimes...." This condescending missive, reeking of bias against and prejudice toward Dr. Corsi, who has written two books that rose to number one on the *New York Times* Best Seller list and twenty others in all that made it onto this same prestigious compendium of literary works, contrasts with Kelly, calling the convicted felon Stone simply an "author," without disparaging him. Is it that with Stone's connections to Trump, Kelly thought that someday he might want this convicted felon to approach The Donald for some higher judicial appointment or government post? In fact, Jerry told me that he has ghostwritten books on two occasions for Stone, *The Making of the President 2016* and *The Myth of Russian Collusion*, as Stone's prose left much to be desired.

I therefore, in retrospect, can only conclude that Kelly was throwing a bone to Trump, a friend of Roger Stone whom the president had hinted he would ultimately pardon. Lest we forget, The Donald put Kelly on the federal bench. And if anyone is "self-described," perhaps Jerry should now feel free to refer to Kelly, given his frivolous dismissal orders and unnecessary putdowns, as a "self-described" federal judge, since he disgracefully delayed and then issued patently dishonest decisions, which improperly extinguished Jerry's rights, a flagrant violation of the judicial oath he willingly took under 28 U.S.C. 453, that "I will faithfully and impartially discharge and perform all duties incumbent upon me under the Constitution and laws of the United States. So help me God."

I remember federal judge Royce Lamberth telling me that Kelly would be a good Trump judge, smiling that the former was serving as his mentor after confirmation. God only knows what Royce taught him! And, in the wake of the January 6, 2021, uprising, Kelly is following and one-upping his mentor's lead, having not only denied bail to Proud Boy protesters but also outrageously jailed another peaceful protester Doug Jenson for watching MyPillow founder Mike Lindell's symposium on election fraud, among other so-called right wing figures, on the internet! As reported by Associated Press:

> U.S. District Judge Timothy Kelly said that Doug Jensen, 42, of Des Moines, Iowa, had violated the strict conditions that were set when he released Jenson from jail on July 13, including prohibitions on accessing the internet and using a cellphone.
>
> Kelly ordered marshals at the federal courthouse in Des Moines, where Jensen attended Thursday's hearing, to immediately take him into custody as he awaits trial.
>
> Prosecutors had moved to revoke Jensen's pretrial release on Aug. 19, days after a federal officer found Jenson in his garage using an iPhone to watch news from Rumble, a streaming platform popular with conservatives.
>
> Jensen acknowledged that he had earlier watched two days of the cyber symposium sponsored by MyPillow CEO Mike Lindell, an ally of former President Donald Trump who used the event to push false theories that the presidential election's outcome was changed by Chinese hackers.[119]

Wow! This demented judicial moron knows no bounds! One hell of a Trump judge! Good job, Donald! It's bad enough that you associate with the likes of Roger Stone, but will you also now continue to boast of your judicial appointments, who have, as part of the establishment Republican swamp, turned on you and your allies, showing their true colors!

As for the Honorable Dabney Friedrich, she also incredibly summarily dismissed a well-pled defamation complaint, even

---

119. Ryan J. Foley, "Jan. 6 Riot Defendant Returned to Jail for Using Internet," *Associated Press* (September 2, 2021), https://apnews.com/article/technology-capitol-siege-a8b8a146f368d8105533e95f520b105d.

sworn to under oath by Laure Luhn, brought by my severely damaged client. It is well-known that Laurie was the primary sexual abuse victim of Fox News's founder and former CEO Roger Ailes.[120] When Ailes was forced to step down amid massive scandal, his top assistant Suzanne Scott was picked to fill his despicable shoes. It appears Fox News chose a female leader to offset criticism arising from the sexual abuse against Laurie and others, as well as to make sure that the extensive number of Ailes's female victims was not fully uncovered, particularly since many other hosts and television personalities followed the example, most notably Bill O'Reilly, who also was forced to resign. Incredibly, Scott, as depicted accurately in the Showtime miniseries *Loudest Voice*, was Ailes's facilitator and primo enabler, even procuring hotel rooms for him to work his sexually perverse deeds on my client.

Scott, right before the *Loudest Voice* was scheduled to air, not coincidentally gave an interview to the *Los Angeles Times*, the main newspaper in Tinseltown, claiming incredulously that she knew nothing of what Ailes had done to Laurie and the other sexually harassed women.

Scott was obviously trying to blunt what was about to be revealed in living color by Showtime. And by falsely claiming her innocence and non-involvement, Scott defamed Laurie, who was thus publicly called a liar in terms of her abuse at the hands of Ailes. For my client, a woman who has tried to commit suicide on at least two occasions—as she continues to suffer emotionally as a victim of Ailes's sexual abuse and the notoriety and public shaming this caused—it's clear that the damage done to her reputation by Scott is inexcusable.

And, as the past is indeed a prologue, Friedrich in the aftermath of the January 6 2021, uprising, she has reared, like her compromised colleagues of the most corrupt federal court in the land,

---

120. Luhn v. Scott and Fox News, 19-cv-1180 (D.D.C.), https://www.govinfo.gov/app/details/USCOURTS-dcd-1_19-cv-01180.

her ugly head again. As approvingly reported by Associated Press with joy, given its leftist pro-Biden-Harris bent, Friedrich denied bail of a peaceful protester, despite the fact that "(o)ther charges were dropped (by prosecutors) including physical violence in the Capitol grounds or buildings; impeding passage; and parading, demonstrating or picketing in a Capitol building."[121]

Since I wrote the first edition of this book, these three Trump judges, undoubtedly having read my stringing criticism of them in the first edition of this book, in retaliation, rubber-stamped a politicized temporary suspension order concerning me issued by rabidly leftist and establishment judges on the Court of Appeals for the District of Columbia, which sits at the top of the Bar's disciplinary apparatus over the previously discussed disciplinary proceeding involving the Iranian woman host of Voice of America. This woman, Elham Sataki, not coincidentally, was harmed by their colleague Judge Kotelly, who refused to even put her back to work in a satellite VOA bureau in Los Angeles, away from her alleged harasser. In suspending me temporarily as a matter of so-called reciprocal discipline, the three Trump judges failed to accord me with my constitutional right to be considered innocent until proven guilty. As a result, I have been forced to sue McFadden, Kelly, and Friedrich and ask that the case be transferred to another circuit, given the bias and prejudice and thus conflict of interest inherent before the federal court in Washington, D.C.

It is most likely that Chief Judge Beryl Howell, who also was named to my Federal Judicial Hall of Shame, assigned this reciprocal disciplinary matter to McFadden, Kelly, and Friedrich, to create the appearance that Trump judges would not be biased into doing her leftist bidding to try to remove me from practicing law in their Court. Such are the under-the-table unethical "fun and games" that all too frequently take place on the federal bench, particularly in the capital of corruption!

---

121. Ken Ritter, "U.S. Amends Capitol Siege Charges Against Two People, Including One from Tennessee," *Associated Press* (September 28, 2021), https://apnews.com/article/crime-arrests-las-vegas-nevada-tennessee-36b526990a3d8525c247e0796c201c41.

And, talk about infestation of judicial rats in the District of Columbia—where the swamp's actual fury rodents outnumber humans by seven to one— how can one overlook the abdication of judicial responsibility of Trump's own handpicked Supreme Court justices, Bret Kavanaugh, Neil Gorsuch, and Amy Coney Barrett, who refused to even hear a well-pled complaint filed by the attorney general of Texas in the aftermath of the 2020 presidential election, which if successful could have spared us the incompetent, socialist, and criminally minded Biden-Harris regime. To vote to hear the case might have cost them their free entrée into the boudoirs of Georgetown. So much for loyalty to the person who put them on the Supreme Court, much more the Constitution, which provides original jurisdiction for SCOTUS to hear election disputes between the states, which was at issue here. But the justices did not care about the Constitution! According themselves immunity from any liability to the American people, they characteristically did as they pleased, unaccountable to anyone but God, the latter of whom in practice they consider to be only their equal.

Finally, there are two Trump-appointed federal judges from South Florida who are also more than worthy of induction into my Federal Judicial Hall of Shame: Roy Altman and Rodney Smith.

Altman, at thirty-nine, even younger than McFadden and also a former DOJ assistant U.S. attorney, has proven to be obnoxiously arrogant and also wet behind his intellectually dishonest ears. To prove it, he dismissed a complaint I filed for the conservative Jewish activist Laura Loomer, who has taken on anti-Semitic Jew haters, the Muslim congresswomen Ilhan Omar and Rashida Tlaib. When we learned that Altman was assigned to the case, I thought that his "Jewishness" might be an asset, since Laura has been attacked by the leftist media for her strong pro-Israel stance. Laura is now a congressional candidate in Palm Beach County and was defamed by the leftist media publication *New York Daily News* and others.[122] This publication was incorporated as a limited liability company (LLC), and since it was headquartered outside of Florida, I sued in federal court alleging diversity jurisdiction, as Laura was a citizen of Florida.

No sooner had I filed suit, and before the complaint was even served on the leftist media defendants, Judge Altman took it upon himself to issue what is called a show cause order, demanding that I tell him if any of the partners of the LLC were Florida citizens, thus destroying diversity jurisdiction. When my research could not show that any of this was true, and I suggested that Laura be allowed to serve the complaint and the defendants would then assert any defense they wished, Altman rushed to dismiss the case. And in so doing, like Judge Kelly with Dr. Corsi, he intentionally allowed Florida's statute of limitations to run, if we ever sought to refile it—as the case had been filed with only a few days left on the statutory period to file suit.

I then asked Altman to reconsider the dismissal, and he never responded, causing my client to file an ethics complaint against him before the Judicial Counsel of the Eleventh Circuit, which oversees the federal court in Palm Beach. Again, typically, no response from Altman's fellow federal judges, as jurists of a feather flock together and protect their collective nests.

And last year on behalf of myself, I refiled in the same Palm Beach federal court the InfoWars and Roger Stone case that Kelly had previously transferred to the U.S. District Court for the Western District of Texas to get it out of his courtroom. Jerry's case remains in Texas, but being a Florida citizen, I filed a new one on my behalf in the Southern District of Florida. The case was assigned to Judge Altman, and low and behold, in just a few days, well before I could even serve the complaint, he issued one of his now patented juvenile, gratuitous, and premature show cause

---

122. Loomer v. New York Media LLC et. al, 9:19-cv-81555 (S.D. Fl.), https://www.pacer-monitor.com/public/case/30972611/Loomer_v_New_York_Media,_LLC_et_al.

orders disparaging me.[123] Here is how he began his flippant and disrespectful order by mocking my serious claims against Stone: "Larry Klayman was upset when Roger Stone called him 'incompetent' on national television…so he filed this Complaint—which when attachments are included—is 46 pages long."

My complaint was hardly about Stone calling me incompetent but rather about him making many defamatory statements that harmed my reputation, including an outrageous false allegation that I was ousted from Judicial Watch at the time that I left to run for the U.S. Senate because of a sexual harassment complaint. Stone added that anyone could ask Tom Fitton, the current head of Judicial Watch. When I later deposed Fitton under oath, as he obviously had falsely told Stone this, Fitton was forced to admit that this was not true. Fitton has been defaming me for many years since I departed Judicial Watch, and I even have a judgment against Judicial Watch for compensatory and punitive damages in the sister federal court of Altman in downtown Miami.

Following the show cause order, I asked Judge Altman to disclose if Stone, a friend and adviser to Trump, had recommended Altman to the bench, as both live in close proximity in South Florida and likely know each other as a result of both attending Republican events there. Again, as he had in the Loomer case, Altman did not respond, raising more than a legal presumption that my intuition was true. At that point, I voluntarily dismissed my case before Judge Altman and refiled it in state court, where perhaps I could get an ethical and honest judge who, rather than being appointed to the bench by Trump for life, was elected and thus accountable to and removable by the citizens of Palm Beach. Indeed, there are some very good elected state judges in South Florida, and they are generally not inclined to take cases away from the jury.

---

123. Klayman v. Infowars LLC et. al, 20-cv-80614 (S.D. Fl.), https://casetext.com/case/corsi-v-infowars-llc-1.

Given the gross misconduct of Judge Altman, I can only surmise that he does not like either my client Laura Loomer or me, and as strong conservative activists and controversial public figures, does not want us in his courtroom. Or was he doing a favor for Roger Stone, who likely recommended him to The Donald for appointment to the federal bench? And allowing Laura and me in his courtroom may jeopardize his standing in the club of establishment Republican pols and groupies, brain-dead if not blinded by the sun in the Sunshine State. These characters, by and large, are still, for some reason, in awe of Roger Stone, even after his felony convictions on five counts of making false statements to the government, one for threatening witnesses aka witness tampering, and one for obstruction of justice. Stone, to try to resurrect his fallen self and to raise money for himself and his lawyers, continues to sell himself as a close adviser to The Donald.

And as for Altman's disparagement and mocking of me in the InfoWars and Stone case, he also probably wrote his show cause order to try to help his likely "guardian devil" Roger in all of the other defamation cases that Dr. Corsi and I regrettably have had to file against this convicted perjurer who could not tell the truth if his life depended on it. Stone has now predictably used Altman's missive with these other judges to again tar Jerry and his lawyer, meaning me.

Apparently, my prophecy has proven to be true, and the convicted Stone was later sentenced to forty months in a federal penitentiary for lying under oath, witness tampering, and obstruction of justice. Then, after Stone waged a public relations campaign that he would die in prison due to COVID-19, Trump commuted Stone's sentence on the eve of his incarceration and later pardoned him. However, this admitted and proud "dirty trickster" and Mafia admirer is not out of the woods. In the cases that Dr. Corsi and I have brought against Stone for defamation and other alleged illegal acts, his testimony will be given no weight in front of the jury, since according to the Florida Rules of Evidence a convicted felon for making false statements to the government, who had been sentenced to over one year in prison, is to be accorded little to no credibility by a jury. And Stone has also since been sued by the Internal Revenue Service over alleged tax evasion and fraud,[124] as well as the Capitol Police over his alleged involvement with the Proud Boys and Oath Keepers leading up to and during the January 6, 2021, uprising.[125]

The two-faced, immoral, and proudly dishonest dirty trickster Stone has also since, to try to save his own slimy skin, even thrown his "friend" Donald Trump under the bus, proclaiming that the January 6, 2021 uprising at the Capitol Building was illegal if not criminal, after being subpoenaed to testify and produce documents by the rabidly leftist January 6, 2021 Congressional Committee, which believes that Stone has direct involvement in what they wrongly call an insurrection. Here is what has been reported that Stone said by USA Today and a number of other publications:

> "I question the integrity of this inquiry, 'Stone told reporters after a 90-minute session with the panel.' "I stress yet again that I was not on the Ellipse. I did not march to the Capitol. I was not at the Capitol. And, any claim, assertion or even implication that I knew about or was involved in any way whatsoever with the illegal and politically counter-productive activities of Jan. 6 is categorically false."[126]

---

124. United States of America v. Stone et al, 0:210-cv-60825 (S.D. Fl.), https://www.sec.gov/Archives/edgar/data/72971/000007297112000589/wfc_13f-6302012.txt.

125. Robert LeGare and Kathryn Watson, "Roger Stone and His Wife Sued Over Nearly $2 Million in Alleged Unpaid Taxes," CBS News (April 17, 2021), https://www.cbsnews.com/news/roger-stone-sued-2-million-unpaid-taxes/; Kevin Breuninger, "Capitol Police Officers Sue Trump, Roger Stone and Others Over Jan. 6 Invasion," *CNBC* (August 26, 2021), https://www.cnbc.com/2021/08/26/capitol-police-officers-sue-trump-roger-stone-proud-boys-over-jan-6-invasion.html. Smith et al v. Trump et al, 1:21-cv-02265 (D.D.C.), https://dockets.justia.com/docket/district-of-columbia/dcdce/1:2021cv02265/234873.

126. Bart Jansen, "Roger Stone Takes 5th, refuses to answer questions from House Committee Investigating January 6," USA Today (December 17, 2021), https://www.usatoday.com/story/news/politics/2021/12/17/roger-stone-jan-6-committee-deposition/8938595002/.

To the contrary Mr. Stone; the mostly peaceful protest on behalf of someone who you have traded off of for decades, President Donald Trump, was neither illegal nor counterproductive. But you have "principles" only when it suits your selfish self-aggrandisement and nefarious financial and other interests.

Last, but hardly least, is Judge Altman's colleague, Trump-appointee Rodney Smith, who presided over and dithered for an interminable period of nonproductive time on another case I filed for Laura Loomer.[127] Here, Mark Zuckerberg's Facebook, which had previously banned conservative Laura from its site, was sued because it defamed my client as "dangerous" and a "domestic terrorist" mostly for truthful comments she had made about Islam, which persecutes women and purveys hate against gays, lesbians, and transgenders. Finally, after a year of prejudicial delay, he conveniently transferred the case to federal court in San Francisco, although Laura lives and works in Palm Beach, Florida, and a defamation case belongs where the victim resides.

San Francisco, of course, is in the Bay area, the home of Facebook, and is very leftist. Home-court advantage Zuckerberg. Thank you, Rodney, for your impressive federal judicial courage to avoid having my client and me in your courtroom and allowing for us to legally take the "great and powerful" Facebook to the woodshed! And, as a result, Laura, who was severely harmed by Zuckerberg and his leftist minions, was then forced to travel over three thousand miles away from Florida, at great additional loss of time and expense, to try to get justice in a far-leftist court that worships at the altar of Facebook, its "hometown" buddy up the road in Menlo Park! At that point Laura decided to dismiss the case and fight Facebook at some future date in time. To try prevail in this uber leftist court would be a colossal waste of time and money.

---

127. Loomer v. Facebook, Inc., 9:19-cv-80893 (S.D. Fl.), https://digitalcommons.law.scu.edu/cgi/viewcontent.cgi?article=3206&context=historical.

Yes, Mr. Trump, "plus ça change, plus c'est la même chose." Next time, dear Mr. President, if you decide to run and are elected in 2024—which likely will not happen as were you to announce, the rabid leftist Democrat prosecutors in New York City will improperly indict you and your sons over tax issues and this will tie you down in a criminal prosecution—please pay attention to whom you are appointing to the federal bench!

And now, with the total leftist takeover being implemented through its lackeys Biden and Harris, a further mockery is being made of the federal judiciary, as this braindead president continues his practice of appointing mostly those who will satisfy the anti-white, anti-male, and anti-Judeo Christian race baiters who have a hold on his presidency. As reported "lovingly" by the leftist taxpayer funded NPR:

> President Biden has gotten a group of 40 federal judges confirmed in the Senate this year, the most for a new president since the Reagan era—and he is prioritizing diversity among his nominees for these life-tenured posts.
>
> Biden's nominees include the first openly LGBTQ woman to sit on a federal appeals court, Beth Robinson of Vermont, and the first Muslim American to be a judge, Zahid Qurasishi of New Jersey. Biden has also named more Black women to circuit courts, many of them former public defenders, than any other president.[128]

As just one example of Biden's affirmative action judicial selection "prowess," which rubber stamps like Trump also did, names of jurists who are put in front of him by his ethically bereft special interest supporters, is former Obama lower court appointee Judge Ketanji Brown Jackson, a black woman I once appeared in front of on behalf of my client Cliven Bundy in a Freedom of Information

---

128. Carrie Johnson, "Biden Had a Productive Year Picking Federal Judges. The Job Could Get Tougher in 2022," NPR (December 28, 2021), https://www.npr.org/2021/12/28/1067206141/biden-federal-judges-nominations-diverse.

Act (FOIA) case. Incredibly, in the Bundy case Jackson barely knew anything about FOIA, hardly a complex law! Now, she has not only been placed on the D.C. federal appellate court based on her color and sex, but is also reportedly on the short list to be a Supreme Court nominee now that Stephen Breyer has retired.[129]

So much for having the best and brightest on the federal bench. Being black, Muslim, gay, lesbian, transgender or transexual, or whatever as long as one is not a white male, are under the Biden-Harris regime the overriding criteria, as our federal judges and courts sink to a new low.

---

129. Brent Kendall, "Senate Confirms Ketanji Brown Jackson for Powerful Appeals Court: Judge Jackson Is Seen As a Candidate for a Future Supreme Court Vacancy," *Wall Street Journal* (June 14, 2021), https://www.wsj.com/articles/senate-confirms-ketanji-brown-jackson-for-powerful-appeals-court-11623709503.

CHAPTER SEVEN

QUASIJUDICIAL TYRANNY

"Because power corrupts, society's demands for moral authority and character increase as the importance of the position increases."

—John Adams[130]

I f by now you are convinced that Jefferson was right, namely in his thoughts regarding the federal judiciary, unelected by the people and believing that they are installed for life, with immunity from being sued for their wrongs, then you will be more than troubled by other bastions of tyranny lurking and embedded in our legal system.

One such dangerous example, underscoring how too much authority can be abused, is the Office of Disciplinary Counsel of the District of Columbia Bar (ODC), which oversees alleged attorney misconduct. Until just recently, here is what the bar had

130. John Adams, *BrainyQuote*, brainyquote.com, https://www.brainyquote.com/quotes/john_adams_389106.

published on its website, which created a false impression that ODC was evenhanded and nonpartisan:

> "In this capacity, the Office of Disciplinary Counsel has a dual function: to protect the public and the courts from unethical conduct by members of the D.C. Bar and to protect members of the D.C. Bar from unfounded complaints."

Then there are other quasijudicial bodies, such as arbitration panels, who also throw around their power, greased to the hilt by large and powerful corporations, labor unions, and other vested special interests—generally to the detriment of ordinary folk.

TYRANNY AT THE OFFICE OF DISCIPLINARY COUNSEL

ODC is run and managed by rabid leftists, nearly all of whom, a search of Federal Election Commission records will show, have donated heavily to the Clintons and Barack Hussein Obama, Biden as well as other liberal Democrats. Indeed, in recent history, not one of them has given even one cent to a Republican political candidate, presidential or otherwise.

The leftist prosecutors of the ODC are not much different in practice to the prosecutorial team of Special Counsel Robert Mueller—individuals who use the power of their office to try to remove persons whose ideology they despise from the practice of law.

It thus should come as no surprise that in deciding which lawyerly scalps ODC wishes to pursue for alleged violations of the District of Columbia Code of Professional Responsibility, the vast majority are Republicans and conservatives. And it's prosecutors lay off of, if not endorse, prominent leftist Democrat legal counsel, such as David Kendall of Williams & Connolly, who obstructed justice by helping Hillary Clinton, his client, wipe clean and destroy her 33,000 plus emails from her private server, which contained classified national security information. A former District of Columbia lawyer, Ty Clevenger—a conservative activist who was forced for financial reasons to resign from the practice of law by ODC and its minions—had filed an ethics complaint, in the public interest, against Kendall. It was promptly thrown in the circular bin by Deputy Bar Counsel Elizabeth Herman. No surprise, as Herman had contributed to the presidential campaign of Barack Obama, the administration in which Hillary served as secretary of state.

The now sadly deceased and renowned legal scholar and expert Professor Ronald Rotunda, who while alive I came to know as a friend as well as for his expertise in professional lawyer ethics and constitutional law, fought against the politicization of ODC and other state bars, as he too, a conservative, had been a target of the rabid prosecutors in the leftist ODC when he served as a legal counsel on the Select Committee on Presidential Campaign Activities investigating Watergate during the Nixon years. Ron used to tell me that many state bars, most of which are quite leftist-oriented, target conservative lawyers and "want their scalps." But from my experience, none is as overt as ODC in the nation's capital. The equally leftist New York Bar is a close second.

Ironically, I founded Judicial Watch to be a sort of "Hamburger Helper" to the bars of all fifty states, as after seventeen years of legal practice, I had had the misfortune of having to contend with many unethical if not criminally minded lawyers. In this regard, and as just a few examples, I might remind you that the Bonnie and Clyde of American politics are both lawyers, having graduated the same year from Yale Law School and then returned to Little Rock, Arkansas, where they auditioned for their later role as the most corrupt duo to ever occupy the White House. So too were Richard Nixon, Barack Obama, and Joe Biden lawyers as well! Thus, I conceived of the mission of Judicial Watch to not only "watch" judges to prevent unethical conduct but also to combat illegality in the government and the legal system as a whole.

In this age of The Donald and especially "post Donald," where the left has seized total control over the nation, the vicious polarized climate in Washington, D.C., has reached a fever pitch. Anyone who supported and/or represented President Trump is considered and treated by the Left as an enemy of the state, that is a state envisioned by socialists, communists, anarchists, atheists, and radicals of all ideological stripes. Case in point, Rudy Giuliani, who recently was suspended temporarily without even an evidentiary hearing and thus due process by the District of Columbia and equally rabidly leftist New York bars simply over his representation of Trump in post-election lawsuits, which the leftist officials of these bars and others of their ilk call "The Big Lie." On the other hand, if a lawyer who brings cases to try to change society for the better simply toes the line and does not make waves through conservative public legal advocacy or some other provocative means that offends and is seen as a threat by the Left, he or she has a better than good chance of being left alone by ODC. Of course, this latter option does not apply to someone like me, who has had a legal knife to the throats of corrupt leftist politicians, so-called government leaders, lawyers, and judges for decades.

For years during my time as the head of Judicial Watch, I had been subjected to retaliatory politically motivated bar complaints by persons associated mostly with the Clintons. But I always prevailed in the end, since ODC during these years was run by it's now-retired head, Bar Disciplinary Counsel Wallace "Gene" Schipp, a fair and decent man. But in and around the time that Trump ascended to the White House, the leadership changed. Now, a very partisan bar disciplinary counsel named Hamilton "Phil" Fox has taken over, stoking a virtual inquisition against me and other conservative advocates.

Interestingly, Fox came from the law firm of Sutherland, Asbill & Brennan, which was my legal counsel in negotiating my contentious severance agreement with Fitton and the disloyal and paranoid "boys" I left behind at Judicial Watch, when in the fall of 2003 I was leaving to run for the U.S. Senate in Florida. In fact, when Fitton and the other directors breached this agreement and I could not resolve the dispute and regrettably had to file suit against them and the public interest group I founded, it was Fox who actually defended a deposition of his partner, Herb Beller, a tax and corporate lawyer who had negotiated my severance agreement with Fitton and Judicial Watch's outside counsel, David Barmak. Talk about a looming conflict of interest!

So predictably, in the current environment of the swamp, I came to be a target of ODC under Phil Fox, a dyed-in-the-wool leftist lawyer hack who has donated heavily to leftist Democrats, including Obama, whom I had sued many times in the past. And with the help of Tom Fitton, Phil Fox had found a vehicle to try to target me for legal extinction! Of course, an insecure person like Fitton was happy and grateful to be of assistance, since he feared competition from Freedom Watch, which I founded after my U.S. Senate campaign, and was envious that I was a lawyer and he was not—but I believe was also afraid I might someday regain control of my baby. Fox and his venomous, fire-breathing, anti-white-male Deputy Bar Counsels Elizabeth Herman and Julia Porter used Fitton when they set out to remove me from the practice of law, as "conservative public enemy number one."

Fitton had filed vindictive and strategic bar complaints against me, one of which alleged that I had a conflict of interest in representing, after I left to run for the U.S. Senate, donors, clients, and employees of Judicial Watch that either had their monies misappropriated, were abandoned, or were harassed and fired respectively. In fact, I had no choice but to step in to protect these victims from the "enfant terrible," since they lacked the resources to hire a lawyer to remedy the damage that was caused. As just a few examples, it was yours truly, while at the helm of Judicial Watch, that solicited monies from donors so we could buy the building that was being rented. About one and one-half million dollars was raised under my name, but after I left, and now even nineteen years later, Fitton and Judicial Watch still have not even bought the building but instead pocketed the monies. The abandoned client was none other than Peter Paul, whom Judicial Watch had agreed to defend in a criminal matter related to the Clintons. As a result of Fitton breaking this contract, Paul was left without effective assistance of counsel and wound up doing ten years in prison. The employee I represented was Sandra Cobas, the director of Judicial Watch's Miami office. She was harassed and forced out along with other regional directors I had hired.

And how do I know that ODC used Fitton—who is not a lawyer—to try to disbar me? I actually have audio recordings that I made of meetings I had with ODC prosecutors, during which they admitted to not liking the way I practice law—meaning, I held politicians like the Clintons and Obamas, their "heroes," to the rule of law. In the District of Columbia, only one-party consent, meaning me in this instance, is needed to secretly tape conversations. On these audio recordings as well—my "insurance policy"—one of the somewhat less rabid prosecutors at ODC, H. Clay Smith III, albeit a "yes man" who will not challenge his fearless leaders, suggested that I consider resigning from the bar, to avoid the time, expense, and publicity that was about to come my way.

At the time, I did not comprehend why Clay Smith would make such a bizarre suggestion, but in retrospect, I now fully understand. He knew what his office's "Mission Impossible" was! Because what followed were at the time three bogus bar complaints—two of which were filed by the childish and envious

Fitton and all of which I am still litigating at the cost of great time and expense. Fitton, apparently not willing or able to get a law degree and license to practice law, wanted to reduce me to his level so he could compete. I need not belabor these complaints other than what I previously discussed. Suffice it to say I am confident of success, one way or the other, in the end, when all appeals are heard and decided and my countersuits and other strategic endeavors proceed to a conclusion.

I am also confident because I am not one to sit back and take punches from anyone, and in a way, I actually relish holding the corrupt Fox, Porter, and ODC, much less Fitton, to legally account. After all, that is why I founded Judicial Watch and now Freedom Watch: to fight against a corrupt legal establishment. I thus felt duty bound to sue Fox and the female Deputy Bar Counsel Julia Porter and Elizabeth Herman, the "witches" who masterminded and instituted their witch hunt, to try to remove me from the practice of law, just as Special Counsel Robert Mueller had so attempted to remove Donald Trump from the presidency.

I also filed ethics complaints against Fox, Porter, and Herman, as they not only engaged in abuse of process in instituting these complaints, many years after the underlying charges had arisen, but also lied in legal pleadings. To add insult to injury, one of the hearing committee members sitting on the only bar complaint at the time not filed by Fitton, was none other than Michael Tigar and the father of Judge Jon Tigar, an avowed communist who obviously is not unbiased toward me. I suspect that he was recruited by the leftist chair of the committee, Anthony Fitch, to set me up for a fall, such is the putrid witch's and warlock's caldron of the disciplinary apparatus of the District of Columbia Bar.

In the appeal of the recommendation of Tigar and Fitch to have me suspended from legal practice for thirty-three months, my own lawyers, Stephen Bogorad and John Richards, who are both left of center, refused to raise the issue of Tigar's past and his obvious bias and prejudice toward me, so I raised it myself, resulting in their withdrawing from the case out of fear that they would be retaliated against. Such is the power of ODC. Bogorad's and Richard's exit stage left was good riddance. In retrospect, it was a mistake to have retained them. I do not need liberal self-serving cowards representing me. They will be sued for malpractice, breach of fiduciary duty and contract, at a time and place of my legal choosing.

My complaints against ODC and its deputy bar counsels Porter and Herman, as well as the president Esther Lim of the District of Columbia Bar and Mathew Kaiser who heads the Board of Professional Responsibility, which and who oversee ODC and refused to police ODC's misconduct, were filed in federal court in Washington, D.C., and alleged discrimination on the basis of political bias, gender discrimination, and outright illegality. They were assigned to an Obama-appointed judge, the Honorable Randolph Moss and a few other politicized federal judicial hacks. So much for the wheel of fortune in randomly assigning cases.

I immediately learned by having my associate check FEC records that Moss has donated about $38,000 to President Obama and related Democratic interests to grease his nomination to the federal bench. And Judge Moss's former law firm WilmerHale— the same one as Robert Mueller and Jeannie Rhee of Trump witch-hunt-fame—bundled contributions from their partners to contribute a lot more. Incidentally, WilmerHale, through its financial "largesse," was also instrumental in getting its other former partner, Judge Dabney Friedrich, the jurist who dismissed the Laurie Luhn case against Fox News, and its CEO Suzanne Scott, appointed to the federal bench by President Trump. How convenient, this mega-swamp-infested firm now has bookends of federal judges in its pocket on the U.S. District Court for the District of Columbia, one Obama appointee and one Trump appointee. Little luck or prowess is now needed when its lawyers argue before them! Also great for luring clients to retain their firm in matters before the D.C. federal court!

In any event, learning of Moss's payola, I politely asked him to consider recusing himself from my cases against the ODC and its deputy bar counsels, but he refused, claiming and trying to assure me that he could be neutral and fair. But many months later, he dismissed my complaints nevertheless, claiming, as usual, that my allegations of illegality were not "plausible," a staple of federal judges who want to take cases away from juries based on their own irrelevant views.

As with many of the federal judges I wrote about in Chapter Five, I asked for Moss to hold status conferences when my cases were delayed. With the exception of Judge Huvelle in the case that my client Dr. Corsi filed against Robert Mueller, they all hid in their chambers and would, like judicial vampires, not be seen in the light of their courtrooms, and this was even well before the quarantines resulting from COVID-19. Instead, Moss and the others simply issued written orders, probably because they did not want to confront me in person, so insidious, frankly embarrassing and dishonest were their intended "precooked" rulings.

In dismissing my complaint, Moss also used as an excuse the claim by ODC and its deputy bar counsel that they have immunity not just from suit but also ethics complaints. But the immunity they falsely claim was without valid legal basis and shamelessly created by the bar itself through the whim and decree of its Board of Professional Responsibility. This so-called immunity was without a valid legal basis and was illegally put in place in order to protect the Board's minions, such as ODC prosecutors and hearing committee members like Michael Tigar as well as those lawyers and laypersons who sit on the Board. How else can a communist like Tigar preside on a case involving Larry Klayman and try to escape from his "cooked" recommendations—liability free! Blanket immunity such as this will not fly legally, and I have challenged Judge Moss's dismissals in part under this phony guise of immunity with the appellate court. If necessary, I will attempt to take this issue to the U.S. Supreme Court. Of course, good luck in that regard. It was SCOTUS, which like the Board, illegally granted immunity to itself and all lower court federal judges, so they all can do as they please and sleep peacefully at night.

So there you have it! A conflicted and corrupt Bar Disciplinary Counsel, Phil Fox, and his leftist conservative lawyer-hating and anti-Trump deputy bar counsels can flout process, obscure the truth, and subvert ethics and the rule of law by carrying out selective prosecutions of licensed attorneys such as myself. And, to top it all off, they, and their allies on the federal bench such as Judge Moss, who profits from the same claimed immunity from suit, cover for them. What a toxic icing on this filthy cake we have been heretofore duped into believing was a "just" justice system.

But Larry Klayman is not the only conservative scalp sought by ODC, backed up by corrupt federal judges like Moss. Low and behold, Michael Tigar and fifteen of his leftist colleague professors in various leftist law schools around the nation, vindictively filed a bar complaint against Trump's White House Counselor Kellyanne Conway for simple remarks she made on cable news. And Kellyanne, while a licensed lawyer in the District of Columbia, is not even currently on active status and no longer practices law. The Marxian likes of Michael Tigar simply can't resist.... Their ends justify the means, as Karl Marx had put it.

And just in the last year or so on July 22, 2020, all four of the former presidents of the District of Columbia Bar, and other leftist and Democrat lawyers, including those who have previously served as assistant bar disciplinary counsel at ODC, filed a complaint before ODC, against Trump attorney general William Barr. The complaint, which if the past is a prologue, ODC will be pleased as punch to prosecute, seeks to predictably, as has been attempted with yours truly, have Barr, like Giuliani this year, removed from the practice of law. The basis? They are shedding crocodile tears and complaining that Barr made political decisions and publicly commented on ongoing criminal investigations with regard to alleged criminality by those implicated in the Mueller witch hunt. Barr is also being crucified for allegedly speaking dishonestly on cable television, among a host of other alleged professional ethics violations against leftist humanity. This is akin to the pot calling the kettle black, given that these leftist lawyers themselves, contrary to bar policy, publicized their complaint against the attorney general, all with the obvious intent to publicly smear him for political purposes.

And, why is all of this venom necessary when, ironically, Barr failed miserably to bring even one high-level indictment against any of the principal actors who caused the witch hunts of President Trump and his allies? Only one logical answer. The leftist District of Columbia Bar and its even more politically driven ODC and its sister kangaroo court the New York Bar cannot help themselves, as they continue and ramp up their contrived legal crusade against conservative and Republican lawyers.[131] They are an integral part of the conspiratorial cancel culture of leftist despots and tyrants, bent on maintaining a socialist, communist, atheist, and otherwise radical noose around all of our collective necks, ramped up even more during the age of the Biden-Harris regime.

Such is the incestuous cabal of leftist bar disciplinary counsels and federal judges in our national reptilian swamp and Gotham City, bent on removing lawyers from the practice of law who will

---

131. Betsy Woodruff Swan, "Past D.C. Bar Association Chiefs Call for Probe of William Barr," *Politico* (July 22, 2020), https://www.politico.com/news/2020/07/22/bill-barr-bar-association-probe-377272.

challenge their views of what our body politic should be, and worse, public advocates like me who proudly supported President Trump. I, for one, will never roll over to the likes of these Jeffersonian-predicted tyrants, and neither should you, fellow patriots.

THE SCAM OF BIG FIRM ESTABLISHMENT ARBITRATORS

With their superior bargaining power, large corporations, labor unions, and establishment-vested special interest groups, when they enter into contracts with people or companies of lesser means and bargaining power, almost always demand that the agreement contain a so-called arbitration provision, administered by big arbitration firms, like a group called JAMS, to resolve any disputes. These arbitration clauses always contain a provision that designates what law will be used, among the fifty states, to decide the case. You can bet that the chosen state law always favors these powerful entities.

And because individuals do not have the bargaining power of these mega-interests, they usually agree to arbitrate, as the contracts are generally presented to them on a take-it-or-leave-it basis.

In principle, arbitration is intended to be a faster, less expensive means to decide cases, but the parties generally pay for the service themselves. Arbitrators are the equivalent of private bought-and-paid-for judges, the difference being that federal judges are "paid for" with other means, as previously discussed. And the arbitration firms and their arbitrators, chosen by these big interests, feed at this legal trough, like fat and happy pigs, of the business that is sent their way by these big mega-interests. In short, if the arbitrators do not rule consistently in favor of these behemoths, no more business will be sent their way. Convenient, huh?

So it was that when one of my clients, Jackie Beard Robinson, having started a boutique with Melissa Gorga, who she had hit it off with when the television star of NBC's *Housewives of New Jersey* walked into her store in Deerfield Beach, Florida, was forced into arbitration when the two started a joint fashion design business that later broke up.[132]

In retaliation for Robinson having decided to end the business relationship, the television actress Melissa Gorga accused Robinson of stealing merchandise and publicized it on another NBC show, one with personality Andy Cohen.

Prior to the "divorce," Gorga had promised Jackie she would also have a role on *Housewives of New Jersey* to promote their joint venture, and my client, before I came to represent her, had signed a contract with NBC that contained an arbitration provision, designating JAMS to resolve any dispute under New York law. New York is where NBC's headquarters is located. The contract also released NBC from liability for any alleged illegality that would occur into the future.

The problem was, however, that a release cannot apply to events that have yet to take place. And the defamation that Gorga, through Cohen, had maliciously trained on Jackie after the split was clearly exempt from this release, since it occurred after the contract was signed and was not foreseeable in advance.

Having tried to settle Jackie's defamation claims amicably with the payment of damages over my client's loss of reputation for honest business practices, which harmed her and her company severely, our pleas fell on deaf ears at NBC and its sister network Bravo, where Gorga and Cohen had made false and damaging statements about my client.

Knowing that NBC most likely had its designated arbitration service, JAMS, in its "hip pocket," I crafted a legitimate way

---

132. Robinson v. NBC Universal Cable et. al, JAMS Arbitration Ref. No. 1130007593, https://www.law360.com/cases/5a2943ddd426a42c4e000004.

around this "straight jacket" of quasijudicial decision-making and filed a complaint in federal court in the U.S. District Court for the Southern District of Florida. The complaint alleged that Jackie had been defrauded into signing the contract containing a waiver of possible future liability, since Gorga and Cohen had intended to set her up to be defamed. As such, the agreement with NBC was a nullity, and the arbitration provision would thus fall with this voidable contract. Obviously, Jackie and I wanted a jury to decide the case, not some arbitrator that NBC, Gorga, and Cohen effectively had in their hip pocket. Juries, incidentally, are more likely to award large damages, particularly in Florida, which is what lawyers call a "plaintiff's state."

As bad luck would have it, the case was assigned to the now infamous Judge Donald Middlebrooks, of Hillary racketeering fame, the jurist who dismissed my case against the Clintons and their foundation because he, a Clinton appointee, divined in his inner self that my case was not "plausible." His appointment reminded me of the mantra of my uncle Bennie Klayman, after a shot or two of Chivas Regal scotch, that "if I did not have bad luck, I would have no luck at all." Indeed, when I learned that Middlebrooks was the federal judge, I felt like taking a few shots as well, although I no longer drink alcohol.

Sure enough, Middlebrooks dismissed Jackie's case, again claiming that our allegations were not plausible. He slavishly sent the complaint to JAMS, as NBC, Gorga, and Cohen had requested. What was Middlebrooks motivation in again taking an exit stage left, as he had with the RICO case against Bonnie and Clyde? Probably that he did not want to be the federal judge who presided on a case that could tar NBC, a giant in the media, with large damages. Not good for any future publicity that this federal judge may covet from this network in the future should he want a higher appointment from a future Democrat president on an appellate court or wherever, and that is the best scenario short of more sinister possibilities.

In fact, Middlebrooks is not unique. Judges of all stripes don't generally like to have big print and television media as defendants in their courtroom for the same reason. If the past is a prologue, the same is true in taking on the Big Tech giants, Google, Apple, Twitter and their socialist and leftist clones.

After the case was sent to JAMS, an arbitrator was chosen. He was, you guessed it, a retired New York judge who had probably figured out he could make more money as an arbitrator than on the judicial bench. After sitting on the case for nearly a year, during which time he went AWOL for a period of time, I demanded that he finally rule on and deny NBC's, Gorga's, and Cohen's motions to dismiss and allow the arbitration to move forward to discovery and a conclusion. But rather than making any real effort to analyze the facts and law, and in many instances intentionally misstating both in his eventual ruling dismissing the case, he not only "deep sixed" Jackie and her claims but also ordered her to pay the legal fees and costs of NBC, a thirty-billion-dollar-plus enterprise.

Not to take this sitting down, I then sued the arbitrator and JAMS for their fraud, if not gross negligence, in Florida state court in Palm Beach County. As one of their defenses, they claim that federal arbitration laws grant them immunity from liability for their decision-making. And while, in theory, this should not fly, in today's corrupt legal world, any additional outrage is possible, if not likely. Indeed, a lower court state judge has already so held, and the matter is going up on appeal, all the way to the Florida Supreme Court and U.S. Supreme Court if necessary. But don't hold your righteous breath with these corrupted tribunals, infested with leftist and establishment and special interest yes men and yes women.

For more about this quasijudicial corruption, and the analogous sleazy state of state family courts where judges, magistrates, guardian ad-litems, and even opposing legal counsel are virtually all in bed with each other—scratching each other's backs and frequently splitting fees or passing bribes to enrich themselves at the expense of spouses, ex-spouses and their children—read as well my earlier book *Whores: Why and How I Came to Fight the Establishment!*, still available on booksellers online. And take the time to watch a recent Netflix documentary about the conservatorship of Britney Spears, titled "Britney Vs. Spears," which aired on September 22, 2021, where her own father, named a conservator by a compromised and corrupt family court judge, treated her like a caged animal and exploited her for decades. It is a miracle that the poor woman was not forced to commit suicide over her legal enslavement, which only recently ended.[133]

Isn't life great in the big leagues of our justice system? Federal judges, bar disciplinary counsels, arbitrators, and judicial, quasijudicial dishonest and self-serving hacks of all persuasions, and family court legal cockroaches and leaches, can do as they please with little to no consequence. And when they are called to task, they hide behind phony claims of immunity, which almost always sticks, since their colleagues protect them as part of the sleazy club all too prevalent in the so-called legal profession. This is why I, a lawyer of forty-five years since I was sworn in before the Florida Supreme Court on December 7, 1977, ironically Pearl Harbor Day, have always tried to live by the famous quotation of comedian and actor Groucho Marx, who often quipped that "I refuse to be a member of any club that would have me as a member."[134]

---

133. Jem Aswad, "Read Britney Spears' Full Statement Against Conservatorship: 'I Am Traumatized,'" *Variety* (June 23, 2021), https://variety.com/2021/music/news/britney-spears-full-statement-conservatorship-1235003940/.

134. Groucho Marx, *BrainyQuote*, Brainyquote.com, https://www.brainyquote.com/quotes/groucho_marx_122546.

Regrettably, in today's world, Groucho's line is no longer funny, but instead our sad reality!

This rank perversion of our legal system must change if we are to have a republic of laws and not men, as one of our other Founding Fathers proclaimed in advocating for the Declaration of Independence in my birthplace of Philadelphia. His name was John Adams.

CHAPTER EIGHT

REFORMATION OF THE FEDERAL JUDICIARY?

CONGRESS AND THE STATES CAN ACT, BUT DON'T COUNT ON IT!

"When a man assumes a public trust, he should consider himself as public property."

—Thomas Jefferson[135]

By now, you can see that federal judges, not elected by We the People and with supposed lifetime tenure, are the biggest threat to the continued existence of our democratic republic. But wait, the wives' tale that these despots in robes can serve for life is just that. In fact, the Constitution says nothing about lifetime appointment. Article III, Section 1, merely states, "The judges, both of the supreme and inferior courts, shall hold their offices during good behavior."

Simply put, this is not for life. All "good behavior" must come to end.

---

135. Thomas Jefferson, *BrainyQuote*, Brainyquote.com, https://www.brainyquote.com/quotes/thomas_jefferson_157238.

Nor does the Constitution grant immunity to U.S. Supreme Court justices or lower court federal judges. It is totally silent in this regard. Instead, the justices, again unelected by the citizenry, decided conveniently to grant themselves and their children on the inferior courts near-total immunity from being held legally accountable for their actions under virtually any circumstances, however malicious, severe, and compelling! Talk about unchecked "godly" power of the federal judiciary, as Jefferson predicted, and you have more than simple chutzpah; you have unelected, unaccountable tyrants if not criminals in robes. We should rename them the "untouchables," but believe me they are no Elliot Ness. Rather than enforcing the law, they feel free to make up their own law!

Encyclopedia.com summarizes and explains most simply the bogus and legally unjustified evolution of claimed federal judicial immunity:

> Judicial immunity was first recognized by the U.S. Supreme Court in *Randall v. Brigham*, 74 U.S. (7 Wall.) 523, 19 L. Ed. 285 (1868). In *Randall* the Court held that an attorney who had been banned from the practice of law by a judge could not sue the judge over the disbarment. In its opinion, the Court stated that a judge was not liable for judicial acts unless they were done "maliciously and corruptly."

> In *Bradley v. Fisher*, 80 U.S. (13 Wall.) 355, 20 L. Ed. 646 (1871), the U.S. Supreme Court clarified judicial immunity. Joseph H. Bradley had brought suit seeking civil damages against George P. Fisher, a former justice of the Supreme Court of the District of Columbia. Bradley had been the attorney for John H. Surratt, who was tried in connection with the assassination of President Abraham Lincoln. In Suratt's trial, after Fisher had called a recess, Bradley accosted Fisher "in a rude and insulting manner" and accused Fisher

of making insulting comments from the bench. Surratt's trial continued, and the jury was unable to reach a verdict.

Immediately after discharging the jury, Fisher ordered from the bench that Bradley's name be stricken from the rolls of attorneys authorized to practice before the Supreme Court of the District of Columbia. Bradley sued Fisher for lost work as a result of the order. At trial, Bradley attempted to introduce evidence in his favor, but Fisher's attorney objected to each item, and the judge excluded each item. After three failed attempts to present evidence, the trial court directed the jury to deliver a verdict in favor of Fisher.

The U.S. Supreme Court has consistently upheld absolute immunity for judges performing judicial acts, even when those acts violate clearly established judicial procedures. In Stump v. Sparkman, 435 U.S. 349, 98 S. Ct. 1099, 55 L. Ed. 2d 331 (1978), the Court held that an Indiana state judge, who ordered the sterilization of a female minor without observing due process, could not be sued for damages under the federal civil rights statute (42 U.S.C.A. section 1983).

In 1971 Judge Harold D. Sparkman, of the Circuit Court of DeKalb County, Indiana, acted on a petition filed by Ora McFarlin, the mother of a fifteen-year-old Linda Spitler. McFarlin sought to have her daughter sterilized on the ground that she was a "somewhat retarded" minor who had been staying out overnight with older men.

Judge Sparkman approved and signed the petition, but the petition had not been filed with the court clerk and the judge had not opened a formal case. The judge failed to appoint a guardian ad litem for Spitler and he did not hold a hearing on the matter before authorizing a tubal ligation. Spitler, who did not know what the operation was for, discovered she had been sterilized only after she was married. Spitler, whose married name was Stump, then sued Sparkman.

The Supreme Court ruled that Sparkman was absolutely immune because what he did was "a function normally performed by a judge," and he performed the act in his "judicial capacity." Although he may have violated state laws and procedures, he performed judicial functions that have historically been absolutely immune to civil lawsuits.

In a dissenting opinion, Justice Potter Stewart argued that Sparkman's actions were not absolutely immune simply because he sat in a courtroom, wore a robe, and signed an unlawful order. In Stewart's view the conduct of a judge "surely does not become a judicial act merely on his own say so. A judge is not free, like a loose cannon, to inflict indiscriminate damage whenever he announces that he is acting in his judicial capacity."

On appeal by Bradley, the U.S. Supreme Court affirmed the trial court's decision. Judges would be reached for their malicious acts, but only through impeachment, or removal from office. Thus, the facts of the case were irrelevant. Even if Fisher had exceeded his jurisdiction in single-handedly banning Bradley from the court, Fisher was justified in his actions. According to the Court, "A judge who should pass over in silence an offence of such gravity would soon find himself of pity rather than respect."[136]

In sum, the U.S. Supreme Court, not much different today than it was in yesteryear, has taken it upon itself to rule that its justices and those in the lower courts are "above the law!" And their passing off the duty to police the federal judiciary to the U.S. House of Representatives, as the sole remedy to hold these judicial despots legally accountable for the damage they inflict on We the People, is more than a bad joke! In the 233-year history since the Constitution was enacted by the legislative branch and ratified by the states, Congress has impeached only eight judges, hardly what

---

136. "Judicial Immunity," Encyclopedia.com (updated June 2, 2020), https://www.encyclopedia.com/law/encyclopedias-almanacs-transcripts-and-maps/judicial-immunity.

one would call meaningful, genuine, and effective oversight of the judiciary. That is one federal judge about every thirty-one years!

Indeed, as also held in *Bradley* and in the much later cases of *Forrester v. White, 484, U.S. 219, 108 S. Ct. 538, 98 L. Ed. 2d 555 (1988)* and *Pulliam v. Allen, 466 U.S. 522, 104 S. Ct. 1970, 80 L. Ed. 2d 565 (1984)*, the U.S. Supreme Court, giving some ground, merely ruled that federal judges could only be subject to equitable relief rather than monetary damages for their illegal actions—meaning that they could be enjoined from "killing again." This was roughly analogous to finding that O.J. Simpson could no longer be ordered to pay damages for having slit the neck of his ex-wife, Nicole, after he murdered her in cold blood.

Congress, our compromised legislative branch of court jesters, fools, philanderers, closet homosexuals and money changers, could, if it so chose, clarify that the Constitution does not grant lifetime tenure to the federal bench and could override the immunity the U.S. Supreme Court has kindly bestowed on itself and lower federal court judges. Will Congress ever do so? Unlikely at best. But if, with Divine intervention, these corrupted political clowns on Capitol Hill ever have an epiphany, I would propose enacting legislation that also requires this:

In the precursor to this book, I had proposed that candidates for federal judgeships should cease to be vetted by the American Bar Association, a band of leftist lawyers who recommend appointments. (I quit this organization many decades ago.) I further recommended that judicial selection panels could be created with nonbiased legal experts to evaluate the qualification of future federal judges. At the time I thought that persons could be recommended to the president for nomination who will obey the law and the Constitution, independent of their political and social ideologies. That, plus intellect, acumen, and real integrity—not race,

religion, sex and sexual persuasion as under Biden in particular—
must be the litmus test to be a federal judge.

Since then, I have rethought the approach, as the compromised hacks on the federal bench have grown to cancerous levels,
in just months, as set forth in Chapter Five, typified by their despicable if not traitorous conduct after January 6, 2021. As a result,
and given my better experience with elected state judges, particularly in my home state of Florida, I now believe that federal judges
should also be elected, and thus accountable to We the People, as
Jefferson preferred. This should apply not just to the lower federal
courts, but also the Supreme Court.

Second, U.S. Supreme Court justices and lower federal judges
should only be able to serve two five-year terms, renewable after
the first term on the basis of "good behavior," as set forth in Article
III, Section 1 of the Constitution.

Third, there should be a prerequisite that U.S. Supreme
Court justices and federal lower court judges must qualify to run
for office by first obtaining a one-year master's degree in judicial
studies to be taught, at a politically unbiased law school such as
exists at George Mason or Pepperdine Universities, how to impartially analyze cases and issue decisions that instill confidence with
the public. Currently, judicial nominees are plucked from private
practice, corporations, the DOJ, state and federal courts, labor
unions, other establishment entities, and institutions and are
already tainted with their biases and prejudices. For instance, a
lawyer who was a federal public defender would tend to be biased
toward criminal defendants, while a federal prosecutor from a U.S.
Attorney's Office would be biased toward putting criminal defendants in the slammer. In effect, what we have on the federal bench
today are untrained Dr. Strangeloves, who have more than a ten-
dency to think and act as they did before they ascended to the federal bench. This must be remedied and, indeed, in most Western

European countries, there is a special track for those who want to become judges, quite apart from practicing lawyers. We can draw from this experience.

Fourth, for U.S. Supreme Court justices and federal judges on the lower courts to qualify for eligibility to run for office, and to remain on the bench for a second term of five years, they should be periodically psychologically and physiologically tested for mental stability and for drug and excessive alcohol use. Remember the federal judge who pushed me over the edge to conceive of and found Judicial Watch, William D. Keller of the U.S. District Court for the Central District of California in Los Angeles? Keller was not stable during weeks of needless trial when my clients and I had to endure his problematic behavior including offensive rants and signs of alcoholism. For much more about Keller and another federal judge who followed years later in Keller's footsteps, the Honorable Denny Chin of the U.S. District Court for the Southern District of New York, whom I confronted during the Clinton Chinagate scandal, turn to *Whores* for a full expose.

Fifth, federal jurists at all levels, but primarily on the lower benches, should be required by Congress to have what, in effect, is professional malpractice insurance. In this way, litigants who have been maliciously wronged by a federal jurist, with the judge's immunity having been removed, can be compensated for the damage caused by intentionally wrong, grossly negligent, or reckless decisions.

Sixth, there should be an outright prohibition for a federal judicial candidate, either directly or through surrogates, such as a person's law firm, corporation, or labor union, to make political campaign contributions to the judicial candidate. These contributions are, in effect, "legalized bribery" and are given by or for the federal judicial candidate with the expectation that they will return the favor when elected to the federal bench. We must put an absolute end to the buying and selling of our judiciary. Of course, this proposal, like my other ones, may take a constitutional amendment given the U.S. Supreme Court's ruling in *Citizens United v. Federal Election Commission, 558 U.S. 310 (2010)*, which found that the "right" to contribute to political campaigns is protected by the First Amendment, frankly a very specious ruling. But where the integrity of our federal courts is at issue, an exception should be mandatory.

As just one further example of this current corrupt judicial "racketeering enterprise," a recent nominee, the Honorable John McConnell, who is now miraculously a federal judge in Rhode Island, a state infested with Mafia-connected and other unsavory politicians such as Senator Sheldon Whitehouse of Justice Kavanaugh confirmation "shame," contributed over $475,000 to various Democratic Party politicians and entities, including President Obama, to land him his new job! Now he is politicking to have the Federalist Society banned from making recommendations of judicial nominees to President Trump, a proposition I might, in jest, actually agree with, given the hacks this pseudo-conservative cabal put on The Donald's desk to rubber-stamp for nomination.[137] Again, Google Federal Election Commission records and see for yourself how Judge McConnell legally bribed his way onto the federal bench. It's breathtakingly bad!

Fellow patriots and readers of this work, I am also open to your suggestions on how a newly constituted legislative branch can enact legislation that provides a better chance that those who ascend to the federal bench through political patronage no longer be permitted to wreak havoc on John and Jane Doe, meaning

---

137. Carrie Severino, "Far-Left Obama-Appointed Judge Launches Political Attack on Conservative Federalist Society," *Fox News* Opinion Piece (May 23, 2020), https://www.foxnews.com/opinion/carrie-severino-far-left-obama-appointed-judge-launches-political-attack-on-conservative-federalist-society.

ordinary folk like you and me who are not part of the self-styled new American nobility.

But again, do not hold your good breath! Turn to the next chapter to learn what else can effectively be done, through our own God-given powers and rights, to restore equal justice, morality, and ethics to our currently dying republic! This proposition has a good chance of success if We the People, like our Founding Fathers, are not afraid to take on a tyrannical sovereign and wake up from what President Jimmy Carter once called an American malaise. After his defeat to then-Governor Ronald Reagan in 1980, the "Gipper" reawakened America, as We the People must now undertake on our own, with God's Divine Providence. After the leftist takeover under Biden—Harris and Pelosi and other leftist stooges—there is no one but ourselves that in this morally and ethically bankrupt and dangerous world can be counted on! And, God will only help us if we help ourselves!

CHAPTER NINE

MAN THE BARRICADES!

Now It's the People's Turn!

"Let us never forget that government is ourselves and not an alien power over us. The ultimate rulers of our democracy are not a President and senators and congressmen and government officials, but the voters of this country."

—Franklin Roosevelt[138]

During the years, months, and days leading up to the first American revolution, colonial leaders used their oratory and writing skills to unite the masses and prepare them for the perilous road ahead in creating a new nation, free from the tyranny of the British crown. None was more moving than Patrick Henry, who declared: "Is life so dear or peace so sweet as to be purchased at the price of chains and slavery? Forbid it, Almighty God! I know not what course others may take, but as for me give me liberty, or give me death!"[139]

---

138. Franklin Roosevelt, Franklin D. Roosevelt Presidential Library and Museum, http://www.fdrlibrary.marist.edu/_resources/images/msf/msf01180.
139. "The Avalon Project—Documents in Law, History and Diplomacy" (Lillian Goldman Law Library, Yale Law School), https://avalon.law.yale.edu/18th_century/patrick.asp.

In today's world, the predicament that the citizenry of our great republic find themselves in is not much different. Over the last 246 years since declaring independence for the first time, the nation has degenerated—ethically, morally, spiritually, and legally—to the point that, in retrospect, the rule of King George III looks benign by comparison. Indeed, if the king had had the powerful mass surveillance capabilities of today's executive Deep State intelligence agencies—the NSA, CIA, DIA, and FBI—our Founding Fathers would have never made it to Philadelphia to sign the Declaration of Independence. They would have been picked up, arrested for sedition, imprisoned, and executed before they got there.

King George III was Mother Teresa compared to those who think they can rule over us as despots and tyrants today. The king was not a socialist, he was not a communist, he was not an atheist, he was not a radical black, he was not a radical Muslim, he was not a radical member of the Marxian Jewish left, he was not a radical gay, lesbian, transgender or transsexual and he was not bent on destroying the Judeo-Christian foundation of European and American society.

Today, we are far more worse off than on July 4, 1776!

John Adams and his learned revolutionary colleagues like Jefferson and Benjamin Franklin understood that lasting liberty, once obtained, was fragile. In this regard, Adams declared just days before signing the Declaration that it would not matter how many times we changed our form of government or rulers, without ethics, morality, and religion, there would be no lasting liberty.

The time has come again, as Jefferson foretold, to shed the blood of patriots—not violently this time, but, if possible as a first resort, peacefully and legally—to right the sinking ship of state. Federal judges have taken away from We the People our God-given rights to use the law to settle disputes with the sovereign—a sovereign infested with Deep State actors in the executive branch and greedy court jesters and bribed clowns in the legislative branch who do as they please to feather their own rotting nests, not the will of us peasants.

So, the time again has arrived, as Benjamin Franklin most aptly put it: "We must, indeed, all hang together or, most assuredly, we shall all hang separately."[140]

But how can we ordinary Americans, those of us who cannot and do not act as if we are a privileged and protected class, and those who subvert not just our Constitution but the rule of law in general, wage a second American revolution—which with the leftist takeover must now more aptly be called a counter-revolution— meant to clean the rats' nest of unethical and immoral political and social disease that, like a growing cancer, has come to be embedded into what once was our government and other institutions? One important way is for the citizenry to take legal matters into their own hands.

Short of violent revolution—which will surely come to pass if we do not succeed—there is only one strong legal mechanism that can and must be invoked: the so-called "citizens' grand jury," by which Americans themselves can enforce just manmade law and the law of our Creator. This is our only viable peaceful recourse to hold our establishment elitist "rulers" accountable in order to clean house. Over the years, impeachment has not worked nor has any other means to address crimes at the highest levels of executive, legislative, and judicial branches of government.

In this regard, the Fifth Amendment to the Constitution establishes that "no person shall be held to answer for a capital, or otherwise infamous crime, unless on a presentment or indictment of a Grand Jury." A proper understanding of this requirement's effect begins with the common law, since, as Supreme Court Justice

---

140 . Benjamin Franklin, *USHistory.org*, https://www.ushistory.org/valleyforge/history/franklin.html.

Learned Hand stated in *In re Kittle*, "we took the [grand jury] as we found it in our English inheritance, and he best serves the Constitution who most faithfully follows its historical significance."[141]

The grand jury dates back at least to 1166, under the Norman kings of England. These earliest grand juries were convened to provide answers from local representatives concerning royal property rights but developed into a body of twelve men who presented indictments at the request of either private individuals or the king's prosecutor.[142] The Magna Carta granted individuals the right to stand before a grand jury to be charged of their crimes.

By 1681, an important characteristic of the grand jury had developed: the rule of secrecy. This characteristic set up the grand jury as a bulwark against government abuse. Grand juries were designed to exclude all outside persons, including the government's prosecutors, ensuring that all phases of an investigation (not just deliberation) remained secret. Thus, English grand juries functioned to prevent prosecutorial abuses by blocking the king's attempts to prosecute.

This tradition was continued and expanded by colonial grand juries. In America, the grand jury originally began as a defense against the monarchy and was arguably even more independent than the English grand jury of the 1600s. American grand juries initiated prosecutions against corrupt agents of the government, often in response to complaints from individuals. For example, a Massachusetts grand jury refused to indict the organizers of the Stamp Act rebellion.[143] Four years later, another Massachusetts grand jury indicted some British soldiers located within the city boundaries for alleged crimes against the colonists but refused

---

141. Kittle, 180 Fed. 946, 947 (S.D.N.Y. 1910), https://case-law.vlex.com/vid/180-f-946-s-594627878.

142. Susan W Brenner and Gregor G. Lockhart, "Federal Grand Jury: A Guide to Law and Practice," (Thomson Reuters 1996), 4, https://worldcat.org/identities/lccn-no96057194/.

143. Roger Roots, "If It's Not a Runaway, It's Not a Real Grand Jury" (33 Creighton L. Rev. 821, 832), http://www.defendruralamerica.com/files/RunawayGrandJury.pdf.

to treat certain colonialists who had been charged by the British authorities for inciting desertion in a like manner. Similarly, a Philadelphia grand jury condemned the use of the tea tax to compensate British officials, encouraged a rejection of all British goods, and called for organization with other colonies to demand redress of grievances.

By the dawn of the twentieth century, the powerful role of the grand jury had become established law. In 1902, a Minneapolis grand jury, acting on its own initiative, hired private detectives and collected enough evidence to indict the mayor and force the police chief to resign.

In *Frisbie v. United States*, Supreme Court Justice David Brewer declared that "in this country it is for the grand jury to investigate any alleged crime, no matter how or by whom suggested to them, and after determining that the evidence is sufficient to justify putting the suspected party on trial, to direct the preparation of the formal charge or indictment." [157 U.S. 160 (1895)][144]

Again, in *Hale v. Henkel*, Supreme Court Justice Henry Brown stated that "we deem it entirely clear that under the practice in this country, at least, the examination of witnesses need not be preceded by a presentment or indictment formally drawn up, but that the grand jury may proceed, either upon their own knowledge or upon the examination of witnesses, to inquire for themselves whether a crime cognizable by the court has been committed." [201 U.S. 43 (1906)][145]

More recently, in *United States v. Williams*, now deceased Supreme Court Justice Antonin Scalia, writing for the majority, held that:

---

144. Frisbie v. United States, 157 U.S. 160 (1895), https://supreme.justia.com/cases/federal/us/157/160/.
145. Hale v. Henkel, 201 U.S. 43 (1906), https://supreme.justia.com/cases/federal/us/201/43/.

The grand jury's functional independence from the Judicial Branch is evident both in the scope of its power to investigate criminal wrongdoing and in the manner in which that power is exercised. 'Unlike [a] court, whose jurisdiction is predicated upon a specific case or controversy, the grand jury "can investigate merely on suspicion that the law is being violated, or even because it wants assurance that it is not." [504 U.S. 36, 48 (1992) (quoting *United States v. R. Enterprises, Inc.*, 498 U.S. 292, 297 (1991)]¹⁴⁶

Speaking of the origins of the grand jury, Scalia also found that:

> the grand jury is mentioned in the Bill of Rights, but not in the body of the Constitution. It has not been textually assigned, therefore, to any of the branches described in the first three Articles. It is a constitutional fixture in its own right. In fact the whole theory of its function is that it belongs to no branch of the institutional government, serving as a kind of buffer or referee between the government and the people. Although the grand jury normally operates, of course, in the courthouse and under judicial auspices, its institutional relationship with the Judicial Branch has been, so to speak, at arm's length. Judges' direct involvement in the functioning of the grand jury has generally been confined to the constitutive one of calling the grand jurors together and administering their oaths of office. [Id. at 47]¹⁴⁷

Although the customary practice for summoning a federal grand jury is by a court (see Rule 6 of the Federal Rules of Criminal Procedure, or FRCP), such action is mandatory "when the public interest so requires." Regardless, the FRCP does not preclude citizens from exercising their own rights to impanel grand juries under the Constitution.¹⁴⁸ Thus, it is clear that if citizens themselves can

---

146. United States v. Williams, 504 U.S. 36 (1992), https://supreme.justia.com/cases/federal/us/504/36/.
147. Ibid.
148. Marbury v. Madison, 5 U.S. 137 (1803), https://supreme.justia.com/cases/federal/us/5/137/; establishing the doctrine of judicial review.

impanel a grand jury, and if a true bill of indictment results, the courts are technically required to commence proceedings, and the executive branch is required to enforce the court's edicts. However, if the courts refuse and the executive branch does not carry out its duties by, for instance, arresting the criminally accused, Americans do have a right to make "citizens' arrests," hold trials, and legally mete out punishment in their own right. Indeed, this is what occurred in the western part of the United States, in particular, during our early years as a nation, before there was a developed federal court system and executive branch. Just summon the ghost of Wyatt Earp, now resting in a grave in Colma, California, and he will tell you what can be done!

Given the increasingly corrupt and treasonous actions of our public officials, which have nearly destroyed our republic, and the complete corrupt breakdown of the justice system as run by the government, the time has come for us Americans to rise up and use the God-given rights left to us by our Founders. We can do this by using citizen-empaneled and administered grand juries to hold the highest levels of government in all three branches accountable for the crimes that have driven our nation to the brink of extinction.

And once these indictments come down, citizen courts can try the accused, obtain convictions where there is proof that a crime has been committed "beyond a reasonable doubt," and then impose just sentences that can be meted out. Of course, the dilemma, given the current massive power of our corrupted government, is how to enforce those sentences peacefully and legally. While peaceful means may not prove possible, We the People must try to maintain order and not overstep our bounds, acting as the sovereign has acted. After all, the tyrannical, insidious, and unbridled misuse of government power, without federal judges who will step in to protect the populace, is what has gotten us to this regrettable crossroads!

Importantly, there is a body of authority, mostly state, that citizens can make "citizens' arrests." The term has commonly been defined by the Merriam-Webster Dictionary to be simply "an arrest made not by a law enforcement office but by a citizen who derives authority from the fact of being a citizen."

While one would not expect California to be at the forefront of codified statutory citizen's arrest laws, it is the most "progressive" in giving authority to its citizens to enforce the law. For instance, California Penal Code 837 Section 837 provides:

A private person may arrest another:

1. For a public offense committed or attempted in his presence.

2. When the person arrested has committed a felony, although not in his presence.

3. When a felony has been committed, and he has reasonable cause for believing the person arrested to have committed it.[149]

While most states have differing provisions for making citizens' arrests, it is clear that the concept is firmly wedded in Anglo-American law. In common law countries such as our own, it derives all the way back to medieval England, where sheriffs asked regular citizens to take into custody persons who broke the king's law. In the current-day United States, whose law derives from Great Britain, only North Carolina and Washington state do not have citizens' arrest laws.

In short, legal authority exists to carry out sentences through arrests for felonies, even if it may not totally square with the law of any particular state. And when an arrest is made to carry out a sentence that calls for incarceration, the common

---

149. California Penal Code Section 837, https://leginfo.legislature.ca.gov/faces/codes_displaySection.xhtml?lawCode=PEN&sectionNum=837.

law and statutory practice has been to turn the lawbreaker in to established legal authorities.

And that is the dilemma. Ask yourself, what would happen if Hillary and Bill Clinton were arrested by We the People for their myriad felonies and then turned over to the Deep State executive branch DOJ? Would we citizens be permitted, without having to face serious bodily injury or death ourselves at the hands of trigger-happy FBI agents, to take them into custody? Once in custody, would the DOJ's U.S. Marshal Service and the Bureau of Prisons confine them to prison for the term decided by a people's court?

In today's world, this scenario is more than unlikely, since the DOJ has become compromised and corrupt, in effect the Gestapo of the Left, as previously detailed in Chapter Three. As a result, angry masses may resort to taking matters into their own hands, free from any legal constraint, if the cancerous decay in our body politic continues to worsen. Indeed, January 6, 2021, given the ever-increasing tyranny of the Left, will look like a warm-up act. And then we are back to July 4, 1776, or, worse still, the bloody French Revolution, which broke out in 1789, the year our Constitution was enacted. The French thus began where we left off!

Regardless of the consequences, the American people must attempt to use citizens' grand juries, people's courts, and citizens' arrests, and do so in a nonviolent way. If not, the alternative of another violent revolution forecast by Jefferson will become reality.

In this age of pandemics, such as COVID-19, the nation is rapidly approaching the breaking point. As just one example among many, state governors in particular have used faux dictatorial power to effectively imprison the populace in their own homes and now impose draconian vaccine mandates. As a result, he citizenry is becoming increasingly defiant. People no longer have faith that the government has their best interests at heart, much less can be believed at all. I for one, a post-World War II baby boomer

who has lived through the lies of President Johnson during the
Vietnam War, President Nixon's Watergate caper, the forty plus
Clinton scandals, the senseless Iraqi and Afghan wars of President
George W. Bush triggered by Deep State intel community false-
hoods that Saddam Hussein had weapons of mass destruction, the
racial division resulting in violence stoked by President Obama,
and the witch hunt of Robert Mueller and the ensuing impeachment of President Trump over alleged Ukrainian collusion—all
based on frauds—and now the total leftist takeover through its
stooges Biden, Harris, Pelosi, and Schumer—feel it is no wonder
that we no longer can believe anything that this tyrannical government feeds to us. And we certainly cannot believe what we see,
hear, and read in the media—both left and right—which manip-
ulatively feeds at the profitable trough of their scandal industry.

While the riots, looting, theft, and destruction ignited by the
police killing of George Floyd in Minneapolis, Minnesota, are
demonstrative of the near total breakdown not just of law and
order, they are, in a way, understandable. Respect for those who
claim to govern us has hit rock bottom. The government is no
longer to be trusted or believed! There is a saying about how one
can tell if a lawyer is lying? Answer, his or her lips are moving. It is
not a wonder that most government officials are both lawyers and
liars. This, tragically, is the one thing the Right and the Left now
have in common.

To top it all off is the misinformation if not fraud that continues to be spewed by Big Pharma and the present government
about COVID-19 and the short-, medium-, and long-term side
effects of the unproven vaccines, which are not really vaccines
at all. New disclosures reveal that they do not provide absolute
immunity but are rendered ineffective only after a few months.
Indeed, just last fall, former Chairman of the Joint Chiefs of State,
National Security Adviser and Secretary of State Colin Powell died

of COVID-19 after having been fully vaccinated, showing that it is not very effective, if at all; he is just one of many tragic examples. Despite this, government officials, comprised of both Democrats and Republicans, continue to try to ram them down our collective throats. It's a cabal of politicians and the so-called vaccinemakers, raking in trillions of dollars, with likely kickbacks to the politicians and others who push them on the public, that drives this money train of deceit. And the public is catching on, particularly since now there is a full-court press to have our school children, grades K through 12, subjected to the unknown consequences of the COVID-19 vaccines.

So where does the citizenry turn in such a state of affairs? Like our Founding Fathers, who coalesced the colonies and joined them as one in fighting against and vanquishing a tyrant, the American people are rapidly reaching the point where, as Popeye used to say in the cartoons of my youth, "Enough is enough and enough is too much!"[150] This fictional character then took on and vanquished Brutus. We can do the same, only for us, it's no longer fiction but reality! Let us start with citizens' grand juries, and indeed, I have.

Just a year or so ago, I convened a citizens' grand jury, and summoned grand jury testimony from my brave client, Dr. Jerome Corsi, who Mueller and his prosecutorial staff attempted to coerce into lying to implicate President Trump in Russian collusion crimes. Dr. Corsi implicated Mueller in the crimes of attempting to suborn perjury and obstruction of justice, to name just a few. Sure enough, the citizens' grand jury, which you can watch in action at www.freedomwatchusa.org, returned a True Bill of Indictment, using procedures similar to those employed by DOJ attorneys. Next up will be Mueller's criminal trial, where I will seek his conviction along with a prison sentence. The same can and will be done for the other felonious public officials of modern lore,

---

150. Popeye, ACM Digital Library, https://dl.acm.org/doi/10.1145/226650.226653.

the James Comeys, the Andrew McCabes, the James Clappers, the John Brennans, the Bill and Hillary Clintons, the Barack Obamas, the Joe and Hunter Bidens, and other politicians, government officials, and federal judges of all stripes!

Indeed, in the last months we have also indicted Joe, Hunter, and James Biden, Joe's felonious brother, over their massive bribery racketeering scheme that laundered millions of dollars from Communist China, Ukraine, and Russia into the family's coffers, with a ten percent share for Joe himself, according to Tony Bobulinski who for a period was Hunter Biden's business partner. See www.freedomwatchusa.org for Bobulinski testimony.

Braindead Joe Biden has also been indicted for negligent homicide and manslaughter, much more treason, over the surrender of Afghanistan to Taliban, Al Qaeda, and ISIS terrorists, as well as the killing through a drone strike, designed for the Biden-Harris regime to look tough after thirteen GI's and hundreds of Afghans were killed at Kabul airport, of ten civilian Afghan aid workers and seven of their young children. So, too, has Dr. Anthony Fauci been held to criminally account for his lying to the American public and collaboration with the Wuhan Lab that, through U.S. grants under the Obama-Biden regime, over the creation of the more than probable COVID-19 bioweapon and thereby causing a worldwide pandemic.

Dr. Anthony Fauci was also indicted and will soon be tried for his having lied under oath about his involvement, during the Obama-Biden administration, in funding dangerous gain of function research by the Chicom Wuhan Lab which produced the likely COVID-19 bioweapon, as well as his apparent general criminality in providing false and misleading information to the public about the virus and the so-called vaccines. Satirically, but in all dead seriousness, Freedom Watch named Fauci as Criminal of the Year for 2021, a takeoff of *Time Magazine*'s Person of the Year, for his felonious acts that have resulted in sickness and the deaths of millions not just in the United States, but worldwide.

Ilham Omar, the anti-Semitic and Islamic terrorist connected congresswoman from Minnesota, has also been indicted over alleged immigration fraud in marrying her brother, tax evasion, and federal election fraud. Our so-called government, even under Trump, did not address this, so We the People must now mete out justice.[151]

We are also holding to account many of the federal judges for violating their sworn oath of office, as detailed in Chapter Five. They, and others being prosecuted, such as Attorney General Merrick Garland and FBI Director Robert Wray, who have even sicced their FBI and federal prosecutors on parents complaining about critical race theory and perverted ideologies being taught their children, are implementing and furthering the tyranny and lawlessness running rampant in the land. No one who has so perverted, disrespected, defiled, and dishonored our once just system of justice, will be spared the legal executioner's citizen grand jury sword.

In this regard, and hardly last, there are George Soros financed and elected state and local district attorneys such as Philadelphia's Larry Krasner, Los Angeles's George Gascon, Chicago's Kim Fox, San Francisco's Chesa Boudin, son of convicted Jewish Marxist Weather Underground domestic terrorists Kathy Boudin and David Gilbert, and later adopted son of convicted Weather

151. J. Patrick Coolican and Stephen Montemayor, "New Documents Revisit Questions About Rep. Ilhan Omar's Marriage History," *Star Tribune* (June 23, 2019), https://www.startribune.com/new-documents-revisit-questions-about-rep-ilhan-omar-s-marriage/511681362/; Dave Orrick, "Ilhan Omar Under Scrutiny: First Marriage, Then Fidelity, Now a Federal Campaign Complaint. And at State Fair Death Threat," *Brainerd Dispatch* (August 29, 2019), https://www.brainerddispatch.com/news/government-and-politics/4636131-Ilhan-Omar-under-scrutiny-First-marriage-then-fidelity-now-a-federal-campaign-complaint.-And-a-State-Fair-death-threat; Clare Foran, "Rep. Omar Ordered to Reimburse Campaign Committee After State Board Finds Spending Violations," CNN (June 7, 2019), https://www.cnn.com/2019/06/07/politics/ilhan-omar-campaign-finance/index.html.

Underground domestic terrorists Bill Ayers and Bernardine Dohrn, and a host of other Soros backed leftist district attorneys who have stoked and largely caused the recent crime wave by refusing to prosecute felons, particularly minority ones, and furthered the release of violent criminals from prison. They too will be indicted, tried and convicted of violating their oath of office and intentional and reckless endangerment of the citizenry, designed to destabilize and throw the nation into chaos, as part of their apparent conspiratorial plan to destroy our Judeo-Christian heritage and to install and cement a Marxist dictatorship in its place.[152]

More indictments by our citizens' grand juries are planned and the accused will now be served with the indictments and notice of the charges, be arraigned, and then tried in a people's court. A citizens' judge has already been chosen and trials will begin in the near future. And, when we obtain likely convictions and sentences meted out, We the People will summon the police and the military rank and file to conduct the arrests and incarcerations. I honestly believe they will come to the aid of the citizenry, after years of having been disrespected, defunded, and exposed to death with their hands tied behind their backs by state and local politicians, and in the case of the military it's politically appointed brass, as well as being maligned, assaulted, battered, and even killed by the card-carrying members of the radical left.

Couple this with Freedom Watch's ongoing Third Continental Congress, begun at Independence Hall's Visitor Center on July 5 and 6 of 2021, which is continuing, and there are plans in the works for We the People to pull the plug on our corrupt and terminally ill government on life support, and declare independence

---

152. Allan Smith, "Parents Guilty of Murder and Raised by Radicals, Chesa Boudin is San Francisco's Next District Attorney," NBCNews.com (December 16, 2019), https://www.nbcnews.com/politics/elections/parents-guilty-murder-raised-radicals-chesa-boudin-san-francisco-s-n1101071; Isabel Vincent, "How George Soros Funded Progressive 'Legal Arsonist' DA's Behind US Crime Surge," *New York Post* (December 16, 2021), https://nypost.com/2021/12/16/how-george-soros-funded-progressive-das-behind-us-crime-surge/.

again in 2022. Simply figuratively erecting an electrified fence around the D.C. swamp to keep the criminals at bay and locked up will work no better than it did at Jurassic Park, where maneating dinosaurs—the early animal kingdom equivalent of the likes of political T-Rexes Biden, Harris, Pelosi. Shumer, and McConnell—found a way to eventually escape. As with the Second Continental Congress, We the People must with all due speed lay the groundwork to form a new government—not a new nation—where our newly minted elected leaders and judges will not be bought and paid by political hacks and criminals, rolling around enriching themselves at the public trough squealing like pigs in shit.

Leave the criminals of the Democrat and Republican Parties in the swamp to wallow in their excrement and let us, with God's Divine Providence, erect a new government, with nominated and elected officials—rather than appointed—to carry out the vision and creation of our Founding Fathers. We did this once before, so why not again! And, if the present government does not like it and moves on us violently, the citizenry has its Second Amendment rights, which include the right to form militias in our self-defense.

If we truly care about the continuation of "one nation under God," the people must be prepared in the words of former President John F. Kennedy, long ago broadcast in his inaugural address on January 20, 1961, when it was thought that communism was on the rise—it has now fully arrived—"we shall pay any price, bear any burden, meet any hardship, support any friend, oppose any foe to assure the survival of liberty."[153] JFK, who I continue to admire in many ways, was no Joe Biden, Kamala Harris, Nancy Pelosi, Chuck Schumer, Bernie Sanders, Alexandria Ocasio-Cortez, Ilhan Omar, or Rashida Tlaib, and their leftist socialist, communist, and otherwise leftist hordes, to be most kind! As then a Democrat, JFK

153. John F. Kennedy, "Transcript of President John F. Kennedy's Inaugural Address (1961)," *Ourdocuments.gov*, https://www.ourdocuments.gov/doc.php?flash=false&doc=91&page=transcript.

had nothing in common with these poor excuses in governance and loyalty to our American way of life.

Man the legal barricades, fellow partisans. The time to act is now before the vision and creation of our enlightened and brave Founding Fathers is destroyed to the point that it metastasizes into stage-four terminable cancer! In the words of the citizens of France in rising up to wage a revolution patterned after our own, "Liberte, Egalite, Fraternite, ou Mort!" Translated, this signifies, "Liberty, Equality, Brotherhood, or Death!"

We the People must now also pattern our second American revolution—now a counter-revolution with the Left's total take-over—after the first one. If we are smart and wage it correctly, we will not have to fire a shot, as we are dedicated to "Live Free or Die!", the battle cry of the colonies.

CHAPTER TEN

THE JURY'S VERDICT: GUILTY AS CHARGED!

TIME TO JUDGE THE FEDERAL JUDGES AND OTHER ARROGANT LAWLESS GOVERNMENT ELITISTS

"With us, all the branches of the government are elective by the people themselves, except the judiciary, of whose science and qualifications they are not competent judges. Yet, even in that department, we call in a jury of the people to decide all controverted matters of fact, because to that investigation they are entirely competent, leaving thus as little as possible, merely the law of the case, to the decision of the judges."

—Thomas Jefferson to A. Coray, 1823, ME 15:482[154]

J efferson was the most insightful and eloquent Founding Father. He understood the absolute need to have juries composed of ordinary citizens decide cases before the courts, not unelected judges who would inevitably grow so power-infused and hungry that they would become despots. Jefferson thus opposed lifetime

---

154. Thomas Jefferson, "From Thomas Jefferson to Adamantios Coray, 31 October 1823," Founders Early Access, https://rotunda.upress.virginia.edu/founders/default. xqy?keys=FOEA-print-04-02-02-38371823; A. Coray was a Greek intellectual and author.

tenure. And, indeed, there is no such thing embedded into our Constitution. Instead, Jefferson pressed to have federal judges elected by the citizenry:

> It has been thought that the people are not competent electors of judges, learned in the law. But I do not know that this is true, and, if doubtful, we should follow principle. In this, as in many other elections, they would be guided by reputation which would not err oftener, perhaps than the present mode of appointment.[155]

Most states elect judges, and I can tell you from my forty-five years of experience as a licensed Florida lawyer, the jurists there are far superior (and that is to be most diplomatic) to the greasy political hacks that my clients and I, and you as well, have been forced to endure in the federal courts. By and large, federal judges are catapulted into office because of their own political monetary contributions and those of the senators, presidents, and special interest groups, which include large law firms, corporations, and labor unions, who want their yes men and women on the bench.

And while Jefferson saw the need to elect federal judges, and to allow juries to decide cases rather than "the king's men and women," he also, in principle, respected their legitimate role:

> The judiciary…is a body which, if rendered independent and kept strictly to their own department, merits great confidence for their learning and integrity.[156]

Notice the "if" in this last Jeffersonian word of wisdom: "if" rendered independent.

---

155. Thomas Jefferson, "Thomas Jefferson to Samuel Kercheval, 5 September 1816," *Founders Online*, https://founders.archives.gov/documents/Jefferson/03-10-02-0255.

156. Thomas Jefferson, "From Thomas Jefferson to Archibald Stuart, 23 December 1791," *Founders Online*, https://founders.archives.gov/documents/Jefferson/01-22-02-0410.

And that is the problem today. The federal judges and the justices of the U.S. Supreme Court, whose official duties, in principle, were designed to protect us from the tyranny and illegal actions of the other two branches of government, have become rubber stamps to these corrupted institutions and the special interests who greased the skids to get them on the bench. In effect, our government, if one can stretch to call it that anymore, has become one big power-hungry, happy family, defying the will of the people and enriching themselves with more power and money—not much different from the money changers of the temple in ancient Hebraic days.

I have not written this work to brag about my accomplishments over the last twenty-eight years since founding Judicial Watch and Freedom Watch, however few, given the state of affairs on the federal bench and quasijudicial organs that are supposed to mete out just law. I do not boast, as the head of my former public interest watchdog group does daily, spewing forth in press releases "news" of the "latest Judicial Watch victory." This generally amounts to little more than obtaining documents under the Freedom of Information Act and then begging the same Deep State that resisted its production, overseen by the DOJ, to bring about justice. By now, you know that it ain't going to happen, period.

No, I cannot and will not, like those on Fox News and the other cable networks, boost my ratings in the conservative community by spewing forth fake bullshit rather than the cold hard truth, raking in more contributions to Freedom Watch, as these networks do with their advertising revenue, particularly during the current COVID-19 pandemic and the aftermath of the debacle in Afghanistan, to name just a few tragedies. I am not proud of my "accomplishments," given that I, not for lack of trying, was unable to put more than a dent into the ethical, moral, and lawless slide of our beloved nation into a cancerous sea.

It's time for the unvarnished truth, fellow patriots, and this book seeks to give it to you, no holds barred. I will no longer be a part of the so-called scandal industry. Instead, I call on you to join me in waging a second American revolution—now a counter-revolution—peacefully if possible, lest the nation explode into a sea of deadly violence ala the French Revolution.

I have put forth various suggestions on how we can embark on this journey before all is lost. And I ask you to join me in this quest. You and I are the superheroes who, as part of our own Justice League, must peacefully and legally defy the establishment's conventions and set the nation on a new course. As former U.N. Ambassador Alan L. Keyes writes in the foreword, we cannot lose sight of God's hand in all of our endeavors, and He will be with us all the way to a real victory.

And this must begin if we are, as Jefferson foretold, to avoid having to spill the "blood of patriots" yet anew, by fashioning a new method to select federal U.S. Supreme Court justices and judges on the lower courts, even if we have to tinker with the Constitution to do it. And, indeed, I have already summoned modern-day learned people, experts, and scholars in the mold of Jefferson, Franklin, and Adams to Philadelphia, my birthplace and the birthplace of liberty, to a new Third Continental Congress that you can watch and hopefully join at www. freedomwatchusa.org! You and my colleague, former U.N. Ambassador Keyes during the presidency of Ronald Reagan and twice presidential candidate, were among our delegates to chart and implement a new path to wage a counter-revolution and restore the nation to that shining city on a hill envisioned in the Book of Isaiah and later by President Ronald Reagan.

Many so-called conservatives, who like to feed at the trough in profiting from the ongoing scandal industry, say that fine-tuning the Constitution for amendment is dangerous, as the Left will seize upon this to rewrite it entirely and turn the nation into a social-ist if not communist state. Notwithstanding that the Left has no "standing" to be a part of our counter-revolution, I say, what do we have to lose? Thanks to our runaway despot federal judges and other corrupt government officials, the rule of law and its over-riding Constitution, much more the divine guidance of our God, have, in any event, been totally defied and trashed. It's thus time changes that are needed short of amendment, as well as consider and act on the bigger task of fine-tuning our seminal document.

Time is short, as the republic has been thrust into a crisis with the COVID-19 pandemic and other burgeoning crises under the Biden-Harris regime. And the pandemic was thrust upon us by an adverse foreign power that has our defeat and destruction in its grasp. And there will be more attacks from the outside on our nation, be it with terrorist copycat bioweapons, dirty bombs, or even a nuclear holocaust, accidental or otherwise. Even worse, there will be more assaults from the inside, by radical leftists, anar-chists, fascists, and the domestic terrorist groups Antifa and Black Lives Matter, to name just a few of many.

It is not enough to bring class-action lawsuits against some of the barbarians now inside our gates, such as the one I recently filed on behalf of the American people in Dallas, Texas, against the Communist Chinese for the death, sickness, and huge financial destruction they have caused to our nation by releasing what is likely a bioweapon in the form of COVID-19. Or another one I filed against the Biden-Harris Justice Department and its FBI over their Gestapo tactics. Nor is it sufficient to file a criminal complaint at the International Criminal Court in The Hague, Netherlands, to put China's President Xi Jinping and his Politburo comrades in the slammer for life, where they belong, as Freedom Watch and I have also done, along with another one against Joe Biden for crimes against humanity over the killing of ten Afghan civilians and seven of their young children with a premeditated drone strike. These actions are necessary, but they are only a few of many that We the People are duty-bound to pursue with God's speed!

And, we must fine-tune our Constitution and reaffirm it. Here are a few proposals that are being debated and will be soon voted on by our Third Continental Congress:

1. Explicitly incorporate the Ten Commandments into the Constitution.

2. Remove any claim of immunity from federal judges and Supreme Court justices, much less government officials, for their intentionally harmful or reckless actions.

3. Insert a recall provision to remove a president and other government officials short of having to bring impeachment proceedings, or to avoid having to invoke the hapless 25th amendment, which requires a president's own handpicked cabinet to remove him, when the chief executive officer is as mentally and physically impaired if not debilitated as President Joe Biden, as impeachment and conviction have never worked. We cannot, as just the current state of affairs underscores under Joe Biden and his cackling witch of a sidekick Kamala Harris, be saddled with another three years of this fatally destructive president and his rabidly leftist minions, for instance.

4. Elect and not appoint cabinet secretaries, to avoid corrupt political hacks taking hold of federal departments.

5. Require that our budget always be balanced and not in debt.

6. Expand the concept of legal standing to sue to allow the citizenry to legally challenge unconstitutional acts by government officials and judges, even if the complaining party is not personally affected, thereby making us all private attorneys general.

7. Make it clear that there is a right to life and that killing the unborn is murder.

8. Making it clear that there is no right to gay marriage, gay adoptions or surrogate procreation by gays, lesbians and transgenders of children in the Constitution, and that there are only two sexes, male and female.

9. Making it a felony to cross into and enter the United States without proper immigration clearance and granting dual authority to the border states to enforce the immigration laws.

10. Banning the use of hard narcotic drugs such as heroin, cocaine, methamphetamine, ecstasy, and mushrooms and making this a felony, as their usage is a danger to the community and the nation as a whole.

11. Making it clear that vaccines and other medications cannot be forced on the citizenry.

I welcome more suggestions from you, fellow patriots, which will be put before our ongoing Third Continental Congress, in which we welcome your earnest participation.

We must confront and vanquish these barbarians at our gates, and now even within our gates, to avoid going the way of ancient Rome. We must, as Benjamin Franklin argued in defeating an early tyrant, King George III, all hang together, or separately we will all hang. And this means urgently exhausting all avenues of peaceful and legal recourse before we collectively decide whether stronger Jeffersonian measures are needed. And, most urgent and important, we need to declare independence again, set up a new government and take our capital out of the swamp of Washington, D.C., which is indelibly infected with stench and governmental vermin and actual rats. I propose returning our new government to the scene of where it all began, at Independence Hall in Philadelphia. That is the real deal, not the Disneyworld imitations of ancient Greek buildings such as the Supreme Court found in the swamp. Genuine Americana, like the White House, can be deconstructed and reconstructed, moving them away from the rotting and putrid decaying rat infested banks of the Potomac.

That is the message of this book, It Takes a Counter-Revolution: Wake Up America! So don't "forget it," and wake up, Americans, get up off the couch, come out of retirement if you are old, enlist if you are young, and rededicate your lives if you are middle-age. Put your martini down, turn off cable news, and enlist in our Justice League, our citizens' grand juries, and Third Continental Congress at www.freedomwatchusa.org to save our great republic, now threatened primarily by our compromised and cowardly federal judges and other governmental whores who are, by and large, bought and paid for, and who sacrifice our well-being, curtail our freedoms, and forsake our protection for their own corrupt ends.

The jury has come in! Guilty as charged! Now it's time, long overdue, for We the People to mete out the sentences and reform our nation, with a new government, with new leaders and new political parties, and a new capital in Philadelphia or for that matter any place other than what has become the reptilian corruption infested hellhole commonly known as the swamp!

It's time to wake up America, get up off the couch, and not just worry about our future, but actively do something about it! You and I are not Alfred E. Newman of Mad Magazine fame, although the country and the world have indeed gone "mad." The crisis we are in is deadly serious, the republic is on life support, and it's time to pull the plug on our terminally ill government and its federal judiciary and put them out of their misery for the benefit not just of you, but your children, grandchildren, and future generations!

CHAPTER ELEVEN

THE TIME HAS COME TO GET A DIVORCE AND TAKE CUSTODY OVER THE NATION!

"Every citizen should be a soldier. This was the case with the Greeks and Romans, and must be that of a free state."

—Thomas Jefferson[157]

BOLSHEVIK POWER GRAB COMES TO AMERICA! COUNTER-REVOLUTION AT HAND!

During the last few years, America was at the height of the protests over the death of an African American, George Floyd, a convicted five-time felon, one of those convictions for

---

157. Thomas Jefferson, "From Thomas Jefferson to James Monroe, 19 June 1813," *Founders Online*, https://founders.archives.gov/documents/Jefferson/03-06-02-0188.

armed robbery—at the hands of the Minneapolis police. Judicial Watch, Inc., the public interest group I founded, wrote the leftist Democrat mayor of the District of Columbia, Muriel Bowser, and demanded that she paint the motto that I coined during my ten years at the organization on the city streets: "Because No One Is Above the Law." It was a clever publicity stunt, given that my former group does little to enforce the law, other than to mainly just obtain documents under Freedom of Information Act Requests, useful to get Tom Fitton on Fox News and thus boosting its fundraising appeals to the public. It then begs the government to do the job of We the People. Indeed, our Founding Fathers did not ask King George III for help against his own tyrannical regime! Instead, they took it upon themselves to enforce colonial law and the law of God. In so doing, they founded a new free republic of the likes not heretofore known to mankind.

Today, our once-free republic is not just under siege but has been occupied by Bolsheviks, instigated by a radical cabal of leftist communists, socialists, anarchists, atheists, and other radicals of all colors, sexes (in today's world there is no longer even a biological distinction between our God-given sexes), and sexual persuasions. And, they are not only destroying private and government property, such as police stations, but also looting, burning, and killing. As just one example, two thirds of the private enterprises on Beverly Hills' most famous street, Rodeo Drive, were trashed and robbed. It was turned into a crime scene by criminals of all sorts.

Around the same time as Judicial Watch's letter to Mayor Bowser, as a testament to how my public interest group does the work that I used to do when I ran Judicial Watch, and for that matter the work that DOJ should do but doesn't, I appeared before the U.S. Court of Appeals for the Ninth Circuit in a case I had filed four years ago—yes, way ahead of the downward curve—against members of Antifa and the University of California at Berkeley and the city itself.

At the outset of the hearing, in providing background to the panel of three federal judges in a Freudian slip of the tongue, I referred to the date that my brave gay woman client, Kiara Robles, was attacked by Antifa on the Berkeley campus as February 1, 1917. When I saw the jurists laughing at how I had said 1917 instead of 2017, the year the assault actually occurred, and poking me for being 100 years off target, I responded in jest that whenever I think of the university and the city I think of the Russian Bolshevik revolution.

My quip to these establishment federal judges, ironically, hit the mark. With the then-ongoing occupation of sectors of Seattle and the maiming, assault, and destruction that was targeted in full force at localities and states all around the nation, indeed we were then the midst of an attempted and now all but successful forceful leftist takeover. It is the result of not only ultra-leftist benefactors like George Soros who finance many of these radicals, and the race baiters, conmen, and radical black Muslims like the so-called Reverends Louis Farrakhan and Al Sharpton, but also white communist and socialist organizers and vigilantes who see an opportunity to reduce the republic to ash and then build a country back up Marxian style.

We are thus living through a period not unlike what Russia experienced in 1917, and what Ayn Rand predicted in her famous book *Atlas Shrugged*.

What is making matters worse, is that not only the police who have been ordered to lay down their arms by reflexive government leaders and leftist Soros financed and elected district attorneys, but the local mayors and state governors in particular are taking an exit stage left and allowing this Bolshevik revolution to gain traction. Couple this with the corrupt DOJ and its FBI essentially dumping off responsibility to the do-nothing localities and state authorities to prosecute these criminals, and we have dangerous chaos, as the leftist cancer continues full force to become potentially terminal.

In the socialist state of California, for instance, it is not a prosecutable crime to steal less than $950.00. In Los Angeles alone black hoodlums and others are simply walking into stores, loading up trash bags, and walking out with goods, with no contest from security much less the police. And on Tinseltown's Melrose Avenue, gunmen confront café dwellers and rob them in broad daylight, without any resistance from either the patrons or law enforcement. Then there is Chicago, Philadelphia, New York City, Seattle, Portland and Miami, which have become literally killing fields, with murder rates skyrocketing, with little to no law enforcement. Why is this? Because tens of thousands of cops in those and other American cities quit or retired, not wanting to be accused of being racist and prosecuted for doing their jobs!

We at Freedom Watch and a new public interest group, America's Sheriff, I formed with America's Toughest Sheriff Joe Arpaio—I would like to think I am America's Toughest Lawyer—are using our resources to also bring legal actions to protect police and other law enforcement who have been victimized, such as in my birthplace and the birthplace of our republic, Philadelphia, by what is, in effect, reverse racism, where white cops are fired based on what the leftists falsely consider to be racist tweets and social media posts on private accounts. And, we have other legal actions in the works to restore equal justice under the law—no matter what one's race, ethnicity, gender, or religion may be. Our Framers wrote and enacted a Constitution on the bedrock principle that all men and women are created equal. But in today's warped and sick world, all people are not treated as equal, particularly if you are a white male cop or, for that matter, white and male in general!

So, while I tip my "white hat" to my former colleagues at Judicial Watch for its high-profile publicity stunt, let me take it into the real world of the moment. What exists now is not any semblance of "Because No One is Above the Law," but instead "Because There Is No Law!" Taking a page from the group I founded, I too had written to Mayor Bowser to demand that she have this painted on Pennsylvania Avenue right in front of her office. Predictably, she did not respond, as there is no government accountability anymore, even though District of Columbia law requires equal treatment for political speech in public places.

The bottom line: even assuming good intentions among small minority in the public sector, no one in government, or for that matter in the private sector as well, is or wants to be in charge, as the barbarians storm and enter the gates of our civilization, much as occurred in ancient Rome before its demise.

This is why the teachings of this book are so important. Without federal judges and government officials, including federal and state prosecutors, who will enforce the law without regard to politics and their personal biases, prejudices, and predilections, the citizenry is left defenseless, and bloody revolt is just around the corner—as counter-revolutionaries from the extreme right, such as the Klan, neo-Nazis, and others posing as militias will fill the void and "take care of business" in reprisal.

Thus, fellow patriots, digest the bitterly frank words of this work and take up legal and peaceful arms by joining me and Freedom Watch and now America's Sheriff to return the rule of law and respect for our Constitution, much more our Judeo-Christian values, to our sacred shores. The preservation of godly values do not include millions of unborn babies being killed, so-called critical race theory being preached to our children that white people are racist from birth, or erasing the God-given distinctions between man and woman, much less normalizing homosexuality, gay and lesbian lifestyles, transgenderism and transexualism, which are thrust in our collective faces and pushed on us relentlessly by the Left. While all people should be treated with respect, this march toward "anything goes" historically has destroyed civilizations. Just ask the Greeks and the Romans!

And in my opinion do not think for an instant that God is not watching and sending us a message with our current pandemics and crises that either we shape up and honor the word of the Lord, or He will make sure that we ship out! God has done this before, so why not now with the ever-increasing immoral, depraved, perverted and unethical decay that is foisted upon us primarily by the Left.

In my various walks of life, I have encountered few people who even realize the potential consequences of our current sad state of affairs. Most believe that it is just a passing phenomenon, and are living in "La La Land." But like those who sat on the deck of the Titanic clueless and listening to eerie chamber music as the boat sank to the bottom of the sea, our ship of state has nearly already hit rock bottom. If you want to see your children and grandchildren, much less yourselves, relegated the dark reaches of Davy Jones's socialist and increasingly communist, and atheist locker, then continue to do nothing and party on! If not, join our cause for freedom and liberty.

In the days leading up to July 4, 1776, most colonialists were content to live under the king. The populace was generally rich, fat, and happy. The British Crown's primary oppression was over-taxation to pay for the rest of the king's empire. But our Founding Fathers convinced the citizens that they could not be content, as there was a massive dictatorial storm brewing on the horizon, which would get much worse over time. Like our enlightened and God-inspired forefathers, we can educate, coalesce, and unite the colonies again, meaning those who now live in our fifty states. In fact, in today's world, the storm is no longer brewing, as it is already here! What the citizenry faces now is much worse than anything experienced in the days, months, and years leading up to July 4, 1776.

To those of you who are seniors and retired, and to the young and middle-aged, if you want a free country, now is the time to wake up, America, before it is too late! It is no longer time to be entertained by the likes of Sean Hannity and Fox News. The destruction and total leftist hold on this nation is simply not entertaining. Now is the time to act and to act strong. In the words of the great pamphleteer Thomas Paine in his seminal work *Common Sense*, written and distributed widely during the lead-up to our first revolution, we do not need or want any more summer soldiers and sunshine patriots! We do not need those who, for self-promotion and profit, simply talk a good game! Instead, we want fellow warriors who will put words to action, will risk all and stand up to and vanquish the cancerous tyranny at hand that grows daily!

If we turn to God's divine grace and honor Him and His Son, and act now, I am confident we will prevail and preserve and protect the vision and creation of our greatest of Founding Fathers, Thomas Jefferson. As God proclaims in the Old Testament Book of Isaiah, the Tarnished City, with righteous, and courageous counselors and judges, and an honest and earnest government, we can be returned to a Faithful City!

But time is of the essence and there is much hard work to do! Let us begin by being bold, going for broke and again declaring our independence, establishing a new government not bound by the corrupt past run by political, governmental and judicial whores, fine-tuning our Constitution, taking our capitol back to Independence Hall in Philadelphia where it all began or at least someplace other than the swamp, and leaving the court jesters and money changers in the District of Columbia to commit more crimes against each other, nominating and electing new leaders and judges, establishing new and more than two vibrant and competitive political parties, and above all looking to the heavens to get us through these dangerous times, when the nation has been taken over by leftist barbarians who have entered our gates with their mission to destroy all we hold dear! America must not be turned into an immoral, unethical, sick and perverted, lawless and godless Marxist state! I, for one, will not accept this! And neither can you if you care about your children, grandchildren, and future generations of proud and free Americans!

Give us liberty or give us death, in the renewed and powerful words and deeds of Patrick Henry and our Founding Fathers, who are beckoning all of us from their graves to wake up, get engaged, stand up to tyranny, and preserve a free republic, which they gave their blood, sweat, and tears to create. Jefferson, Adams, Franklin, and the rest of our Founding Fathers pledged their sacred honor, gambled with their fortunes, and risked their lives to form the greatest nation the world has ever seen or experienced. Now We the People must have their unbridled courage to take back the nation from the Bolshevik barbarians and other leftist radicals who have entered our gates, taken total control over our lives, and are bent on destroying all we hold dear, as one nation under God!

ABOUT THE AUTHOR

Larry Klayman, Esq., founder and former chairman of the successful non-profit foundation Judicial Watch, has dedicated his career to fighting against injustice and restoring ethics to the legal profession and government. He was born and raised in Philadelphia, graduated with honors in political science and French literature from Duke University, and later received a law degree from Emory University. He is the only lawyer ever to have obtained a court ruling that a U.S. president committed a crime, which occurred during his tenure at Judicial Watch. He became so well known that NBC's hit drama series *The West Wing* created a character inspired by him, named Harry Claypool of Freedom Watch. In 2003, Mr. Klayman left Judicial Watch to run for the U.S. Senate. After his Senate race, he established Freedom Watch. As head of that organization and his law firm Klayman Law Group, P.A., he now divides his time between South Florida, Los Angeles, and Washington, DC.